Mayada,

DAUGHTER OF IRAQ

Mayada,

DAUGHTER OF IRAQ

One Woman's Survival
Under Saddam Hussein

Jean Sasson

DUTTON

DUTTON
Published by the Penguin Group (USA) Inc.,
375 Hudson Street, New York, New York 10014, U.S.A.
Penguin Books Ltd, 80 Strand, London WC2R 0RL, England
Penguin Books Australia Ltd., 250 Camberwell Road, Camberwell, Victoria 3124, Australia
Penguin Books Canada Ltd, 10 Alcorn Avenue, Toronto, Ontario, Canada M4V 3B2
Penguin Books (N.Z.) Ltd, Cnr Rosedale and Airborne Roads, Albany, Auckland 1310, New Zealand

Penguin Books Ltd, Registered Offices: 80 Strand, London WC2R ORL, England

Published by Dutton, a member of Penguin Group (USA) Inc.

First printing, October 2003
10   9   8   7   6   5   4   3   2   1

LIBRARY OF CONGRESS CATALOGING-IN-PUBLICATION DATA
has been applied for.

ISBN: 0-525-94811-2

Printed in the United States of America
Set in Weiss
Designed by Jaye Zimet

PUBLISHER'S NOTE
Names of certain individuals portrayed in this book have been changed to protect privacy.

Obituary: Reproduced with permission of The Times of London 02.11.1936
Speech: Reproduced with permission of Curtis Brown Ltd, London on behalf of Winston S. Churchill. Copyright Winston S. Churchill 1921.

This book is printed on acid-free paper. ∞

To Samara

and all the shadow women of cell 52

CONTENTS

Meeting Mayada

Distant places have always called me. So when I received an opportunity to travel to one of the most exotic and dangerous parts of the world, I accepted the challenge.

I was a young woman in 1978 when I left the United States to work at a royal hospital in Riyadh, where I remained until 1990. While living in Saudi Arabia for twelve years, I developed a strong network of friendships with Saudi women. Through these friendships, I began to understand what it meant to be a woman in a male-dominated society, with little recourse or protection from individual acts of violence and cruelty.

Since that first trip I have traveled throughout the Middle East: Lebanon, Egypt, Jordan, Syria, Israel, Palestine, the United Arab Emirates, Iraq and Kuwait. Everywhere I went I would speak to women and children. I would visit the hospitals. I would visit the orphanages. I would attend parties. Thinking back on my success at getting to know the locals, I believe they were as intrigued by me as I was by them.

My only frustration was that many of the Middle Eastern lands I visited were plagued by hardship; but regardless of the palpable poverty, the people I came to know always extended a welcoming gesture, cheerfully opening their homes and hearts to an American traveler.

After the 1991 Gulf War, the entire Middle East became even more tumultuous, but particularly Iraq. I'd been interested in the Iraqis since the Gulf War, curious about the people who had lived through wars and sanctions brought about by their own president, Saddam Hussein. Propelled by this interest, I decided to visit Iraq in the summer of 1998.

As the author of a book critical of Saddam, I knew that I would never be issued a visa by a government official, so I wrote directly to the Iraqi president and sent him a copy of my book, *The Rape of Kuwait*. In the letter I told Saddam that I hadn't agreed with his invasion of Kuwait, but that I was concerned about the well-being of ordinary Iraqis who were living under the sanctions. I wanted to see for myself how the Iraqi people were faring.

Within three weeks, I received a telephone call from Baghdad informing me that my visa would be granted through the Iraqi U.N. Mission in New York.

I packed my bags with wartime supplies—canned goods, flashlights and candles—and left for Baghdad on Monday, July 20, 1998. With the U.N. sanctions in place, planes were not allowed to fly into Iraq, so I would have to start my voyage from a neighboring country. Considering the distance to Baghdad from other major cities in the area, and the unrest that still plagued the northern and southern regions of Iraq, Jordan appeared to be the perfect place to start my journey.

The nation of Jordan was created by Great Britain after World War I, during a refashioning of the weakened Ottoman Empire. Today, Jordan occupies an area just over 37,000 square miles (roughly the size of Indiana) and is home to four million people, the majority of whom are Palestinian. The tiny country serves as a highway between Syria and Saudi Arabia, connecting the Syrian city of Damascus and the Saudi Arabian holy city of Medina, in much the same way it served as a natural meeting point for the caravan trails of antiquity.

Seven hours after boarding Royal Jordanian Airlines flight 6707 from London, I arrived at Jordan's Queen Ali International Airport, a forty-five-minute drive from the capital city of Amman.

The dilapidated baggage area of the airport reminded me that Jordan is considered by many to be nothing more than a place to wait for the next connection. Yet Jordan is a land of compelling contrasts—from Aqaba, the source of T. E. Lawrence's extraordinary adventures, to the gravel plateau of the Syro-Arabian desert, where Bedouin tribes from centuries past graze their animals, to the legendary Petra of the rose-red Nabatean tombs, where elaborate buildings and tombs were carved out of solid rock by a nomadic tribe.

After a rapid pass through Jordanian customs, I stepped outside the airport. It was still quite warm—the hot July sun had set only moments before the plane touched down.

I studied the waiting crowd and soon spotted a middle-aged Arab man in well-worn beige trousers and a blue shirt, who held a large white sign with my name written in bright blue letters. I settled into the backseat of his rather exhausted-looking Peugeot 504 station wagon for the forty-five-minute drive to the Inter-Continental Hotel in Amman and, after a few moments of polite conversation, sat back and quietly stared out the window.

Twilight had set in, and the local desert plants projected their sharp outlines against the peony-pink sky. As is their custom, many Jordanians had driven to the outskirts of the city, where they spread their colorful Oriental rugs on small mounds of dirt for their evening picnics. Dozens of small fires blazed, lighting up the shadowy silhouettes of women grilling chicken on spits. Tiny firelights flashed as Arab men gestured and emphasized with their lighted cigarettes, and small shadows scooted here and there as children played in the endless sand. I lowered the car window and heard the crackling of the fires mingling with the muted voices of family gatherings, and for a fleeting moment I wished to belong to one of those families.

Amman is an appealing city set among seven hills. We soon arrived at the Inter-Continental, which is in the heart of the diplomatic

area set atop one of those hills. I had selected the hotel for no particular reason, other than the assumption that it was a safe place with decent food where I could purchase supplies and organize the 650-mile
land journey to Baghdad.

That first evening I slept fitfully. After several telephone calls
the next morning, the Jordanian owner of Al-Rahal arrived at the
Inter-Continental in a white Mercedes. His quote for the Amman–
Baghdad–Amman round trip was $400 U.S., with half to be paid prior
to departing Amman and the other half to be paid prior to departing
Baghdad. I paid him the first $200, and was told to expect a four-
wheel-drive vehicle the following morning at 5:30. I would be driven
by a Jordanian named Basem.

The people I met that day were rather startled when they discovered that I was traveling alone into Iraq. There were legitimate reasons for their concern. The summer of 1998 was a time of enormous
tension between Iraqi President Saddam Hussein and the United Nations' chief arms inspector, Richard Butler. Mr. Butler was a persistent
character, a man determined to discover and destroy Iraqi weapons,
and he had earned the nickname "Mad Dog Butler," coined by Saddam Hussein himself. Hussein was equally relentless and unwavering
in his quest to protect his long-sought and well-guarded weapon
supply, of course, and Western news reports made it apparent that
Richard Butler was clearly exasperated with the lack of cooperation
from Iraqi officials. Everyone in the area feared that *something* unpleasant was bound to happen between the aggressive dictator to their east
and the determined foe to their west. In light of the rising tension and
Saddam's growing animosity, few members of the American media
even considered travel into Iraq that summer, and those who did usually chose to travel in disguise, generally under the pretext of working
with humanitarian organizations.

But I have always embraced adventure, and I find it best to travel
alone. So it was with great anticipation that I departed Amman at the

appointed hour—I felt the sense of an adventure beginning to unfold dramatically.

Amman was soon behind us, and we passed through the Zarqa district before coming to the Al-Azraq oasis, known for its bumpy, potholed highway. The narrow road, churning with large trucks and buses, stirred terror in my heart. My mouth dried with apprehension as I noted the large number of charred bus and truck carcasses by the roadside—they resembled huge beasts who had suffered agonizing deaths.

For long hours, Basem and I traveled through land so endlessly monotonous that it appeared to have been scoured clean by high winds. We traveled at eighty miles an hour, yet seemed incapable of escaping the flat beige of the dusty land and its wretched little trees and thorny plants.

The terrain remained rough, but eventually and dramatically changed shape and color to round, black-lava boulders that sparkled under the midday sun. Unfortunately, we soon reentered the monotonous, featureless terrain of stark, sandy flats.

As the morning wore on, we sped closer to the Iraqi border. From the days of ancient Mesopotamia, the country now known as Iraq has played a pivotal role in the entire region, and as a result has been invaded and conquered many times. From the Mongols to the Ottomans to the British, many foreign powers have attempted to make the beauty and convenience of Mesopotamia their own. With the end of World War I, the British created the modern nation of Iraq, forcing Kurds, Sunnis and Shiites to come together unnaturally as one.

After crossing the border and easily passing through Iraqi customs, my heart began to pound with excitement. Before long the ancient Euphrates River came into view. We passed through the region called Al-Anbar, an area dominated by Iraqi Sunnis, chiefly from the Dulaimi tribe. These people sided closely with Saddam Hussein. Even after the senselessness of the 1991 Gulf War, Saddam was so warmly received by the people of the area that he reacted in an uncommon manner for a man burdened with paranoid impulses—he emptied his revolver into the air, leaving himself defenseless.

Finally, after eleven hours of riding, the low ridge of Baghdad came into view, with palmtops and rooftops rising above the flatland. In silence I gazed at the small beige houses, which, after the bleak desert, assumed the dimensions of a great civilization. Small mosques with huge domes were scattered across the skyline. Homes with balconies and courtyards peered tantalizingly from small cross streets. Occasionally I saw a straggle of scrawny violet or white flowers struggling to grow under the shade of a palm tree.

Street corners were crowded with pedestrians threading their way through busy city streets. Sadly, the old, quiet streets of Baghdad had turned chaotic, with aging autos on bald tires dawdling behind limping buses that belched black smoke. I knew that the wars and sanctions brought about by the Iraqi government had isolated the Iraqis from the rest of the world, so the sight of generally somber-faced people wearing worn clothing was not a surprise. When we stopped at traffic lights, I studied the Iraqi faces, knowing I was in the midst of a nation of people who had lived unimaginably dramatic lives. An Iraqi man or woman close to my own age of fifty years would have witnessed rebellions and revolutions, the crowning of kings, numerous government coups, the discovery of oil, the promise of great national riches, wealth wrecked by brutal wars, a repressive police state and crippling sanctions.

With the dying light I heard the voice of the muezzin calling Muslims to the sundown prayer. I looked up to see a small citadel facing the street. The muezzin's low-pitched, musical voice soared from the top of the citadel as the sun slowly set. Basem turned in at the Al Rasheed Hotel. I had arrived safely.

Iraq was a fascinating study in contrasts. Although repressed, the Iraqi people were surprisingly open and friendly. The employees at the Al Rasheed Hotel were unfailingly polite, bringing me photographs of their family members and showering me with small gifts that I knew they could barely afford. Employees at the Ministry of Information invited me into their homes, where I ate their food and met their friends. The guards outside the Ministry followed me to my car to tell me stories of their families. The mothers and fathers of children dying from leukemia at a nearby hospital shared small snacks when I visited the children's wards. My new driver, hired through the manager of the Al Rasheed, accepted no other employment during my stay and sat for hours in the lobby in case I needed anything. And after three unfamiliar men knocked on my door during the first night of my stay, the hotel management provided a full-time guard outside my room.

But the most wonderful part of the trip was yet to come. Two days after arriving in Baghdad, I met the unique and unforgettable Mayada Al-Askari, a woman who has become closer to me than a sister.

My good luck in meeting Mayada owed much to my determination that a woman, rather than a man, would translate for me while I visited Baghdad. After my first day in the city, I wondered why no one from the Ministry of Information had paid me a visit—I had read many stories about their intrusions on foreign guests. By the second day, I had grown impatient and had my driver take me to the Ministry, where I planned to request a translator. I was told that a man by the name of Shakir Al-Dulaimi headed the Ministry's press center.

I walked into Shakir's offices and joked that I had heard that foreigners were followed by Iraqi minders, but that no one seemed to know I was in town. Wasn't I important enough for a minder? Shakir seemed amused, and told me that if I liked, he would have an Iraqi man accompany me.

Because I was interested primarily in Arab women's issues, and knowing from my years of living in the Middle East that no Arab woman would speak openly in front of an Arab man, I told Shakir that I would have to decline his kind offer. I insisted that I would only accept a female translator. After some friendly bickering, Shakir raised his hands in the air and shrugged, an Arab sign of friendly defeat, and agreed to my demand. (I later learned that official government policy was to hire only male translators.)

I returned to Shakir's office the next morning, where I met an Iraqi woman modestly dressed in an ankle-length garment, her face framed by a black scarf. She was average height and slightly overweight, her face was pale with rosy cheeks, and expectation shone from her light green eyes. We studied each other. She then looked at Shakir and back to me.

The woman seemed kind, and I smiled hopefully, hoping that she might be my guide for the duration of my stay in Iraq.

She acknowledged my smile with a tentative one of her own.

Shakir looked at me and announced, "Jean, here is your woman."

In a pleasant and lightly accented voice, she said, "I am Mayada Al-Askari." She told me later that she hadn't been employed by the Ministry for several years, that the men in charge would almost exclusively hire male translators. I felt glad—and I think she did too—that I had reacted stubbornly to Shakir's original suggestion.

Mayada and I became fast friends. I quickly discovered that she spoke fluent English and had a wonderful sense of humor. She was the divorced mother of a fifteen-year-old girl named Fay, and also had a twelve-year-old son named Ali. Mayada shared my passion for animals—she was the proud owner of two house cats, one of whom had just given birth.

Over the next few weeks I discovered that Mayada was a daughter of the ancient land of Mesopotamia, known to the modern world as Iraq. She was proud of her country, for good reason—for much of its history, Mesopotamia was an ancient paradise with great glory. The culture produced artists, poets and scholars, and some early rulers were mighty builders who were devoted to literature and good works, and who gave the first established laws and freedom to the world.

Although many Mosopotamian reformers strived to improve the lot of the nation's citizens, these judicious rulers were often violently overthrown by tyrants who embroiled the country in violence for generations. Long before the rule of Saddam Hussein, continuous conflict raged across Mayada's land. Blessed with two major rivers in a region known for deserts, a desirable geographic location connecting busy trading centers, and great wealth, Mesopotamia was a prized target. From the ancient Sumerians to the Mongols to the Tamerlane to the Persians to the Ottomans, the country was repeatedly conquered and lost.

To understand Mayada's family, one must know something of the rule of the Ottoman Empire, which dominated the entire Near East from 1517 to 1917, and Iraq itself from 1532 to 1917. This vast empire included Asia Minor, the Middle East, Egypt, part of North Africa and even a sliver of southeastern Europe. And in every region they conquered, the Ottomans appointed like-minded allies to govern. The sultans of the Ottoman Empire were Sunni Muslims, so they were inclined to appoint members of the Sunni sect to positions of authority. This gave the Sunnis, who were a minority group, authority over all other Iraqis, including the Shiite majority. The Ottoman rulers thus set the stage for a permanent pattern of ethnic tensions across Mayada's country. But as long as the Ottomans remained in power, these tensions tended to simmer beneath the surface, rather than erupting into chaos. Once the Ottoman Empire buckled, festering hostilities exploded, and those same unstable forces are still alive upon the land.

The Ottoman Empire collapsed after World War I, the death knell sounded by the Sultan's decision to side with the German forces during the war. With the collapse of the Ottomans, there was great hope that Arabs—who had tolerated human rights abuses for centuries under Ottoman rule—would be able to build free nations and live lives of dignity. Unfortunately, their torment did not end with the demise of the Ottomans because the British and the French already had their armies poised to fill the abyss. The Arabs were shocked to discover that their new European conquerors believed themselves the rightful owners of every resource in the region, rather than the Arabs. And so the circle of dispossession continued. The British felt more at ease with the Sunni guardians, and so the Sunni minority continued to rule the Shiite majority.

These enormous shifts in the fortunes of the Ottoman Empire drastically shaped the lives of Mayada's grandparents and parents, for their lineage led directly back into the heart of the Ottoman palaces. Both of Mayada's grandfathers had lived as respected citizens of the vast empire and were witnesses to the disintegration of Ottoman rule following the Allied victory in World War I. And in their hope for prosperous and free Arab nations, both grandfathers were also involved in the formation and governing of the new Arab states of Syria and Iraq.

Mayada's paternal grandfather, Jafar Pasha Al-Askari, was an extraordinary man who served as the Commander of the Arab Regular Army, fighting with T. E. Lawrence and Prince Faisal to help defeat the Ottoman Empire. Mayada's maternal grandfather, Sati Al-Husri, was celebrated throughout the Arab world as a genius and the father of Arab nationalism, and was one of the first scholars to call for Arab rule over Arab lands.

Like her parents and grandparents before her, Mayada was born a Sunni Muslim. The Sunni sect is the majority sect of the Islamic faith worldwide, although it is the minority sect in several Arab countries, including Iraq. Mayada's mother, Salwa Al-Husri, was the daughter of Sati Al-Husri, while Mayada's father, Nizar Al-Askari, was the son of the famed warrior and government official Jafar Al-Askari.

Mayada's family's home was a popular "political house," and visits and telephone calls from politically connected world figures were common. Because she was a beloved daughter and granddaughter, her family helped guide her life down a path of learning and privilege; she was expected to pursue a career in medicine or art and to live a life of culture.

But Iraqi political conflicts tended to dramatically alter every carefully laid out plan. In 1968, when the Baath Party came to power, most intellectuals fled to neighboring countries, but Mayada's father was dying of cancer and receiving treatment at a local hospital. Mayada's family decided to remain in Baghdad.

Despite Saddam Hussein's rule, which became more tyrannical with each passing year, Mayada lived her life in Iraq. She grew up in Iraq. She pursued a career in newspaper reporting in Iraq. She was married in Iraq. She gave birth to two children in Iraq. She survived the Iran-Iraq war. She survived the Gulf War. She survived the sanctions. Mayada suffered through nearly every phase of modern Iraq's turbulent history. Despite these hardships, she always believed that she could live out her life in Iraq, the land that she had loved since her childhood.

On one occasion, we were visiting the children's ward in a hospital in Baghdad. I was so overcome by the misery of those children listlessly handling the special toys I had given them that I had to fight my emotions. Just as I was about to break down in tears, I felt the comforting touch of Mayada's hand on my shoulder. She was sorry to witness my sadness. Then a nurse came into the room and without preparing the children for the needles, began to give them their shots. At the sight of so many screaming children, I became desperate to stop their crying and I began to dance and sing, hoping to take their minds off the painful needles. My foolish behavior brought a few weak smiles from the children and loud laughter from their parents, since I have no talent for dancing or singing.

Mayada asked me to step outside the hospital. I was shocked when she began to confide in me how she detested Saddam Hussein, and her one dream in life was to live to see the end of his rule. She said what we all knew, that he was the main reason for the misery of those children. Not only had the dictator started the wars that brought on the sanctions, but she claimed that Saddam was so eager to lay the blame for infant deaths on the sanctions that he was known to hold back medicine from the hospitals—he might, for example, allow only one cancer drug to be issued for leukemia patients who clearly required two or three different drugs to battle certain cancers. Saddam was also known to display empty baby coffins on the streets, in an effort to inflame the world against the United States.

Afraid that a Saddam loyalist might overhear, I was frightened for her safety and tried to calm her down, but nothing I said could stop her tirade.

I had seen with my own eyes that Iraq had been turned into a big cage by Saddam Hussein. It appeared that every Iraqi was waiting to be arrested and tortured for one state-imagined violation or another, but Saddam's rule seemed permanent, and I had little hope that the Iraqis would know freedom anytime soon. When I asked Mayada why she didn't leave to go to Jordan and live with her mother, Mayada justified her loyalty to her country—but *not* to Saddam Hussein—when she explained that she *must* live in the country of her father's grave. As an Iraqi, she belonged in Iraq—regardless of danger.

My visit to Baghdad was fleeting, and after only a few weeks Mayada and I had to say goodbye.

It was a sad day when I left Baghdad, but from our first meeting, Mayada and I knew that we would be friends for life. After I arrived back in the States, we settled seamlessly into our long-distance friendship. We wrote letters and telephoned each other, keeping in touch on a weekly basis.

A year after our first meeting, Mayada disappeared. There was no answer at her home telephone. I received no response to my letters. But just as I was feeling desperate, she called me. She was home in Baghdad, and she told me that she had been in "the can"—that she had been in prison. I knew better than to ask specific questions, and it was only after she fled to Jordan that I was able to learn the full story of her arrest, torture and escape.

After her arrest, a chain of events set this book in motion. In 1999, Mayada escaped Iraq. In 2000, her daughter, Fay, escaped Iraq. In 2001, New York and Washington, D.C., were attacked by terrorists. That same year, President George Bush sent American forces to root out terrorist factions. In 2002, Bush determined that the Iraqis had suffered enough under Saddam Hussein, and in early 2003, coalition forces removed Hussein from power. That year, Mayada decided that she wanted the world to know the truth about Iraqi life, the truth as told by someone who had seen Iraq from every angle, from Saddam's palaces to Saddam's torture chambers. After discussing the possibility of this book for weeks, Mayada asked me to write the story of her life, and I agreed.

While writing this book I have come to know and love many members of Mayada's family. These great men and women played vital roles in the creation of modern Iraq, and although those wonderful people who came before her are now gone, I am comforted by the fact that all of the history of modern Iraq flows through Mayada Al-Askari's genes, and it is through this remarkable woman that the real truth of modern Iraqi life will stream through the ages.

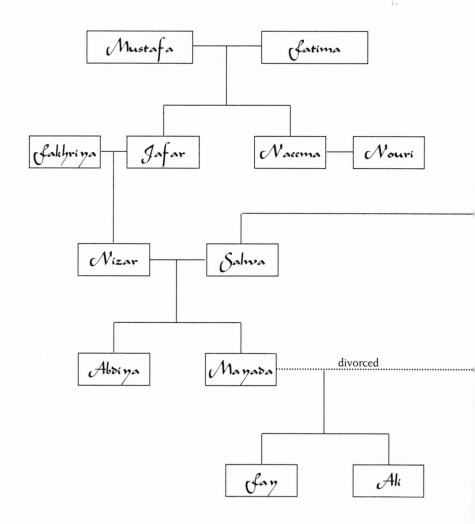

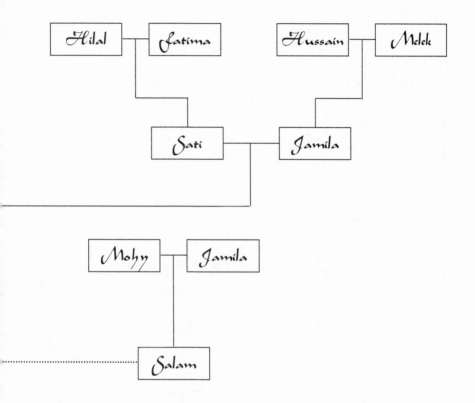

MAP OF IRAQ

MAP OF IRAQ AND NEIGHBORING COUNTRIES

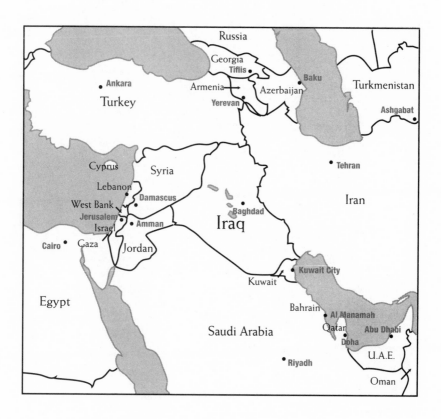

MAP OF PRISON

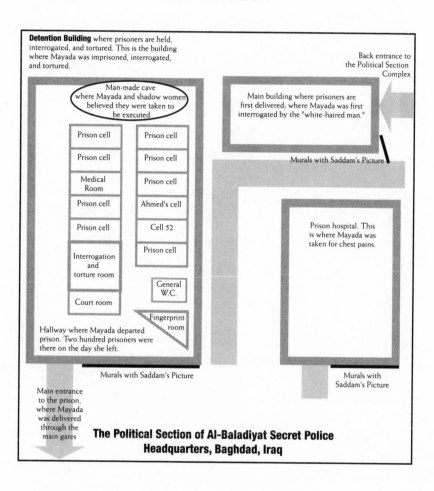

Detention Building where prisoners are held, interrogated, and tortured. This is the building where Mayada was imprisoned, interrogated, and tortured.

Back entrance to the Political Section Complex

Man-made cave where Mayada and shadow women believed they were taken to be executed

Main building where prisoners are first delivered; where Mayada was first interrogated by the "white-haired man."

Prison cell	Prison cell
Prison cell	Prison cell
Medical Room	Prison cell
Prison cell	Ahmed's cell
Prison cell	Cell 52
Interrogation and torture room	Prison cell
	General W.C.
Court room	

Murals with Saddam's Picture

Prison hospital. This is where Mayada was taken for chest pains.

Fingerprint room

Hallway where Mayada departed prison. Two hundred prisoners were there on the day she left.

Murals with Saddam's Picture

Murals with Saddam's Picture

Main entrance to the prison, where Mayada was delivered through the main gates

The Political Section of Al-Baladiyat Secret Police Headquarters, Baghdad, Iraq

Mayada,

DAUGHTER OF IRAQ

1

The Shadow Women of Cell 52

At about 8:45 on the morning of July 19, 1999, Mayada Al-Askari was driving to her office at full speed. Mornings at her print shop were always the busiest time of the day, and from the large number of orders that had streamed into her shop the day before, Mayada knew this morning would be an especially hectic one. When she opened her business the year before, she had purchased the finest printers in Iraq, and for this reason, the work produced at her shop was considered the best in the entire Mutanabi area. As a result, Mayada had more business than she could handle. She accepted a wide variety of jobs, designing logos and writing text for milk cartons, boxes and bottles. She printed books as well, as long as the print order arrived with a stamp of approval from the Ministry of Information. Mayada ran such an efficient business that many other printing houses in the district outsourced their work to her, their competitor, and passed off her work as their own.

Mayada glanced at her watch. She was running late. She careened around corners, but made certain she didn't exceed the speed limit. She glanced through the windshield at the sky. It was growing dark with blowing sand, looking much like a foggy day in England.

The wind was beginning to gust, rising and falling in heated blasts. July was an unpleasant month in Iraq. Mayada yearned to escape the heat and fly to the mountains of Lebanon for a holiday, but she no longer had extra money for vacations, so she pushed those thoughts aside. She parked her car on the street and stepped to the sidewalk. To keep the wind from stinging her eyes and irritating her throat and lungs, she tilted her head down and placed her hand over her mouth, walking rapidly. To her relief, the door to the shop was unlocked. Mayada's dedicated staff was already at work. She had a committed group of employees, and not only because she paid higher salaries than most other printing offices. They were simply a well-educated, serious bunch.

Mayada took a quick look around the office. Hussain, Adel and Wissam were already at their computers. Her eyes strayed to the little kitchenette at the back of the shop. There was Nahla, making coffee. Nahla smiled and walked toward her, holding out a cup. Before Mayada could raise the cup to her lips, she was approached by Hussain and Shermeen, both talking at once about the graphic design projects they were working on. They were interrupted by a new client who rushed through the unlocked door, anxious to start a conversation with Mayada. The young man said he was a Tunisian student and that he had been referred to her by another shop owner in the area. He wanted her to translate and prepare a questionnaire for him. Mayada was discussing his job when the front door flew open and three men strode into her small office. Her heart skipped a beat, sensing instantly that the men were too rigid to be customers.

The tallest of the three men asked, "Is your name Mayada Nizar Jafar Mustafa Al-Askari?" His question astonished Mayada, for few people knew her full name. She used "Mustafa" particularly rarely, though it was a name she bore proudly. It harked back to her great-grandfather Mustafa Al-Askari, who, like her grandfather Jafar, was an important officer in the once-great Ottoman army.

Mayada stood quietly, searching the eyes of the men before her.

For a moment she considered fleeing or lashing out, but her father was dead and she was divorced. Mayada did not have a man in the family to protect her. She uttered a weak reverberation that sounded enough like "yes."

The tall man curtly informed her, "My name is Lieutenant Colonel Muhammed Jassim Raheem and these are my two colleagues. We will search this place."

Mayada found her voice by this time and managed to ask a simple question, "What are you looking for?"

The lieutenant colonel lifted his neck only a little and the loose skin swung one way and then the other before he answered, discharging each individual word like so many bullets: "You tell us."

Mayada was silenced. She did not know what words or actions might save her as the three men began to tear her small business apart. Waste bins were emptied; the undersides of the chairs were scrutinized; telephones were opened with screwdrivers. Then the men seized her cherished computers and printers. Mayada knew she would never find the funds to replace them as she watched the men load the computers into the trunks of their two white Toyota Corollas, the choice vehicle of the Iraqi secret police. Helpless, Mayada slowly crumpled the Tunisian student's papers she held in her hand, watching as the men destroyed her future.

She took a quick look at her frightened employees. They had gathered in a corner of the room, not daring to breathe. Nahla's face was pale and her lips trembled. The Tunisian student tittered, rubbing his hands, his face filled with regret that he had come into her shop.

Mayada did not doubt she was the next item to be loaded into the ominous automobile and she begged the lieutenant colonel for one phone call. "Can I please call my two children and tell them where you are taking me?"

He gave her a sinister look, then shouted, "No!"

She spoke as gently as she could. "Please. I must call my children. My children have no one but me."

Her heartfelt plea failed to touch the man. "No!" He snapped his fingers and his two cohorts surrounded her.

Sandwiched by the two men, she was led away. At the front door of her office she turned her neck and looked back, wondering if she would ever return.

From the backseat of the Toyota, Mayada saw the sympathetic eyes of a passerby steal frightened glances at her before he scurried away.

As the Toyota sped through the busy streets of Baghdad, she grew lightheaded. She willed herself to concentrate on the orange and yellow sky outside that swirled with billowing dust. The sandstorm now fully cloaked the city. Normally her only concern when churning sands approached Baghdad was to protect her home by blanketing windows and shoving papers under the doors. She would wait out the fury of the windblown sand and then seize a broom and dust cloth to fill small buckets with sand, which she emptied into her garden. Mayada's stomach plunged.

She glanced out the car window and watched as tattered but once-proud Iraqis passed. Twenty years ago when she was a young woman, Iraq had hummed with promise. The country boasted splendid avenues, fine shops, beautiful homes and a promising future. But under Saddam, Iraq grew diminished and dilapidated. Corruption clogged every government department. Iraqis were even reduced to standing in long lines for miserly tins of flour, oil and sugar distributed as rations in exchange for Iraqi oil exports under the U.N. 661 agreement.

It was a bitter time for nearly every Iraqi. Even Mayada's mother, Salwa Al-Husri, a strong, intelligent woman intent on supporting Iraq, could no longer maintain her faith that Iraq would soon rebound. Salwa had finally given up on her country and left to live in nearby Jordan.

Mayada's real troubles began after she divorced her husband, Salam, in 1988. The year after, she had left her job as a newspaper columnist and gone into the printing business for herself. But the Iraqi dinar had been drastically devalued and she lost everything. Once again, and in a weakened job market, Mayada was seeking employment. After the wars and the sanctions, few Iraqis had jobs. But for women, the challenge of finding work was even more daunting than for men. An unspoken government policy kept as many men working as possible, but evinced no concern for women who did not have a husband to support the family.

With two children to support and on the verge of complete financial collapse, Mayada asked God for a small miracle.

Her miracle came in the human form of Michael Simpkin, a television producer for Britain's Channel 4. He sought Mayada's mother in Amman and asked Salwa's assistance to meet Prime Minister Tariq Aziz or Minister of Defense Sultan Hashim. Salwa's contacts and influence in Iraq were deep, and she still knew the private telephone numbers of high Iraqi officials. She placed a few calls and established Michael Simpkin as someone government bureaucrats should meet. The British journalist met with Aziz, Hashim and Saad Qasim Hamoudi, the man responsible for foreign relations in Saddam's palace.

Salwa also encouraged Simpkin to meet her daughter Mayada while he was in Iraq, and Simpkin paid a visit to her home on Baghdad's Wazihiya Place. While there, Simpkin told Mayada he needed to hire an interpreter. Once he learned of Mayada's credentials as a journalist and heard her fluent English, he hired her, agreeing to pay her salary in U.S. dollars.

Simpkin's TV program, "War for the Gulf," was a success, and the moment the British journalist departed Baghdad, Mayada formed a plan to go back into business. She had been capable of running her own business, which was destroyed only because of Iraq's precarious financial situation. The business failure had been no fault of her own. She would simply try once again.

She had never been so joyous as on the day she slipped her dollars into her handbag and entered a store to purchase six computers and three printers. The joy surpassed even that of her wedding day, when in an elegant white suit she felt beautiful for the first time in her life.

With her dollars and her determination, Mayada reentered the world of commercial printing. With time, and after long hours each workday, her small business grew profitable. She was feeding and educating her children, without any assistance from anyone. With her success, Mayada came to believe that the worst of times were now behind her.

But she should have known better, she told herself now. Over the past few years, Baath officials had become increasingly suspicious of printing companies, because printed flyers were proving a popular method of attacking Saddam's weakening government. Although she took great care to keep her business above official reproach, innocence alone did not keep one safe.

When she leaned slightly forward and looked through the front window of the car an awesome fear such as she had never known gripped her mind. She was on the way to the "Darb Al-Sad Ma red," the "road from which there is no return."

She knew by the route the car was following that she was being taken to Baladiyat, the headquarters of Saddam's secret police, which also served as a prison complex.

Mayada had never before been inside this compound, but during the time the prison was being built, she had frequently passed the construction site in the mornings on her way to work. Never in her wildest dreams did she imagine she would one day be imprisoned there. But the unimaginable day was now upon her and she feared that death awaited her at Baladiyat.

Within minutes, the main entrance of the prison compound came into view. The automobile passed through a huge, grotesque black gate decorated with two hanging murals. In the gold-plated murals, Saddam overlooked the Iraqi people as they toiled in fields, factories and offices.

The driver stopped directly in front of a large building with small windows centered high atop the structure. Mayada went weak with dread, and when the two men lifted her from the Toyota, she noted the black sand clouds had completely obscured the sky. Her fear made her dizzy but she closed her eyes and took a deep breath, admonishing herself to remain in control of her senses. She found use of her muscles and forced herself to look up. The face of Saddam Hussein stared back from every compass point.

Mayada had been in Saddam's presence more than once. She had even stood close enough to the man to note the dark-green tribal tattoo he once wore on the end of his nose.

Baath party slogans were plastered on posters everywhere. "He who does not plant does not eat." Mayada couldn't help but wonder if she would ever be hungry again. As they pulled her into the building she looked upward to say a small prayer. "God, keep Fay and Ali safe and return me to them."

A man on either side of her guided Mayada up the stairs. At the top, emaciated men in torn, bloodstained clothing squatted on the floor, their hands bound behind their backs. Every face was bruised black; some faces still streamed with blood. No one squatting in the hallway spoke, but Mayada felt an aura of sincere compassion follow her awkward progress as she was dragged down the hall and into a nearby room.

By this time Mayada was stumbling and weeping in absolute terror.

Unlike many Arab women who were long burdened by cruel fathers and other men, Mayada had never known male dominance or masculine outrage. Her father, Nizar Jafar Al-Askari, had always been a gentle man. He never once favored the idea of sons over daughters, even though in Iraq a man surrounded by females is often pitied.

When Mayada was born, her father felt concern even for the reaction of Scottie, the much-loved black Scottish terrier he'd acquired in England. Mayada's father lifted Scottie in his arms and took him into the nursery to sniff at Mayada's feet. He advised Scottie that the feet of his daughter had been designated as his limit for the time be-ing, but that one day soon Mayada would be old enough to play with him as his companion.

Deep in Saddam's secret police headquarters, Mayada was over-whelmed by the wish to have her peaceful father by her side. She had never felt so alone in forty-three years of living as she did at that moment.

Someone shoved her from behind and Mayada was propelled into a room with a fierceness that loosened her sandals. She barely man-aged to catch her footing without sprawling on the floor.

A man stood behind a desk and shouted into a telephone. The skin on his face was youthful but his hair was completely white.

He slammed the phone down and glared at Mayada, then shouted, "And what do you think you were going to accomplish by this treason?"

Mayada began crying even harder at the word "treason," for she knew that such a charge would mean certain death in Iraq. She clutched her hand to her throat and sputtered, "What do you mean?"

He screamed loudly, "You lowlifes have the guts to print leaflets against the government!"

She did not understand this charge. Her small print shop had never been asked to print leaflets criticizing the government, and even if it had, she would have refused. She knew such a thing would gain the attention of Saddam's secret police and would end in the deaths of every man, woman and child associated with her shop. Only revolutionaries with a mind to overthrow Saddam became in-volved in such unlawful activities. She was a law-abiding citizen who was careful to stay far out of reach of political controversy.

As she stood there petrified, the white-haired man shouted, "Take this lowlife woman away! I will tend to her later!" Mayada feared what he meant, but her thoughts shifted to Fay and Ali. In Iraq, when a family member is arrested, the family's children are often taken away to be tortured, as well. Mayada summoned all her courage and asked the white-haired man, "Where are you sending me?"

He looked at her and shouted, "Detention!"

Mayada's background gave her the courage to ask, "Can I please make one phone call?"

Mayada was well-born, and knew that every Iraqi was aware of the prestige associated with her family. Operating on instinct, she delivered her own threat by adding, "My mother is Salwa Al-Husri."

The man's foot was raised inches from the floor, and he paused in that silly position to look at her. As he considered his response, he continued to hold his foot elevated. At any other time in her life Mayada would have laughed at his ridiculous posture, but the moment was wholly devoid of humor. Still, she felt the smallest glimmer of hope. Was it possible that the white-haired man did not know who she was? His apparent utter surprise gave her hope that her words might change the course of events.

She told him, "Sooner or later you will have to answer to someone. My mother has many contacts at the highest ranks."

As in slow motion, he placed his upheld foot back on the floor. But she could see that he was still thinking. Without a word, he handed her the telephone.

Her trembling hands were so pale she wondered if somehow the blood had left them. She took the phone and dialed her home, praying that her children would answer, praying that they had not been taken. The phone rang and rang.

There was no answer.

Without looking into the man's face, she fought her panic and dialed a second time, hoping that in her jumbled mental state she had misdialed her home number.

As the phone continued to ring, the man stood and watched, tilting his head first one way and then another.

Suddenly he grabbed the phone from Mayada's hands. The fears of every bombing raid she'd endured during the war years could not compare with her terror at the idea that the secret police might lay a hand on Fay and Ali. But she would be left without an answer. With a smirk, the white-haired man gestured for her to leave.

Mayada had to make a second pass of the prisoners still squatting in the hallway, and she steeled herself with the knowledge that she was now one of them. And worse, no one outside Baladiyat knew where she was.

The two guards pulled matching, black-tinted sunglasses from their pants pockets and placed them across their eyes. They crowded around her, walking along with solemn expressions and nudging her shoulders with their hands to urge her forward. She was escorted out of the building and across the prison grounds.

Since she had never been to this compound before, she found herself comparing this new center of operations to the old secret police headquarters, a place she had visited a number of times during the 1980s, when family friend and mentor Dr. Fadil Al-Barrak worked there as Director General. At that time, she'd had no idea that the place she visited held such horrors. As far as Mayada knew, Dr. Fadil, as she called him, was a man in charge of Iraq's security, a man who protected Iraqis from dangerous opposition groups or internal terrorists. When she visited Dr. Fadil at the secret police headquarters, she went there to discuss his books or to explore her writing career.

But now Mayada felt overwhelming guilt for benefiting from her family's relationship with Dr. Fadil—she now understood that he had presided over a place where thousands of Iraqis were tortured to death. She now knew that she had deceived herself about the reality of her government's shameful activities, and that in her youthful naïveté she could not see her country as she should have. She compared long-forgotten things that she suddenly remembered from the old headquarters with what she was now seeing at this new center. Everything was different, and the new buildings reflected those changes.

When Dr. Fadil was Director General—or, as he was called by everyone in the secret police service, "Al-Sayid Al-Aam," or "Mr.

General"—the secret police headquarters was in Al-Masbah, close to Park Al-Sadoun, a Baghdad area that was once inhabited by Jews and Christians. The homes in that area were built in the old Baghdad style, with ornate shutters and large balconies, and generous gardens where laughing children would play games of hide-and-seek and hopscotch.

One beautiful Iraqi morning, government officials had unexpectedly arrived and confiscated those fine old homes from their owners, then built a high fence around the neighborhood and turned the area into a warren of buildings and streets with hidden chambers.

Dr. Fadil, who had ruled over the entire department and answered only to Saddam, had built himself a modern office in the midst of these old homes. The ground floor of his office building was a garage filled with new Japanese automobiles, which Mayada knew had been given as gifts by Saddam Hussein. Dr. Fadil's office was furnished with a huge mahogany desk and a dark leather couch, with two lofty chairs and glass coffee tables. The ceiling was constructed of small metal squares decorated in a pop-art image so dazzlingly bizarre that Mayada imagined it suitable for a dance club. His huge office had every modern convenience, including numerous monitors on which he could view every aspect of the rambling prison. Dr. Fadil's office also boasted such luxuries as video machines, which were then very rare in Iraq, as well as a small movie screen on which he invited close friends to view the latest Hollywood movies. He even had a large swimming pool constructed at his office.

In the spring of 1984, Dr. Fadil had been promoted and transferred to the Iraqi Intelligence Service, and his new offices were located at Sahat Al-Nosour, in the Al-Mansour area. Mayada had visited him in his new headquarters at various times until 1990, when Saddam ordered Fadil's arrest. She knew that if Dr. Fadil were still in charge she would be a welcomed visitor to Baladiyat, rather than a frightened prisoner.

Mayada and her two guards arrived at a solid block of concrete buildings. As she passed through the door she was taken into a spherically shaped office to the right of the entrance hall. There a small-boned man with a wrinkled face sat behind a circular desk. She eyed him closely. His face was wrinkled by worries, not by time. She could not explain how she knew that the man had been aged by what he had seen, rather than by the number of years that had passed, but somehow she knew.

He suddenly spoke. He ordered her to give him her possessions. He registered each item calmly: a ring, a watch, a wallet with 20,000 Iraqi dinars (about U.S. $10), a workbook with assignments for printing and design, a telephone book, a compulsory identification card, her keys and, finally, a note from her daughter Fay reminding her not to forget the luncheon date they had made for that day.

Another man suddenly came out of nowhere, grabbed her right hand and crushed her thumb onto an inkpad. He stamped an impression of her thumb on the list of her belongings. A second man then came into the room, and the two guards took her to the prison cells.

After passing a double door, she found herself in a long corridor lined with cell doors. The men stopped in front of the third door on the right. Mayada stood nervously while the thickset man unlocked the heavy padlock and gestured her to enter. Then she saw it. "52." Terrified, she cried out, "Noooooo."

She trembled in disbelief as she reached out toward the number. They were going to lock her into cell number 52. Her eyes began to prickle, then her flesh began burning from her toes to the top of her head. The number 52 pressed against her heart like an iron fist—52 was an unlucky number that had pursued her family for generations. Her beloved father had died at age 52, in room 52 at the Nun's Hospital. Her father's father, Jafar Pasha Al-Askari, had been assassinated at age 52. And now she was being locked into cell 52. Mayada felt certain that her arrest was as good as a death sentence. No! She could *not* enter that cell. No one could make her. She planted her feet firmly on the floor and looked around for something firm to cling to.

The pock-faced guard shouted. "Go in!"

Mayada's voice was jerky, the words she spoke almost inaudible. "I cannot. I cannot."

The guard's jaw tightened. *"Go in, I said!"*

The second man gave her a violent shove.

Mayada flew sprawling into cell number 52. She groped at the cell wall with her fingers to keep from falling. Her vision blurred as she slid her fingers over the cool wall.

She heard the slamming of the door and the click of the lock behind her. She was trapped. With her palms pressed hard against the wall, Mayada regained her balance. She stood in the middle of a small, rectangular cell.

Flushed and panting and confused by the fluorescent lights on the ceiling and the dancing shadows all around her, she broke into tears when she realized that the shadows were not actually shadows at all. The images formed into women, and one of the women walked toward her. In a voice filled with kindness she asked, "Why are you here?"

The woman who moved toward Mayada stood silent, aside from her question, giving Mayada time to gather her wits. She made an effort to respond to the woman's simple question, but could not speak. Instead, she flapped her hands and arms up and down. She did not know why she responded like this, and she worried what the other women must think. Genuinely frightened, she was afraid that the other women would call the guards to take her away to a mental ward. To avoid that fate, Mayada made a great effort to clear her lungs, which were bursting with tension. She struggled to force saliva onto her swollen tongue and into her dry mouth; she had had no water to drink since her morning arrest. She blinked her eyes several times in an attempt to adjust to the light. Mayada was too confused by the poorly lit interior of the cell to tally the indistinct silhouettes that she now knew were other prisoners, but she believed there were more than a dozen dark "shadow women." For some reason, their presence gave Mayada a feeling of unexpected consolation.

She later learned that she was prisoner number eighteen in a cell meant to hold eight prisoners, but as Mayada looked around at the overcrowded rectangular cell, that number might as well have been eighty. A toilet had been purposely placed in the cell's one spot that lay in the direction of the Kaaba in Mecca, the point toward which she was supposed to take her five daily prayers. This was an intentional insult against every Muslim, because all Islamic architecture takes great care to locate toilets as far away as possible from the direction of the Kaaba.

Mayada's mind was now moved from her thoughts of prayer by a terrible stench. She had never smelled such a disgusting odor, even during the worst of the war, when rescuers were tugging at burned bodies that had been concealed under concrete ruins for days. The cell's vile odor was so overwhelming that she could only imagine that it must have arisen from vomit covering the floor. She was so convinced that she stood in piles of filth that she lifted her sandals and examined the soles, but they were clean. She cautiously inhaled and decided that the odor was everywhere. She could only assume that the stench of lentils cooking in the prison kitchen had seeped through the cement of the cell, where it merged with the scent of unwashed bodies and the strong stench of the frequently used toilet.

Before turning her attention to the woman who had spoken, Mayada took another long look around the cell. Red, black and gray graffiti was scrawled on the walls—she hoped that the red messages weren't written in blood. She saw a glimmer of sunlight coming through a tiny barred window at the top of the back wall. Two iron benches that she presumed were bunks ran along the sides of the room.

The owner of the sympathetic voice stepped closer and a hand gently touched Mayada's shoulder. "Why are you here, little dove?" she asked.

Mayada looked into the woman's face and saw that she was beautiful. The woman's skin was extremely fair. She even had a few freckles scattered over her delicate nose. Her vivid green eyes shone.

The beautiful woman spoke again. "I am Samara. Why are you here?"

Other shadow women stepped forward to listen, and the expressions on their faces conveyed compassion for Mayada.

Mayada looked into their faces and shared the official explanation for her arrest. "The white-haired man told me that my printing company had printed something against the government, but that is not true. I have printed *nothing* against the government."

Hearing her own words caused Mayada to crack. The faces of her two children flashed before her eyes. She was going to take Fay to a luncheon and then to the dentist. Ali needed to go to the barber shop. Afterward they were going grocery shopping. Now she was frantic that Fay's infected tooth was hurting.

Only two days before, they had celebrated Fay's sixteenth birthday. Mayada had spent more money than she possessed to make her daughter happy. She had arranged for a birthday celebration in the Alwiya Club, a fashionable social club in Baghdad. Mayada's own grandparents and parents had held many celebrations in that club, so it was always fun to party there, a small way of anchoring Mayada and Fay and Ali firmly to their past.

Now, with her arrest, all of their lives were jeopardized in a way that would have seemed unbelievable yesterday. Mayada could no longer restrain the sorrow eating away at her and she cried out, "My children! There is no one to take care of them!"

Samara took one of Mayada's hands into her own and said, "Listen, you need to build a wall around everything you left behind. For now, you must think only about saving yourself. Otherwise, you will go crazy."

Mayada couldn't think normally, and she knew that nothing would ever make her stop worrying about her children. But something told her to take a deep breath and to listen. Samara could help her survive. Mayada nodded, but tears continued to stream down her cheeks. Mayada winced when she noticed for the first time that other than Samara, every face looked pale and hopeless.

It was clear that Samara was a practical woman when she ignored Mayada's tears and asked her, "Are you hungry? We will share what we have with you."

"No. Thank you. No, no." The thought of eating was nauseating.

Samara was so kindhearted that she insisted, "You must keep yourself strong. During the interrogations they try to break our spirit along with our bones."

When Samara saw a look of complete terror wash over Mayada's face, she placed her hand on Mayada's back. "Put the thought of your children in a little compartment for now. Surely someone on the outside will tend to their needs. Think only of yourself until you get out of here. They will bring us some lentils or rice soon, and if you do not want to eat now, I will save you a plate. But here is some advice." She leaned toward Mayada and whispered in a conspiratorial tone, "Never eat the eggplant. They served eggplant soup a month ago and we were all poisoned and could do nothing but lie on the floor writhing in pain for many days. We later heard that many prisoners died, although everyone in our cell survived."

Samara's advice chilled Mayada, and she thought she was going to collapse. Then, at first quietly but growing in volume, Mayada heard the most exquisite voice drifting through the cement walls of the prison. A male voice was reciting Surah 36 of the Quran, Al-Yasin. In the Muslim faith, it is believed that whoever recites those particular verses is granted the blessing of a wish. The beautiful voice was chanting, "For that my Lord has granted me forgiveness and has enrolled me among those held in honor!"

Mayada leaned her head against the gritty cell wall with the other shadow women and listened to the soothing verses.

The voice continued with the words of consolation, "Verily the companions of the garden shall that day have joy in all that they do. They and their associates will be in groves of (cool) shade, reclining on thrones (of dignity)."

A tall woman with big brown eyes muttered, "They are going to kill that poor soul if he doesn't stop."

Samara looked at the brown-eyed woman and said, "Roula, pray for him."

Her curiosity aroused by the superb voice she was hearing, Mayada lifted her head and asked, "Who is that?"

"That is a young man named Ahmed," Samara answered. "He's a Shiite who has been arrested because he converted to the Wahhabi sect."

The strict Wahhabi sect originated in Saudi Arabia. The Iraqi government forbade Iraqis from joining the group, which was considered dangerously radical by most other Muslims.

A third shadow woman, sitting on a metal bunk brushing her long red hair, added, "Ahmed has been here for six months. Every evening he recites the Quran. Every evening they take him out and beat him. His screams shatter the walls of our cell but the moment they return him to his cell, he begins reciting once again. He is very defiant." She nodded her head sadly.

"Yes, Wafae," Samara noted, "and he steadfastly recites even as they are beating him."

Mayada was now so exhausted that her legs could no longer support her frame. She slowly slipped downward, until she sat crumpled on the cool cement floor like some of the mentally disturbed beggars she had seen sitting on Baghdad street corners.

The other shadow women gathered around Mayada, and three or four lifted her from the floor and led her to one of the iron beds, as though she were a helpless baby. They tenderly sat her down, and she felt the comforting touch of a cotton cloak as it was laid upon her shivering body.

Iraqis can readily gauge the social status of another Iraqi, an intuition no prison cell can erase. Despite her exhaustion, Mayada overheard one of the shadow women, addressed as Asia by a second woman, whisper, "This may be our lucky night. With one of the well-born bunked in this cell, perhaps the guards will increase our quota of food."

Mayada was so dispirited that she lay in silence while the shadow women continued to gently question her. She did not wish to appear ungracious, but she could not find the strength to utter a single word in response to their inquiries.

Samara settled on the floor beside the iron bed and began to tell Mayada her story. "I am a Shiite. Despite the guaranteed difficulties awaiting Shiites at every official Iraqi corner, I am proud of my background.

"I've been told by family members that I was born an unusually pretty child. My maternal grandfather favored me from the first moment. So he asked my father to let me carry his name forward. My parents agreed, because they had more children than they could feed." Samara smiled. "Besides, I was but another daughter, not as valued as my brothers. So my official Iraqi identification papers were issued in the name of my grandfather, rather than my father's." She added proudly, "I grew up a bit of a legend in the region because many people claimed that I was very beautiful."

Mayada nodded in understanding. Iraqi society values nothing more than great beauty. And this shadow woman was a raving beauty.

"When I reached puberty, many men asked my grandfather for permission to marry me. So I was married at an early age to the best man of the lot. I had known him from childhood. He was a good man. And, although we were poor, we had no troubles until the Iran-Iraq war began. As you know, Shiites were not given the advantage of any government benefits, yet our men were expected to slip on their army fatigues with the enthusiasm of someone enticed with a plate of gold."

She turned her green eyes toward Mayada. "My husband, like every other man in the village, dutifully went off to war. I was grateful that he was allowed to come home several times a year, but his war breaks meant I became pregnant each time he visited." Her eyes suddenly narrowed. "Several days after the birth of my third child, I received word that my young husband had been killed during an important battle. Whether the battle was important or unimportant, nothing mattered to me but the fact my husband was dead. I was a young woman left alone with two sons and a daughter to feed. I became sleepless with worry.

"A few weeks after my husband's death, the government returned a coffin that they said contained his body. The accompanying official warned us not to open the coffin. We assumed the man was protecting our feelings, that he had been maimed. I didn't want to see my husband. I was afraid he had been so disfigured by those Iranian artillery shells that my eyes would be haunted by the sight of him. But one of my husband's brothers insisted that the coffin be opened." Samara turned to stare at Mayada. "When my husband's brothers disobeyed government orders and opened the coffin, what do you think they found?"

Mayada shook her head and asked, "What did they find?"

Samara's mouth flew open. "The coffin was filled with dirt!"

"Dirt?"

Samara clenched her jaw. "Yes. Dirt. Can you believe it?"

"What did you do then?"

Samara gestured, raising a hand in the air. "What could we do? If we complained about that dirt, then everyone would have been arrested for disobeying direct orders."

Samara continued, "The family had the burial service and everyone cried. We could never stop mourning, wondering if my husband was truly dead, or if he had been taken prisoner by the Iranians and was rotting in some Iranian cell. To this day, the truth of my husband's body remains a mystery."

Samara bristled at her memory. "That is Iraq for you."

Mayada sat silent and motionless, a great sadness overwhelming her.

"Then a second man proposed marriage soon after we buried that dirt. I was lucky once again. My second husband was a reasonable man who was kind to my poor, fatherless children."

Mayada looked thoughtfully at Samara. Most Arab women widowed and left with three children would have a difficult time finding a husband willing to assume the responsibility of another man's children. But this woman's flawless beauty was so striking that many men would want to marry her, Mayada was certain.

"We only had one problem. My second husband was not comfortable with the fact that I carried the name of my grandfather, rather than the name of my father. In his opinion, it was a sign of a father's shame that his daughter would owe immediate allegiance to another, even to her mother's father. So to make him happy I changed my official papers, in precisely the way the town officials advised."

For just a moment, Samara's face wore a sorrowful expression, then she smiled and patted Mayada on the arm. "You see, after the Iran-Iraq war and the Gulf War and U.N. sanctions, my husband found it impossible to find any work. Then by 1997 we were so desperate that we decided to leave the children with my first husband's family and go to Jordan. We had heard of other couples who had done this. So we bought cigarettes at a cheap price and sat on the pavement of Al-Hashimi in downtown Amman. We made a nice profit on those cigarettes. Not only were we able to support ourselves, but we had money left over to send back into Iraq, to help his family and mine. But we were stupid. We were so caught up in making enough money to feed everyone that we neglected our official papers. We overstayed our visa. We found ourselves stranded in Jordan. We didn't know what we were going to do. But after the sad death of His Majesty King Hussein in February 1999, his son Abdullah, the new sovereign, graciously pardoned all Iraqis without proper papers. In our desire to remain legal, we decided to return to Iraq in order to get our passports stamped. Our desire was to return to Amman after a visit with our family in Iraq." Her voice became wistful. "We loved Amman. I felt as free as a bird in that place."

She sighed deeply. "And so we came back to Iraq. I remember that trip like it was yesterday, even though so much has happened since then. I admit that my husband and I were feeling particularly happy on that day. We were relieved that our documents were in order and we knew we would soon see our loved ones. It had been nearly two years, you know. We made plans to treat his family and mine to some special fish and rice. But those dreams failed miserably. The minute we stepped inside Iraq, we were asked to step aside at the Iraqi border station. We were both startled and frightened. Despite our cries of innocence, we were detained and led away to prison. We were held in a shared cell in the Al-Ramadi secret police headquarters, the one near the Iraqi/Jordanian border. For six weeks. I was not tortured during our stay at Al-Ramadi. But my poor husband was beaten daily. After two weeks had passed, his torture got worse. The torturers at that place began to hoist him to the ceiling by his hands. Some days he was thrown back into our cell unconscious. I had nothing there. No water. Nothing. I remember I used to spit on his face to try to revive him."

Samara looked at Mayada. "I really did that. I spit on my poor husband's face. But that spit was out of love, not hatred." She tilted her head and looked to the ceiling. "We would have done anything to stop his torture. But how could we stop the torture if we did not know what it was we were accused of doing? Strangely enough, the guards didn't even know. When my husband asked them what it was he had done, they said they didn't know. The only thing they knew was that orders had come down to arrest us. But no cause for the arrests had been given, even to them.

"I truly thought my husband was going to die from those beatings. But just when I thought, this is the end for him, we were transferred here, to Baladiyat. But then there was another big shock. They separated us. Now I haven't seen my husband since March." She counted on her fingers. "Four months. It's been four months now. I don't know if he's dead or alive. And as far as I know, not a single member of my family or his knows where we are. They probably believe we're dead. Or, perhaps the government has returned a couple of dirt-filled coffins claiming that our bodies are inside." She then leaned down and whispered, "During my first interrogation here at Baladiyat, I finally discovered why we had been arrested in the first place."

Samara paused and took a cup of water offered by Wafae, the shadow woman with the long red hair, and held it against Mayada's lips.

Mayada insisted, "No. No. Really. I can drink nothing. Later."

Samara frowned but drank from the cup before continuing with her story.

Samara looked around at the peeling walls. "When I was called in for interrogation, I thought perhaps government officials had discovered we were innocent of all wrongdoing. The officer who questioned me was so polished and polite and nothing like the men who had imprisoned us at the border prison. He even asked me to sit down and have a cup of tea. He treated me like I was the lady of the house and he was the servant."

Samara continued. "This is what he asked me: 'Tell me, would you like to wear some earrings or would you like to wear some pantaloons?'

"I began to relax. His behavior convinced me that he was going to present me with a government-sanctioned gift for all the hardship I had endured. But I was embarrassed at his talk of pantaloons. I told him that ladies from my region did not wear pantaloons, but I let him know that I would be pleased with earrings, something I could sell for cash in Baghdad to buy presents for my children.

"He seemed relaxed, as well. He leaned on the edge of his desk. He smiled at me and then stood up. I thought he was going to get the earrings. My heart leaped with hope when he said, 'Our esteemed guest requests earrings, and earrings it will be.'

"I sat there like a fool with a big smile, but that smile left my face in a hurry. That man called in his assistants and they began to tie me up. They bound my hands and feet to the chair I was sitting in. Then, imagine my horror when they hooked a battery charger up to my ears. Before I could protest, that polite man turned the electricity on full force and stood there laughing at my pain and terror. The pain of that torture was far beyond that of childbirth. Each time the pain eased slightly, he flipped the switch again and again. Suddenly he stopped and I thought the nightmare was over, but then he said that in his opinion my feet needed some attention."

Samara held one small foot up in the air and Mayada thought that she had never seen such delicate white feet. But when Samara flipped her foot to the side, Mayada gasped in horror. The bottom of Samara's foot was crisscrossed with vivid scars of red that cut deep into her flesh.

Samara said, "Those pantaloons he mentioned now came as a surprise. As I sat there limp, waiting for the wood-like taste in my mouth to disappear, one of his assistants entered with a big pair of black pantaloon-like slacks that they slipped over my legs. I was picked up in the air and laid down on a special table. Those pantaloons were used to restrain my legs and feet. Then my feet were bound together in a wooden restraining device. That same evil man began to beat the soles of my feet with a special stick, and I soon found out what it was they believed I had done. He shouted at me as he beat my feet, 'Why did you change your name? Why did you change your papers? Who are you spying for? Is it Israel? Is it Iran?'"

Samara surprised Mayada with a smile and said, "For many weeks I had to lie in bed like a baby and couldn't even hobble to the toilet. The beatings took all the flesh from the soles of my feet. Then they became infected and I believed I was going to die. But I slowly recovered, and now I can walk again. Since that first day, I've been called in on a daily basis. Some days they just question me. Other days they beat me on my back. Then the next day they beat me on my feet. Sometimes they will put me on the electricity. They ask the same questions. I give the same answers."

Samara bent her head over her drawn-up knees. "I've told them over and over. I am a simple woman. Fate made me the favorite of a doting grandfather. This grandfather wanted me to carry his name. My second husband asked me to go back to my father's name. And that is the only reason I changed my documents. That is the whole story."

Samara's face crumpled. "They have told me that I will stay here until I confess to being a spy, but I have nothing to confess. I am not a spy, and no matter how many times they shoot me with electricity or how many times they beat me, I will never say I am something I am not."

Samara was in an impossible situation. The men of Baladiyat would not stop the torture until she confessed to spying for Iran or for Israel, yet if she admitted such a thing, whether true or false, she would be put to death.

Samara looked at Mayada and smiled widely. "The only positive thing that has happened to me in the last week is that my torturer has been transferred to oversee a prison in Basra, and the man who has replaced him is not as obsessed with the stick or with the electricity. Be glad for that, because the first man was so evil that I believe if he were bitten by the most poisonous snake, the snake would die!"

At that moment Mayada felt a rushing pain down her arm and into her chest. It was the first time she had ever suffered such throbbing, but she knew such running pains were the symptom of a heart attack. In the next second, her fingers began to go numb. She reached for Samara and told her, "I believe I am having a heart attack. Can you get a doctor, please?"

Samara leaped to her feet and grabbed an empty pot made of iron. She ran to the metal door and began banging with the pot and shouting, "We need help!"

After a long moment someone came to the door and opened the little slot. "What is the problem?"

Samara shouted, "I think this new woman is having a heart attack!"

Mayada suddenly realized that none of the shadow women even

knew her name. She tried to push herself up on her arms to gain their attention. She wanted to tell the women something of herself, so that if she died she could depend on any woman released to search out her children and relieve them of the anxiety of not knowing how their poor mother had left this earth. She told them, "Please, please listen. I am Mayada Al-Askari and I live at Wazihiya Place and my phone number is 425-7956. If I die, or if I do not return, please have someone call my daughter Fay and tell her what happened to me."

One of the shadow women scrambled to find a small piece of charred wood they kept for such a purpose. Samara grabbed it from the woman's hand and asked, "Repeat the information." Samara wrote the details on the wall with the charred stick. She told Mayada, "Do not worry. You will return to your children. But if for some reason you do not, your children will be informed, by the first woman to gain freedom, that you were here."

The man had left without saying what he might do and Mayada suffered the sinking feeling that she was going to be left to die. But in a few minutes two new men arrived, although it was clear they had been interrupted while eating. One was still chewing and the other was using his fingers to pull some food caught between two teeth. The one chewing swallowed, and asked, "Who is the troublemaker?"

Samara told him, "It is not a joke." She then pointed to Mayada. "That woman is having heart problems."

The man sighed with irritability, and marched toward Mayada. He stood and stared at her face for a minute, then took his finger and poked her in the chest as if he could that way ascertain the seriousness of her condition. He shouted for Mayada to get up and follow him. Samara and another shadow woman who was tall and strong came to Mayada and pulled her to her feet. Slowly the two women walked to the door with Mayada before releasing her to the two men.

The hospital was only one building away, but Mayada had to pace her steps due to the escalating chest pains. One of the two men kept whining about his supper growing cold and the second complained about her rate of speed. He asked her why a young woman walked with the gait of an old woman. Since Mayada believed she was going to drop dead of a heart attack, she voiced her opinion of their conduct, telling them that they should be ashamed to treat an ill woman this way. Her bold words won her a slap on the side of the head from one man and a shout from the second man.

Mayada and her guards finally reached the hospital. Although the exterior of the building was new and modern, the interior was untidy and filthy. The two men led her to an examining room.

One of the guards said, "I'll go find Dr. Hadi Hameed," before walking away.

The other guard stood at the door, watching her.

The guard quickly returned with a white-coated doctor who was walking with his head down, staring at his feet. His demeanor gave her the impression he was elderly. But when he raised his face to her, she saw that he was a young man with a handsome face and dark eyes. The doctor startled Mayada when he expressed concern for her situation. Then he politely asked her to sit up on the examining table, and he proceeded to take her blood pressure. The doctor looked at Mayada with worry in his kind eyes, and told her what she already knew: Her blood pressure was dangerously high. Searching his caring face, Mayada reminded herself that her prison experience might cause her to adopt an unreasonably simple view of human nature. She must remember that many Iraqis were forced against their will to join the Baath party. These same people were coerced to accept government jobs that were unsuitable for anyone with a compassionate heart. She believed that this doctor was one of those people.

He proved Mayada right when he glanced over his shoulder and noted that the two men had stepped away. The doctor spoke to her in a low voice. "There is nothing wrong with you that release will not cure. But since your fate is not in my hands, I will give you some tablets that I believe will settle your heart." He then turned to open a drawer in a metal cabinet and selected a packet of small pink pills, handing them to Mayada and instructing her, "Put one under your tongue and let it dissolve. Anytime you feel a chest pain, you should do the same thing." But he cautioned, "Do not to take more than one pill every few days if you can avoid it. These pills cause severe headaches."

The pill was already in her mouth. She nodded.

The doctor turned away and began to document her visit.

As the pill dissolved, Mayada looked around the room. She noted that the examination table was covered with black plastic, and the plastic was covered with the heavy dust of that morning's sandstorm. That sand might now work in her favor, Mayada mused. This doctor's caring manner had given her an idea. Confident enough to take a risk, she used her finger to write the telephone number of her children's grandfather—who had remained friendly to her and the children even after the divorce—in the dust. Mayada then appealed to the doctor's kind heart. She asked him, "Dr. Hameed, please call this number and tell whoever answers that Mayada has been taken to Baladiyat. Tell them to call my mother, Salwa, in Amman. She will know what to do." Mayada stared at the young doctor.

Dr. Hameed gazed at Mayada for a long moment. His expression clearly displayed the internal battle raging between his head—which warned him of the dire consequences of discovery—and his heart, which was shattered by the human despair he was forced to witness. Dr. Hameed stared down at the number Mayada had written in the dust. She breathlessly watched his lips move. He was memorizing the number, Mayada realized. The doctor looked over his shoulder once again, then picked up a cloth to wipe the dust and the digits from the plastic. He gave no sign as to whether his head or his heart had prevailed. Yet Mayada knew that whether he called or not, he *wanted* to have the courage to call. She must remember that the two of them—and all Iraqis—now lived in a terrible time, and this good man could be tortured to death for deviating from Baathist Party rules of conduct.

Mayada opened her mouth to ask if she could rely upon his humanity. But at that moment, the two guards returned, insisting that they must return her to her cell. Mayada froze, fearful that Dr. Hameed might be so anxious about the safety of his own loved ones that he would tell these men of Mayada's request for assistance. But the doctor said nothing. Instead, he looked her straight in the eyes and said, "You will be better, so go back and try to get some sleep." His words gave Mayada hope that he would make the call that might save her life.

The men rushed her back to cell 52, although she asked them to walk slowly to accommodate her chest pains. But the two paid no heed. The rapid pace made her heart throb, and she was surprised at the sense of relief she felt upon reentering cell 52.

Samara rushed to Mayada's side and helped her back to the bunk, and several shadow women gathered around to make her comfortable. Mayada was given a folded blanket for a pillow, while another was placed between her and the cold bunk. A third blanket covered her body. The women had been served their supper while Mayada was in the hospital. As promised, Samara had saved her a plate, but Mayada could not eat.

The women began talking about their own lives. Mayada learned that a woman named Iman was a Shiite from the south. Another woman named Safana was a Kurd. Another nameless woman was a Sunni from Baghdad. They asked Mayada to tell them everything she had seen while outside the cell. Mayada sighed heavily as she told them she could not yet speak, but that tomorrow she would gladly answer all their questions.

One of the shadow women spoke up and asked the question that Mayada had been expecting since relating her family name. "Just tell us, are you related to the great Jafar Pasha Al-Askari?"

Mayada paused, thinking about her answer for a moment. She considered denying the fact, because people would often begin to behave as though she considered herself better than others, which was not the case. And some people, upon hearing of her lineage, would turn into devoted enemies for no reason at all. Still others would shift their normal behavior and treat Mayada with reverence, as if she were a member of a royal family. But looking into the kind eyes of the simple women who shared her cell, Mayada was struck with a deep certainty that they would remain the same considerate women, no matter whose bloodline she shared. "Yes," she admitted with a weak smile, "Jafar Pasha was my grandfather, the father of my own father, Nizar Al-Askari."

The shadow woman reached down and touched Mayada's cheek with a decided tenderness and told her, "My grandfather once met your grandfather when he came to the south collecting votes for King Faisal I. He always said Jafar Al-Askari was a great Iraqi. Many times I heard him say, 'If only we had men like Jafar Pasha still among the living, we Iraqis could have avoided this nightmare.' "

As if those words had unleashed their voices, the other shadow women began to exchange memories of a time when Iraqis had hope for a better future. Mayada overheard several others declare quietly that Jafar Pasha had made beneficial differences in the lives of their own families, too. Samara looked down at Mayada and smiled. "We will repay that great man by taking good care of his granddaughter."

2

The Four
Black Doors

Throughout history, there have been great men who united them-
selves with important moments. During and after World War I, Jafar
Al-Askari, Nouri Al-Said, King Faisal I, Lawrence of Arabia and Sati
Al-Husri were such men. Three of them were closely related to
Mayada, and she knew their lives as she knew her own.

In 1918, at the end of the Great War, 400 years of Ottoman
power had finally ended. No government ruled Iraq, and the Iraqi
people found themselves with a chance for a new beginning. The British and French governments, which had helped them defeat the Ottomans, promised freedom for all Arabs. And compelled by this dream,
Jafar, Nouri, Lawrence of Arabia, and Faisal risked their lives many
times.

But no man was more daring than Mayada's grandfather, Jafar
Al-Askari.

It was perhaps a twist of fate that Jafar Al-Askari was born at the
same time the Ottoman Empire was dying. He entered the world on
June 13, 1885, and his parents, Mustafa and Fatima, were living in
Baghdad, where his father was serving as the Military Governor of
Iraq and the Chief of Staff of the Fourth Army.

Jafar favored his father in every way, with chestnut hair and brown eyes that flashed with gold, and a brilliant mind that allowed him to excel in military strategy, languages and politics.

As a son of an Army Chief of Staff, Jafar received the finest education. And because his father was a military man, that schooling was directed toward the art and practice of soldiering. Then tragedy struck. Mustafa noticed a red mark on his shoulder, a mark the Turks call a "Lion's Paw." Whether the mark was a cancerous melanoma or perhaps even anthrax is unclear, but Mustafa was bed-ridden and soon died a painful death.

Though he mourned the death of his father, Jafar went on to complete his education. While at military school, he met his lifelong best friend, Nouri Al-Said. The two men grew so close that they made a pact to marry each other's sister, and followed through on it: Nouri married Jafar's younger sister, Naeema, and Jafar married Nouri's sister, Fakhriya.

When World War I broke out, Jafar fought with the Ottomans and the Germans, quickly becoming a highly decorated general, but Jafar was so uniquely talented that the British approached him to fight on their side. Jafar refused their appeals until Sultan Mohammed Resat ordered the execution of several of Jafar's friends. He became disillusioned with the Ottoman cause and agreed to the requests of T. E. Lawrence (Lawrence of Arabia) and Prince Faisal of the Hijaz (later to become King Faisal of Syria and Iraq) to join the Arab Army. It was during the war that Jafar and Prince Faisal became close friends. Jafar Al-Askari became the Commander of the Arab Regular Forces. He was the only man in World War I awarded the top military decoration from both the Germans and the British.

When the British occupied Iraq after the war, they had great difficulty keeping Iraqi tribesmen from attacking their soldiers. In order to appease the Iraqis, the British chose to assume an indirect role in ruling the country, and set up a monarchy supervised by the British government. After much discussion and with the encouragement of

British representatives in Iraq, Winston Churchill decided that Prince Faisal, whose father ruled Mecca and Medina, would be Iraq's new king, despite the fact that Faisal had never set foot inside Iraq's borders.

When Faisal arrived in Iraq to take over the country, his close friends and former army commanders Jafar Al-Askari and Nouri Al-Said were there waiting to serve him. Hundreds of Englishmen and Iraqis gathered on the banks of the Tigris River for Faisal's coronation. The proclamation was read in Arabic, announcing that Faisal had won the election of the people, and a band played the British anthem, "God Save the King," much to the shock of the Iraqis present.

Jafar served as Minister of Defense and Nouri served as Chief of Staff. From that first day there were many struggles, but the three men held the country together by sheer determination. Then, in 1933, after only twelve years of rule, King Faisal became very ill with heart problems, left for Switzerland, and died there at the age of forty-eight. Prince Ghazi, King Faisal's only son, became King Ghazi I.

Jafar had lived in London for a number of years, but in 1934, his friend and brother-in-law, Nouri, who was now the Iraqi Prime Minister, appealed to Jafar to return and help him run the government. Nouri explained to Jafar that he faced so many foes in Iraq that he needed the strength Jafar represented by his side. Jafar adored England, where he said he needed only to carry a walking stick—unlike Iraq, where he needed to be armed at all times. Nevertheless, the situation in Iraq was becoming more and more turbulent, and Jafar finally agreed to Nouri's appeal, once again assuming the position of Minister of Defense.

Two years later, in October 1936, Jafar ordered the army to perform a series of routine exercises, but he was met with a surprise. A man that Jafar believed to be his friend, General Bakir Sidqi, Commander of the Second Division of the Army, decided to stage a military coup, the first in modern Iraq.

Three airplanes dropped bombs, and while one fell harmlessly in the Tigris, the other two hit the Ministry of the Interior and the building that housed the Council of Ministers. Another bomb hit the main post office building.

Jafar decided to meet the army and stop it from marching on Baghdad. The British Ambassador Sir Clark Keer was there when Jafar made the vow, and Keer later wrote that Jafar's mission was an act of sheer gallantry, a bravery no other man in the government possessed. King Ghazi was concerned for Jafar's safety, but Jafar said it was his duty to protect the king and the country. As Jafar was leaving, King Ghazi apparently shuddered with a premonition. He ran out of the palace to stop Jafar, but it was too late—Jafar was gone.

Jafar could not know that his friend Sidqi had asked five of his associates to kill him. The first four of the five said they would never kill a man as noble as Jafar Al-Askari. The fifth man however—Captain Jameel, a man who had never met Jafar—agreed to serve as the assassin.

A number of Sidqi's troops met Jafar on the outskirts of Baghdad and told him they would escort him to Sidqi. Jafar was asked to sit in the front seat, and soon realized that something was amiss. He turned in his seat to face the men, saying, "I have a feeling you people are going to kill me. But I am not afraid of dying. Dying is the natural end of every human life. I tell you, however, that if you start killing, you will be held accountable for all the hardship you will put this country through. You will create a river of blood."

When the car stopped at Sidqi's camp and Jafar got out, Captain Jameel shot him in the back. Jafar lived only long enough to turn around and cry out, "Noooooo!" A hasty grave was dug in the sand and Jafar was buried. Bakir Sidqi swore his men to secrecy.

When Jafar failed to return to the palace, the country descended into chaos. Jafar had been the glue that held the government together. Sidqi took over Baghdad and forced King Ghazi to name a new government.

The Arab world was shocked that Jafar Al-Askari was dead. Sadly, Jafar's prediction that Iraq would become a river of blood came true. Sidqi was soon assassinated by officers loyal to Jafar. The royal family remained at the head of numerous rotating governments, as one military coup followed another.

In 1958, the royal family invited Mayada's parents to accompany them on a holiday before returning for the wedding of the king, Faisal II, but Mayada's mother, Salwa, insisted that Mayada have a French Dior gown for her role as flower girl in the wedding.

Mayada was only three, but her mother had arranged a fitting at a French Dior shop in Geneva. The family was in Europe when they heard that General Abdul Karim Qasim, an army officer, had ordered a number of soldiers to surround the royal palace. Over a loudspeaker, they ordered the family to step outside. It was only 7:45 in the morning, but soon afterward, the kitchen door at the back of the palace opened and the royals began to spill out. The officers shouted for the family to step toward the little garden at the side of the palace and stand next to a huge mulberry tree. The royal family lined up, along with the servants. The very young king, confused, kept saluting the officers.

A captain by the name of Al-Obousi shot at the king, splitting his skull open. Everyone else then opened fire. After the massacre, the bodies of the family were dragged to a van, and a crowd began to loot the palace.

As the van passed through the palace gate, a man at the gate jumped into the van and stabbed all the dead bodies. The van was then stopped by a military jeep, whose soldiers took the bodies of the young king and the regent. Crowds had begun to gather, and to pacify the angry mob, the driver threw them the body of Faisal's regent, which was promptly stripped naked, dragged across Baghdad and hung from one of the balconies at the Al-Karhk Hotel. The crowd then cut off his hands, arms, feet, legs and genitals, ripped open his mouth, then dragged what remained of his body to the Ministry of Defense and hung it there. A young man from the crowd then took a dagger and ripped open his belly and several men in the crowd draped the regent's intestines around their necks, like necklaces, and danced in the streets. Finally, someone took the regent's body, splashed it with gasoline and set it on fire. The remains were thrown in the river.

The young king was taken to the Al-Rasheed Military Hospital, where the doctors pronounced him dead. His body was temporarily buried on the hospital grounds, to avoid a similar mutilation by the crowds. Other family members were also buried there.

Prime Minister Nouri Al-Said, the uncle of Mayada's father, was on the run. He had heard about the massacre and knew there was nothing he could do but save himself. Nouri was an old man by then, but the crowds nevertheless wanted him dead, as well. A neighbor, Um Abdul Ameer Al-Estarabadi, urged Nouri to escape to the Um-mara tribes, who would give him refuge. Nouri put on a woman's abaaya (cloak) for camouflage. Unfortunately, Nouri and the neighbor decided to stop along the river in Abu Nawas, and someone in a passing mob spotted a man's shoes beneath a woman's abaaya. Sensing something was amiss, they seized Nouri. He was bound and tied to the rear of a car and dragged through the streets of Baghdad.

The mob threw Nouri's lifeless body into the street, where cars took turns running over him. Others used knives to cut off his fingers. Later, a well-known lady from a good family in Baghdad went around to parties showing off one of Nouri's fingers in a silver cigarette box. Baghdad had been turned upside down.

After Nouri's family heard about the killing, his son Sabah went to ask for his father's body, so the family could have a proper burial. Sabah was murdered and dragged through the streets, as well.

And as Jafar predicted, the coups continued, finally leading to the emergence of the Baath Party, led by Ahmed Hassan al-Bakir and Saddam Hussein. Its aims were a socialist, secular government that would aspire to Pan-Arab unity and Arab rule in the face of foreign domination.

The Baath Party first came to power in Iraq in February 1963, but was overthrown before the end of that year. A more powerful Baath movement guided by Saddam Hussein returned to Iraq in 1968. For Mayada, the Baath Party had become a never-ending nightmare, the root of so many of Iraq's troubles.

That first night in prison was the longest night she had ever spent. Her eyes wide open, she thought of her family, of Fay and Ali, and blamed herself for not leaving when her mother had warned her that Iraq was finished. Mayada retraced the history of Saddam's Iraq in her mind and realized that while Iraqis were being lulled into tranquility by Saddam's charismatic personality, he was crafting four black doors to contain—and obscure—his evil.

In 1980, Saddam had been the President of Iraq for only a year, and many Iraqis still believed in his greatness, but he was actually plotting the first of two wars that would ruin Iraq.

It was a peaceful September day. Baghdad was still wrapped in the cool of the morning. Mayada and her husband, Salam, were having an early breakfast at her mother's home. She watched him eat and contemplated what he would look like when he was old. She hoped that she would not be around to see his black hair turn gray and his body thicken from all of the eggs, toast, milk and sugar he liked to consume.

Mayada had discovered on their honeymoon that she had made a mistake when she agreed to be his wife. Now she toyed frequently with the idea of leaving him, but women in the Middle East approach divorce with extreme caution. So she had accepted that she would be one of many millions of women who live without complaint in a loveless marriage.

Mayada had another reason for feeling anxious. Salam had recently been drafted into compulsory military service; he was now uncomfortably attired in his army fatigues. He tugged at his sleeves and pulled at the crotch of his trousers, which had been washed only once and were still stiff. He was dressed as a warrior, yet Mayada could not connect the idea of violence with this man now living so intimately with her. As these ideas were working their way through her mind, her mother's house was shaken by a loud "swooooosh," followed by the blasts of lesser reverberations. Dishes rattled, lights flickered and her mother's three brightly feathered finches fluttered nervously from one side of their cage to the other. Fear washed through her body and settled into her stomach. "Salam, are those Israeli planes?"

Salam's face flickered in astonishment while small beads of sweat formed on his skin. His husky voice took on a strange high tone. "No. No. It cannot be."

Mayada's heart beat faster as she waited for the piercing sounds of sirens, but the air around them was silent. Salam moved quickly to turn on the radio, but routine programming filled the airwaves. Mayada was working at the *Al-Jumhuriya* newspaper in Baghdad, so she decided to ring the office. As her hand reached for the receiver the phone startled her with an incoming ring. She lifted the receiver and heard the voice of Dr. Fadil Al-Barrak, a recent acquaintance of her family. Dr. Fadil was the head of the Secret Police, the man that everyone knew answered only to Saddam Hussein. It was uncharacteristic that a soft-spoken gentleman such as Dr. Fadil held a position that placed him in charge of internal security, but soon after Saddam assumed complete power, he had revamped the intelligence organizations. Saddam had said that an ignorant man was less trustworthy than an intelligent man, and had appointed a number of highly educated Iraqis to prominent positions. Dr. Fadil was an enormously powerful person in Iraq, overseeing many security departments, including security affairs, Islamic movements, military defectors sections, economic security, opposition groups, drug affairs and others.

Few people in Iraq had the ear of men in such high positions, but Mayada thought little of it at the time, because her parents and grandparents had always been connected to important world leaders.

Truthfully, though, Dr. Fadil had an unusual relationship with her family. While he had become a family friend, Mayada's mother, Salwa, had never actually invited him to occupy that role. Dr. Fadil was a writer and had come to their family requesting to see the books and papers belonging to Mayada's famous maternal grandfather, Sati Al-Husri.

Mayada's family thought nothing of the request, since Sati's writings on Arab Nationalism and Arab educational programs were frequently used as a reference for many Arab writers. From that simple beginning, Dr. Fadil had become a more frequent guest in their home.

On that fateful day Dr. Fadil skipped his usual niceties. "Is Salam serving in Baghdad?"

Mayada felt a flicker of surprise over his concern for her husband's safety. Dr. Fadil had disapproved of her marriage from the first moment, because Salam was from a very well-known feudal family. His father had owned slaves until 1960, and a revolutionary Baathist like Dr. Fadil deliberately avoided former slave owners. Nevertheless, his closeness to the family had not ended, and he had even given Mayada an expensive piece of jewelry on her wedding day.

"No, he is serving in Al-Mahaweel," Mayada answered, referring to a military base in southern Iraq. Sensing that something unusual was afoot, she asked Fadil what was going on.

He whispered ominously, "This is your pin-up hero waging war against us." She knew immediately what he meant, and also understood that the warplanes had nothing to do with Iraqi internal friction but instead related to the growing tension between Iran and Iraq. Despite the seriousness of the moment, she almost laughed aloud at his mention of her "pin-up hero," for she understood how a foolish incident that meant nothing, really, had so angered this man who considered himself a loyal supporter of her family.

The incident had occurred during her engagement and was directly linked to a 1979 student gathering at the Al-Mustansiriya University in Baghdad. Several bombs exploded during the gathering, killing two students and wounding many others. A week after the bombing there was a huge student march from the University to the Bab Al-Muaadam cemetery, where the slain students had been buried. The demonstration meandered through the city and even passed through the main street close to her mother's home. Two government ministers were heading the march, so there were numerous police cars, secret police and intelligence agents patrolling the entire area. When the demonstration passed by her mother's home, two hand grenades were tossed into the procession. The house next to her mother's home was occupied by the Iranian consulate, and so the Iraqi secret police immediately assumed the violence had originated there.

Mayada's family home was a beautiful one with large balconies. Her bedroom had a wide veranda that extended out above their garden and overlooked the consulate. Security forces had to pass through her bedroom to look out on the balcony, from which they planned to shoot into the home of the Iranian representative.

A few weeks before, Mayada had cut and pasted on her wall a catchy photograph of Ayatollah Khomeini, showing the scowling cleric in his black turban framed against a fuchsia background.

When the secret police burst into her room and spotted the image of their enemy, they were so stunned that they forgot they were in pursuit of dangerous rebels and instead rushed to report her treason to the authorities. The Iranians were saved from a barrage of bullets on that day because the young woman Mayada Al-Askari had posted a picture of the Shiite cleric Khomeini on her wall. Such an offense was considered treasonous by the minority Sunni government. But Mayada was too young and too confident to believe she could be in serious trouble for pasting a photograph on her wall.

When Dr. Fadil was told about this incident, he phoned her. The usual warmth of his voice cooled as he informed her that he would be passing by the house at ten o'clock that evening and to please not toss her precious jewel box here and there for everyone to see. She understood his reference at once, for in Iraq when one wishes to scorn a person they say the opposite, and although Khomeini was called a "jewel box" by Dr. Fadil, the cultural translation meant that Dr. Fadil's enemy was in reality a piece of slime.

Dr. Fadil was a man of his word. He arrived promptly at ten that evening, and although his face was calm, his manner bore a distinct frostiness. A tall man, he stood at his full height as he looked down at

Mayada, and she noticed that his left eye was smaller than his right eye. For the first time, she felt that Dr. Fadil was not exactly the kindly man he pretended to be. He squeezed his lips together before asking Mayada's mother, Salwa, for a glass of scotch. He took a long gulp before returning his full attention to Mayada.

A man so close to Saddam possessed great power within the Iraqi governmental hierarchy, and he had the might to have her crushed like an insect, but he loosened up a bit after the scotch passed his lips and began to lecture her like a schoolmaster about their neighbors, the Iranians. He twisted his glass in his hands as he gathered his words and said, "You should have seen Khomeini when he was deported from Iran. He had nothing and we opened up our country to him. He lived in Iraq for many years as a welcomed refugee and when Saddam approached him to speak to the Shiite people against the Shah, who was doing nothing but trying to topple our government, he refused." The soft-spoken Dr. Fadil surprised Mayada and her mother with a sudden outburst. "The man is nothing more than a Persian with shit stuffed inside his bones!" Visibly struggling to gain control of his emotions, he cleared his throat and lowered his voice. "Behind his pious facade he's conspiring with the imperialists."

Mayada was still naïve in those days, believing that no harm would come her way; she struggled to hold back a laugh but sensed that Dr. Fadil was at a breaking point. His lowered lids couldn't conceal the anger in his eyes, and his olive skin had reddened with passion, but she was still brave enough to say, "I thought the Baath Party preaches democracy, and if this is the case, why can't I hang up the picture of my enemy on the wall? I should have the right to hang any picture I please in my bedroom." When he took a deep breath she saw that he was growing even more serious, and so she tried to ease the moment with lighter words. "The color contrast of the pink and black was what caught my eye." She laughed. "It was the color, not the cleric."

Dr. Fadil was furious at her careless words, and he shouted about her lack of Arab loyalty against the Persian beasts. Her mother was a wise woman and knew the ways of men. She replenished his scotch and murmured, "It is good you are here to guide my daughter. She has no father, you know."

Mayada felt a surge of anger at her mother, cringing at the idea that any other man might consider himself a substitute for her father, Nizar Al-Askari.

She loved her father with a great passion. March 2, 1974—the day her father had died after a long bout with colon cancer—was the saddest day of her life. She could still barely think about her father, and any time the memory of his suffering came to her, sadness would creep through her body like a spreading darkness, and she would actually become ill. But now she remembered the gentle masculine love that enveloped the three women her father loved most, his wife Salwa and his two daughters, Mayada and Abdiya. During his last conversation with his girls, he had been frantic with the knowledge that he was going to die very soon and would be leaving his daughters without a father's protection. He had trembled while telling Salwa that Mayada *must* go to medical school at the American University in Beirut, that he had the funds in a bank in Lebanon for that purpose and that Abdiya should follow her sister. He had looked at Abdiya and called her his "little kitty," and emphasized that education should be her main goal in life. Her father's devotion to learning was understandable because he was a highly educated man who had studied economics at the American University of Beirut and then went on to read economics at King's College at Cambridge, where his tutor was the well-known economist John Maynard Keynes.

With her mother's words still ringing in her ears, Mayada felt an unexpected spasm of hatred toward Dr. Fadil, hatred that he had lived while her own father had died, even though she knew such thoughts were sinful—only God could make such determinations. She watched as her mother placated the man with her soothing words, yet she was thinking that a person couldn't appease ruthlessness for very long. For the first time, she was beginning to suspect that Dr. Fadil had a merciless element to his character previously unknown to her or her mother. She thought back to how other Iraqis reacted to his name and to the fact that she knew him. Some veiled their eyes and glanced away, suddenly remembering long-forgotten tasks that needed their attention, while others lavished on her a respect she had not earned—and in the next breath asked her to intervene and assist them in getting this job or that plot of land.

She wanted to ask him why Iraqis reacted to his name with such obvious trepidation, but her mother furtively pinched her arm and gave her a penetrating look.

Dr. Fadil obviously liked the idea of lending a guiding hand to the granddaughter of the legendary Sati Al-Husri. He smiled and then drank some more scotch. He teased Mayada's mother about the foolishness of children. Before he left the house, he reminded Mayada that without his protection, the discovery of her pin-up hero would have landed Mayada's entire household in prison for an extended term. When Dr. Fadil finally departed at midnight, Mayada grudgingly admitted that her mother was a genius in manipulating such awkward situations.

And it was this same Dr. Fadil, who still remembered that incident, that now informed her that Iran and Iraq were at war. He told her that Iranian planes had entered Iraqi airspace and passed over Baghdad, although he claimed that Iraqi heroes had now chased them back across the border.

After hanging up the telephone, she reported to Salam what she had learned and then watched as her husband blundered through the house gathering a few supplies to take with him to the front. She felt a sickening realization wash over her that Salam might well be the first battlefront casualty. Although Mayada did not wish to be married to the man, neither did she want him to die.

Women in the Middle East generally accept the rituals of marriage and child-raising without question. Mayada was no exception.

By the time she was twenty-three years old, she had considered marriage more than once.

When an attractive man named Salam Al-Haimous walked into her newspaper office to place an ad, the shy-mannered man quickly won her attention. When he saw Mayada, Salam mentioned that they were next-door neighbors. Mesmerized by his gorgeous face, Mayada wondered how she had failed to notice him. But from that day on, she grew more observant. When Mayada next arrived at her home, Salam waited outside to greet her. Despite Salwa's misgivings about the marriage, Mayada and Salam had gained the blessings of both parents within a few months.

As soon as the ceremony ended, the joyous couple left Baghdad for a lengthy European honeymoon. Mayada had traveled the world regularly since she was a child, but Salam had never been out of Iraq. Within an hour of boarding the aircraft, Salam made it clear that as an Arab sheik, he insisted his wife hide her knowledge in front of others. He explained with a grin, "I will handle everything. I am the man."

In Italy, Salam wanted to ride all the trains. Mayada adored the museums. Salam liked the gambling casinos. Mayada browsed the libraries.

Country by country, the marriage quickly unraveled.

In Spain, Mayada discovered that Salam thought Picasso, the world-famous painter, was the name of a food dish.

And with that, Mayada realized she had made the biggest mistake of her life.

Still, she dreaded the thought of Salam risking his life in war.

That September morning was only the beginning of years of crushing losses. The ensuing war between Saddam and Khomeini led to the deaths of 1.5 million men, women and children.

Actually, the source of the hostility had begun when Mayada was only a child. At the time of Mayada's youth, Khomeini was a cranky but unknown religious cleric. Believing that the secular government of the Shah of Iran was ruining the religious life of Iran's Shiite society,

Khomeini was blunt in his criticism of the Shah. An impatient Shah then exiled Khomeini, who fled across the border into Iraq, where he lived for fifteen years in An-Najaf, the Shiite holy city. Khomeini continued to stir up dissent against any ruler not faithfully following the tenets of Islam's Shiite branch—including the regime of his host, Saddam Hussein. In the Middle East, dictators and kings tread softly around the words of religious clerics, for many Muslims are willing to die for such men.

A year before that September bombing, Saddam received a request from the Shah to exile Khomeini from Iraq. In return, the Shah agreed to stop supplying Iraq's Shiite population with weapons. Such a promise was welcome to the new Iraqi dictator, who was a member of the Sunni minority. He distrusted Iraq's Shiite majority, and saw this simple request as an easy way to help solidify his rule. Besides, he was already seething with anger over Khomeini's refusal to criticize the Shah on Saddam's behalf. Saddam quickly moved to deport the disruptive cleric from Iraq. A year later, when Khomeini returned from exile in Paris and assumed control of the Iranian government, he proved that he was actually a devoted enemy of Saddam Hussein. Tensions continued to build, and when the Iraqi Shiites formed a group called "al-Da'wah al Islamiyah," or the "Islamic Call," which was designed to stage riots and call for a fundamentalist government based on the Iranian model, Saddam moved against his own Shiite population, making wholesale arrests in every Shiite village and ordering death sentences for prominent Shiite leaders. The al-Da'wah responded with the attempted assassination of Iraqi Foreign Minister Tariq Aziz.

The long-ago rift between two obstinate opponents, Khomeini and the Shah, had hardened the animosity between the governments of Iran and Iraq. Feeling threatened by this new and increasingly cantankerous enemy at his border, Saddam justified a military attack by rejecting the 1975 Algiers agreement with Iran, which had given that country sovereignty over the Shatt-al-Arab, a narrow waterway that was Iraq's only access to the Persian Gulf. For centuries the two countries had bickered over rights to this waterway, so the sore point was a familiar wound for Saddam to pick.

The war was an eight-year nightmare. Like many Iraqis and Iranians, Mayada and her young children lived like frightened animals, hovering under the dining table or behind the sofa while Iranian bomber pilots broke through Iraqi clouds, eager to kill every living Iraqi. That terrifying time would never fade from her memory even if she lived to be a hundred years old. She would never forget the time the bombs and gunfire became so intense that word spread throughout Baghdad that the Iranians had overrun the city. She had screamed at her terrified babies to get down, to hide under their beds while she rushed through the house locking the doors and moving heavy furniture against the windows, believing that any moment she and the children would be murdered by the victorious Iranians.

The war finally ground to a weary halt on August 20, 1988, when Iran and Iraq accepted U.N. Security Council Resolution No. 598, which called for a cease-fire. Iraqis were so relieved to see the end of the shockingly bloody war that they celebrated by dancing in the streets for more than thirty days.

The Iraqis were still in the process of repairing their damaged infrastructure when a second black door opened and Saddam sent his troops on a desert hike from Baghdad, with orders to invade their tiny Kuwaiti neighbor. This invasion brought the fury of the allied Western nations upon their heads, deluging them with yet another war and leading Mayada to believe that Iraqis would soon swim in rivers of blood. But this second war came and went so rapidly, with the bulk of the Allied bombs precisely hitting their military targets and rarely straying into residential areas, that she felt it a mere skirmish in comparison to the Iranian war. But the moment the war ended, new trouble came from every quarter, with Shiite uprisings in the south and Kurdish uprisings in the north.

Mayada didn't know what would happen next. Her marriage had

been a sham that finally ended in divorce, and now in the midst of war and mayhem she was the sole protector of two young children. She braced for street fighting in Baghdad and rushed to gather extra bread, eggs and water. But to her astonishment, the Allied soldiers quit and simply walked away from their victory without entering Baghdad. This was followed by a short period of idyllic calm, which seemed weird and wonderful after the horror of two wars in only ten years.

The calm quickly gave way to desperation, because the U.N. sanctions lurked behind a third black door. For Mayada, the sanctions were more crippling than the wars. The daily grind of searching market stalls for reasonably priced sustenance to prepare for her two growing children was the most demoralizing task of her life. No pain is more tormenting than to stare into the face of your hungry child and have nothing to offer. She became so desperate that she even sold family heirlooms, such as the jewels in her Turkish grandmother's medal, presented to Melek by the Sultan. Mayada took ancient maps and antique books to the sidewalk vendors and sold them for a pittance of their true value.

There was yet a fourth black door waiting to open, one that Mayada had sensed as a growing shadow from the first moment of Saddam's reign. Crouched ominously behind the seemingly endless cycle of wars and violence was the Iraqi Baath Socialist Party's internal security apparatus, the secret police, which had been put in place by Saddam in 1968, when Mayada was only thirteen. The police state had grown along with her as she had matured into young adulthood, tormenting every Iraqi who passed by Baladiyat or other prisons, the sources of millions of Iraqi whispers such as, "Allah Yostur—God forbid and preserve us."

As she lay in the dark cell, Mayada cursed herself for her false sense of safety. Most Iraqis were terrified that they could be accused of false crimes at any time without the opportunity to offer an explanation of innocence.

But that first night in Baladiyat cleared Mayada's mind about Iraq, and she promised herself that if she got out of prison alive, she would pause no longer than it took her to pack a bag and grab her children. She would leave her home and her country and never return, even if she had to sit on the street corners of Amman and sell cigarettes, just as Samara had done.

All the other women in the cell were sleeping. She began to hear steps outside the door, and other doors began to open and close. As the voices grew more urgent, Mayada wondered if the prison was on fire and expected to see smoke seeping through the small opening in their cell door. For the fourth time in only twelve hours, she feared that her time on earth was ending. But there was no sign of fire. Just as she relaxed, Mayada heard a scream that made the roots of her hair tingle. When the first scream was followed by a second and then by a third, she raised herself on her elbows.

Samara rushed quickly to her side and whispered, "Do not worry. They bring in a fresh shift of torturers during the night."

At that moment a heart-wrenching screech was released throughout the prison. Samara pressed her hand upon Mayada's face and told her, "I know it is difficult, but try to sleep if you can. You do not know what tomorrow might bring, and you will be better prepared if you are rested."

But Mayada could not sleep and lay awake the rest of the night.

Even in prison they had a muezzin, and when dawn came she heard the familiar sing-song call to prayer, bringing comfort to her Muslim heart: "God is great, there are no other Gods, but God; and Mohammed was His Prophet. Come to prayer, come to prayer. God is great; there is no God, but God."

Mayada pulled up from her metal bunk and balanced on top, vainly trying to escape the aura of the toilet. She faced Mecca and prayed to Allah. Mayada asked God to solve her problem and to get her out of Baladiyat as quickly as possible.

Just as she completed her prayers, breakfast was distributed. She watched closely as the women clambered to the door to receive small portions of lentils and bread, and small cups of tea and glasses of water. Samara said, "I will get you a plate."

Mayada said that she couldn't eat, but asked Samara to save her one spoonful of sugar for energy. But she noticed that Samara set aside an extra plate of lentils topped by a slice of bread, obviously in the hope that she could convince her to sample a small portion.

After breakfast, the seventeen women began to take turns using the single toilet. In her modesty, Mayada willed her body to shut down, and she decided that a good side effect of her self-imposed fast would be the lack of need for the toilet.

She sat quietly on the edge of the bunk and watched the women milling about with haste as though they had a busy day ahead of them. A few women paused long enough to give her, their new cellmate, small smiles of encouragement, and Mayada smiled back.

Suddenly the small opening in the door was pushed from the other side and a raspy voice echoed throughout the cell. "Mayada Nizar Jafar Mustafa Al-Askari."

Fear made her knees so weak that she could not stand, but Samara rallied around her and whispered, "This is a miracle! They *never* ask for the prisoner the first day after they are imprisoned, but always make the person sweat out two or three weeks in this pit before the first interrogation."

Mayada did not feel it was a miracle but Samara tried to soothe her. "They do not torture in the early morning. *Never! Never!* You will be questioned minus the torture, you wait and see."

Mayada's body felt so heavy that if she didn't know better, she would have assumed lead had been poured into her bones during the night. It took a little pull and then a little push from behind for Samara to get her to the door.

The man outside blindfolded her, which almost brought Mayada to hysterics, but she swallowed three or four times in quick succession and reminded herself of Samara's words—that there were no torture sessions in the morning hours. A sleepless night combined with an empty stomach caused her legs to wobble. She continually crashed into the sides of the hallways. Someone from behind kept grabbing her by the shoulders to keep her pointed in the right direction, and even then it was impossible to walk steadily. Finally one of the men cursed loudly and yanked the blindfold off her eyes and gestured angrily for her to step forward into a room.

One of the men was short and round, though his fingers did not match his torso. They were long and bony, and he snapped them loudly as he gestured for Mayada to enter. She followed his command.

The room was the size of a small auditorium. Three men in security uniforms, all with mustaches, dark hair and bulldog-like features so indistinguishable that she had to hold her tongue to keep from asking if they were related, sat behind a long desk. She instantly sensed that the man in the middle, with his arrogant stare, was the leader, and she knew she had guessed correctly when he ordered the man sitting to his right to open a new page. He glared at her and told her to sit down. "What is your name?" he asked her, as though he didn't know who he had summoned.

Mayada panicked, thinking that she was about to undergo a trial without legal counsel, or even knowing the charges against her, but she told them that her name was Mayada Nizar Jafar Mustafa Al-Askari, and the designated writer wrote while the leader shouted, "She is known as Um Ali around the Mutanabi and Al-Battawiyeen areas," which referred to the two quarters of Baghdad where the printing houses were located.

She was not surprised that he knew she was the mother of Ali, but was troubled that the name of her son had passed over his tongue.

He suddenly shouted so loudly that she winced. "Write that she is a Sunni who is highly supportive of the Shiite." He continued to glare at her. "You were supposed to have come to us two years ago, but Dr. A. Al-Hadithi spared you, all because your great-grandfather was an honor to Iraq."

She knew that Dr. A. Al-Hadithi held an important post in the Iraqi government, and that his master's thesis had discussed the educational methods used by her grandfather, Sati El-Husri.

With a grin, the interrogator added, "Which, of course, was a pity, for we had looked forward to questioning the niece of that bastard Nouri Al-Said."

She took care not to move a muscle in her face. She was not surprised to hear him attack her father's Uncle Nouri. She had been told by many others that while her grandfather Jafar was much loved by most Iraqis of his day—so fondly remembered, in fact, that it would be difficult to find anyone with even a harsh word to say about him—Nouri was a different story. He had been a tough, pragmatic leader who did what he felt he had to do to safeguard the newly formed country of Iraq. During the many years he had ruled as Prime Minister, he had created many enemies.

The leader leaned over and whispered loudly into the writer's ear, and Mayada took that moment to glance to her left and to her right. She was immediately sorry that she had. The walls around her were smeared with blood. She saw chairs with bindings, tables stacked high with various instruments of torture. She saw electrical cables for battery chargers and a contraption that looked like a bow without the arrows. But the most frightening pieces of torture equipment were the various hooks that dangled from the ceiling. When Mayada glanced to the floor beneath those hooks, she saw splashes of fresh blood, which she supposed were left over from the torture sessions she had heard during the night.

The leader shouted one question after another. "Do you have any computers at home? Have you printed any leaflets calling for the overthrow of our President? Do you hire rebels to do your dirty work?"

She breathlessly answered, "No, no," over and over, telling him, "My shop is for commercial graphic designing and the people who work for me are computer engineers. They are highly educated, and they would never risk their lives through such illegal acts."

The leader threw her completely off balance when he abruptly changed the subject. His voice lowered dramatically and he began asking her questions about her mother. He wanted to know where Salwa was living and what was the last post she had held in the government, and did she plan on returning and using her skills to further the cause of Iraq, and had Mayada spoken with her mother recently and if so, how was the royal family of Jordan?

Mayada sputtered as she answered. "While she was the Director General of Research and Studies in the Bureau of International Relations before she retired, it is common knowledge that my mother is living in Amman. I am not certain when she plans to visit me in Iraq, but I will be pleased to telephone her and ask her that question, if you wish."

The leader laughed loudly and told her, "I see that you are as clever as your father's uncle, Nouri. That man outwitted every opponent until the last day of his life. But his cowardly disguise as a veiled woman couldn't save him from death." Without a pause, he asked her once again to reveal all the illegal information on her computers.

Mayada replied, "I am telling you that there are no illegal documents on any of my computers."

He looked at her from under his heavy eyelids. "That is correct. We have already examined all your computer files and disks. We found nothing."

Mayada had been sitting there swollen with fear, even though she knew that there was nothing in her files but run-of-the-mill printing work, but with his words she deflated like a balloon stuck by a sharp needle. To hear her inquisitor admit such a thing was a relief, a gift as precious as the rarest diamond. For the first time, Mayada felt a small flicker of hope that she might live.

With his statement she grew bold. "When will I be released?"

He laughed, *"Released?* Who said you would be released?"

Mayada was befuddled and stared at her interrogator in despair.

He added, "But you can count your blessings that our beloved leader, Saddam, gave us orders not to use violent methods while talking to females. Those instructions arrived this morning, and they saved you."

The third man, who had not spoken until this moment, suddenly sat upright in his chair and his voice rang first with disappointment and then with indignation at this new information. Mayada saw that he was so irate that she could only guess he held the position of principal torturer and had sat through her interrogation eagerly envisioning the various methods that would make her shriek in pain and despair. Unable to control his frustration, he shouted at her, "I will cook you in a frying pan with grease very soon," which is a common threat in Iraq when someone wishes to inform you that they are going to slowly put you to death.

The leader glared at the third man, and she thought for a moment that the two men were going to clash over her fate, but the third man wilted under the leader's direct gaze.

The leader ordered, "Go back to your cell. We are not finished with you and will call you back tomorrow."

Now she felt brave enough to test his resolve. "If you have found nothing illegal, then why am I here?"

"Perhaps something was missed."

She pushed. "I have children that I raise alone. They need their mother and I must go home to tend to them."

The leader twisted in his seat and looked directly at her. He replied in a spiteful tone, "Your family has lost their power. Jafar is dead. Nouri is dead. Sati is dead. Nizar is dead. Salwa has abandoned you. There is no one to defend you here."

She grew quiet in the knowledge that he was right. Since Saddam's rise to power, Iraq had turned into such a place that her jailers could enter false information into her computers and take that information to their supervisors, and those men would slowly climb the ladder of command, convincing others that she was indeed guilty and worthy of their torture. And, truthfully, who was there to help her? No one—there was no one to turn to, she sadly admitted to herself.

President Saddam's face came to mind, and she speculated what his response would be if she telephoned his palace office and politely asked for his assistance in obtaining a release from Baladiyat prison. She had met Saddam five or six times, and had even had been honored and rewarded by him for her writings. She had been specially selected to translate Nostradamus's writings for Saddam's reading pleasure. He had a great interest in the book, since he believed he was a world figure mentioned in the astrologer's predictions. Mayada had even saved other lives in the past by pleading for personal mercy from Saddam. But she quickly dismissed the idea of placing such a call, for the small pad where she kept his telephone number was hidden in a secret place in her home. Even if she had the number in her pocket and managed to reach his offices, she assumed Saddam would not take her call, for she had not spoken with him since Dr. Fadil had been convicted of treason and put to death.

She stared for a moment at the three men questioning her and wondered what they might say if they knew she had Saddam's private telephone number. But she knew deep down that she was not a close family friend whom Saddam would bother to defend. Besides, he was a paranoid man who had deceived and even killed close family members. If he happened to hear that someone was disloyal, he accepted the accusation without question. She recalled how Saddam had trusted Dr. Fadil for more than twenty years, but that when a false allegation against Fadil was raised, Saddam had been ruthless.

"Go!" The leader shouted at her. "Get out of my sight!"

Mayada looked at him intently for a brief moment and was tempted to ask how it was possible to hate a woman he did not know, but she didn't dare. She collected herself by taking a few deep breaths and then stood and walked slowly to the door, for it was important to her that she hide her fear in front of these men.

The same men waited outside the door to walk her back to the cell, and one of the two appeared to be sleeping with his head resting against the wall. Mayada cleared her throat and both men jumped to attention. When she stepped outside the door, she saw that another prisoner was waiting to go into the interrogation room. He was extremely thin, almost ghost-like, and he squatted on the floor. When Mayada walked out, he stood. Mayada thought then that rather than a ghost, he resembled a swaying palm tree. His face was badly bruised and he had the saddest eyes Mayada had ever seen. A guard pushed him roughly toward the door of the room she had just exited. The guard was exceptionally cruel, cursing him and ordering him to move when it was clear that the man did not have the strength to stand upright. Mayada and the thin man exchanged a look. She had a strong sense that today was the last day of that poor man's life, but she smiled, hoping that somehow the smile of a woman would lift his spirits. He must have thought the same, for he took a big chance that won him a blow to his bruised face when he said, "Contact my family for me. I am Professor . . ." but his words were cut short. He was lifted off his feet and tossed like a bag of dried hay into the interrogation room.

Back in her cell, there was an air of excitement. Two new prisoners had just arrived, bringing their number to twenty. When she heard the news, Mayada searched the cell for new faces. But Samara hustled her to the bunk and asked for every detail of her interrogation. "Tell me everything," she demanded.

After Mayada gave her the full account, Samara leaped to her feet and praised Allah, saying, "Our Mayada has just experienced three miracles. I have been in Baladiyat for four months and I have never heard of such a thing."

Mayada was smiling. Samara was so theatrical. She posed with one hand on her hip and gestured with the other. "Here are the miracles. Number one: The interrogators sent for Mayada the very day after her detention. This, as we all know, never happens. These cruel men always let a new prisoner sit in the cell and suffer for a few days first. Number two: Mayada was not physically mistreated. Again, this never happens. They always like to inflict torture. Number three: No real questions were asked. The interrogator even admitted that Mayada's computers were clean."

Samara then clapped her hands together. "Three miracles. This means our Mayada is not long for cell 52." Samara smiled broadly. Everyone in this cell think of the messages you want to send to your families. Mayada will be released soon." She turned to Mayada. "You will be our carrier pigeon, Mayada. In Baladiyat, freed prisoners are our only method of sending out messages."

Samara was so positively enthusiastic that a small gleam of hope began to grow in Mayada's heart that perhaps her time in Baladiyat actually would be brief.

But just as her spirits began to be lifted by the thought that she would soon see Fay and Ali, the women heard boots running in the hallway and secret police shouting, "His heart stopped!"

It was forbidden, but Mayada dropped to her knees and opened the slit where their food was shoved into the cell. There was the professor. He was lying flat in the prison hallway. Mayada was struck with a great sadness that she had been unable to catch his name, so that someone might notify his family.

She turned and looked at Samara. "Why are they upset that he is dead? They are the ones who killed him."

Samara shrugged and told her what she had already guessed. "With certain prisoners they desire additional information. They are experts at keeping the ones they are questioning one breath away from death. It is a game for them to see if they can push and pull a human back and forth, in and out of the grave. When a prisoner dies one moment before they wish them dead, it is considered a failure."

The tragic end of the professor instantly switched Mayada's mood from sweet anticipation to bitter sadness, and she returned to the bunk and lay quietly. She had been in prison for only one day, yet it already felt like a lifetime.

The sounds of the other nineteen chattering shadow women, crowded in a tiny space, increased to a loud crescendo. The foul smells from the toilet seemed to cling to her clothes and her skin and her hair. Although the day had hardly begun, she was tired. She closed her eyes. Drawn to the power of her memories, she thought about her mother's father, her grandfather Sati, the man who also became a legend in the Arab world. She wondered what her Jido Sati, as she called him, would say if he knew that his precious little granddaughter was locked in the notorious Baladiyat prison.

3

Jido Sati

Lying silent on her hard metal bunk, Mayada recalled the way her maternal grandfather, whom she called Jido Sati, clasped his hands behind his back when he paced in his office or walked in his garden. She remembered how he would rest his index finger against his face while he thought at his desk, his mind ranging far for solutions to weighty concerns. She recalled how he was so neat that every paper in his massive office was organized perfectly, despite its overflowing wealth of books and notes. She remembered how she loved to watch him methodically gather stationery and special pens when he prepared for a journey.

Mayada closed her eyes in Baladiyat and opened them in the village of Beit Meri, the quiet Lebanese mountain resort to which Jido Sati always took the family for holidays at his summer house. Suddenly it was 1962, and Mayada was living with her parents and younger sister in Beirut. She was a young girl, years before the civil war in Lebanon shattered everything.

It was a special summer day. She was seven years old and Jido Sati was an old man of eighty-two, although even at that ripe old age he had the physical appearance and good health of a man twenty years his junior.

Jido Sati had always been known as the family alarm clock because he was the first to awaken every morning at 6:30 sharp. On that day he slipped into the room where Mayada was sleeping with her younger sister, Abdiya. When Jido Sati saw Mayada's eyes flicker in recognition, he whispered so not to wake Abdiya and invited Mayada to join him for breakfast. Flattered to be singled out, Mayada moved quietly from the bed and slipped on the little shiny robe her father had bought her in a special shop for children in Geneva.

The silky pink dressing gown made her feel as sophisticated as her glamorous mother, Salwa, when she was attired in a ball gown for a glittering social event. With that image in her mind, Mayada made a grand entrance into the kitchen, her silken robe sweeping the floor. She laughed happily as Jido Sati pulled out her chair and indicated that his little princess should sit and join him for breakfast. She was finally a big girl and felt proud that she remembered to drink her orange juice without slurping, and to swallow her eggs and toast before speaking. Jido Sati breakfasted on toast, cheese and tea, and offered topics he knew interested Mayada, such as her books, and her sketching and painting. He promised Mayada that one day when she was older, he would indulge her with a special holiday trip to the art-filled city of her choice.

After breakfast they ambled out to the balcony to admire the view. She watched his face rather than the view and looked into his widely spaced, honey-shaded eyes that were a fount of kindness. She had once overheard a woman remark that Jido Sati was not a physically attractive man, but that few noticed because his amazing intellect, wise actions and mild demeanor created such an aura of handsome strength and honor. She listened carefully while Jido Sati gave her a little history lesson. He told her that the small village of Beit Meri had been occupied since the time of the Phoenicians, and that there were wonderful ruins from the Roman and Byzantine periods that she was now old enough to appreciate. He promised that they would visit those ruins during the holiday. Beit Meri was seventeen kilometers from the center of Beirut and 800 meters above sea level, and Jido Sati's summer house was perfectly situated to provide an unspoiled view of Beirut from the front balcony. A second wonderful vista, of the deep valley Hanr al-Jamani, lay beyond the small terrace at the villa's rear.

It was a cool morning, although the bright sun was shining over the mountain ridges, and Mayada stood quietly as Jido Sati stared down at lovely Beirut jutting out into the Mediterranean. He lifted her in his arms to point out some of the larger yachts anchored in the harbor, which belonged to wealthy sheiks from various oil-rich nations. Sati told her that he had been on a number of those vessels for one business meeting or another. One day, he said, he would take the family for a little journey out to sea. Mayada enjoyed a fleeting look at the yachts and knew that someday she would sail away on the blue sea, because Jido Sati never broke a promise. Then she tried in vain to search for the rooftop of their home in Beirut, but was unable to find it in the maze of brightly colored roofs that spread over the sprawling city.

Jido Sati had always insisted upon morning walks, and after surveying the beauty of the surrounding scenery, he called out for Mayada's nanny, an Assyrian Christian woman named Anna. He asked her to dress his granddaughter appropriately for a little walk. Mayada could recall the sleekness of her nanny's long, blue-black hair slipping through her small fingers as Anna pulled a simple blue shift over Mayada's head. She sat and stared into Anna's beautiful green eyes, fringed by the longest black eyelashes she had ever seen, as the woman slid comfortable walking shoes on Mayada's small feet. Properly dressed, she happily followed Jido Sati from the villa and down the staircase, out into the winding road that would take them to Broummana, a nearby village famous for its quaint little cafés, shops and restaurants.

Sati and Mayada walked past a row of multicolored flower beds, and when she leaned down to pluck a bright yellow flower in full bloom, her grandfather gently reminded her that it was not nice to take even the smallest flower without first seeking the owner's permission. But he assured her not to worry; he would buy her a colorful bouquet in Broummana and she could share it with Abdiya. He suggested that the two girls could arrange a nice display for the dinner table.

Mayada reluctantly pulled her hand back from the beckoning flower and recalled a conversation she had overheard between her parents. Her mother said that her father Sati was the most respected man in the Middle East because he had never spoken a lie in his life. He had stood so firmly by his principles of Arab Nationalism, which won him the devoted affection of every Arab, that the British authorities had been fearful of his influence. The British governors had confiscated his passport and escorted him, his wife and children out of Iraq with a stern warning to never return to the land he loved. Every Arab leader had offered Sati citizenship in their respective countries, but he had gently refused; he explained that Arabs should be able to travel from one Arab land to the other without restrictions. Even without a passport, Sati Al-Husri was warmly received in every Arab land not controlled by the British.

Though at Jido Sati's insistence she had not plucked the colorful and fragrant flower, Mayada enjoyed their walk immensely. The trail was canopied by Lebanese pines that lent a nice shade, although the path was a bit too steep for Mayada's short legs. But when Sati noticed that his granddaughter was hiking with some difficulty, he slowed down and took the opportunity to ask her about her favorite subjects at school.

Mayada was a bit of an unruly child. Several years earlier, Jido Sati had suggested to her parents that her rowdy manners might be improved if she were enrolled at the German Kindergarten and Primary School in Beirut, and they had taken his advice. Although the instructors had been very strict, she had benefited from the discipline.

Mayada was startled that he seemed so familiar with her classes and assignments, and she began to wonder if he had somehow slipped into her classes unobserved. She gave a small cry of pleasure when he told her he was so impressed with her drawings that he had bought her a small gift of artist's brushes and paints, and that he hoped she would put on a formal exhibition. Mayada was so excited by the prospect that she wanted to spin around on the trail, return to the villa to grasp those brushes between her fingers so she might begin to make masterful strokes on a canvas. But her grandfather laughed and told her it was important for artists to consider their ideas before flinging themselves into a frenzy of work. He told her he would give her two weeks to plan, paint and organize before showing her work.

Her grandfather kept his word—two weeks later, he meticulously arranged an exhibition of Mayada's art. Adults and classmates alike came to view her drawings, and many people said she would become a world-famous artist. But Jido Sati cautioned her to always remain modest about her accomplishments, and he reminded her that nothing truly mattered but her own sense of satisfaction.

Seven years later, when she was nearly fourteen, Jido Sati died. Soon after, Mayada's mother sorted through the deceased man's important papers, and Mayada was touched to tears when she discovered, neatly packed away in a cardboard box with his most valuable papers, her childish drawings.

Mayada still possessed the memory of that perfect summer morning in Beit Meri. She'd felt a sense of pride to be Jido Sati's only walking companion that day, though every time they passed a villa or encountered people on the trail, the neighbors and townspeople bowed and called out their greetings of honor. Each passerby made a big to-do over her grandfather. She was not surprised at their reaction, because it had been that way as long as she could remember.

After the British themselves had been forced to depart Iraq, the Iraqis had called for Sati Al-Husri to come home. He returned to exultant Baghdad streets that teemed with placard-carrying admirers and a huge celebration that swelled throughout the country. Each time Sati Al-Husri traveled to Baghdad to visit his daughter, Salwa, a festival would erupt and their home along the banks of the Tigris would be filled from early morning until late evening with visitors, each clamoring to pay respect to the man they lovingly called the "Father of Arab Nationalism."

Mayada almost shared the same birthday with her grandfather. Sati Al-Husri was born on August 5, 1879, and she was born on August 6, 1955. It was her mother's ambition that her first child would arrive on her father's birthday. Mayada's parents were visiting Beirut when her mother was due to give birth and Salwa was so driven to make the birthdates coincide that she tried to induce labor by walking long hours through the streets of Beirut with her husband. Years later, her father laughingly told Mayada that Salwa had forced him to walk the entire length of Bliss Street, which was near the American University of Beirut, toward Uncle Sam's Snack Bar, and then back to Sadat Street and to Ain Al-Miraisa. Despite Salwa's efforts, she did not go into labor with Mayada until August 6.

This special link of their birthdays was only part of the ideal relationship between Jido Sati and Mayada. Jido Sati had been extraordinarily committed to his granddaughter since she could first remember, an intimacy that buoyed Mayada, since he was the only grandfather she had ever known. Mayada's paternal grandfather, Jafar Pasha Al-Askari, had been murdered nineteen years before Mayada was born. Although the stirring tales about Jafar Pasha were stimulating to hear, and while her father, Nizar, whom she loved with complete devotion, was utterly dedicated to his father's memory, those stories could not be a substitute for a grandfather like Sati, whom she could see in the flesh and who took an intense interest in every detail of her young life.

In 1879, when Mayada's grandfather Sati Al-Husri was born,

enormous change was coming to the Arab region. Sultan Abdul Hamid II was the sovereign of the vast Ottoman Empire, which had been in existence for close to 600 years. However, the stage was set for the dissolution of the empire—the Balkan peoples were discovering their own national identities and were breaking away from the Ottomans to forge their own nations. Meanwhile, Russia was pressuring the Ottoman borders from the east, while England was marching in on Egypt.

Sati's father, Hilal, one of the Sultan's trusted advisors, was highly educated. He had graduated from the Al-Azhar, Egypt's great theological school, and at the time of Sati's birth served as a Supreme Judge and as Head of the Court of Appeal in Yemen. Hilal Al-Husri's influential family tree traced back to Al-Hassan bin Ali Bin Abi Talib, the grandson of the Prophet Mohammad. This undiluted link to the Prophet's family had been authenticated in Al-Azhar during the sixteenth century.

Sati was born in the city of Lahaj, Yemen, where his father held an important government post. From his birth Sati had been exceptionally close to his adored mother, but his father aggrieved him by continually bringing additional brides into his mother's home. Each time a new marriage took place, Sati would plot his revenge. Sneaking pails of water to the upper balconies, he would wait until the young brides passed beneath to pour the jugs of water on them. His mother was a godly woman and pleaded with her son to curb his mischief. She assured him that Allah would have better things for her in heaven and that earthly challenges were to be met with dignity and grace.

Sati's youthful enthusiasm proved so disruptive that his father sent him to school at an earlier age than most. When he was only five, his mathematics teacher had shown the class how to solve a particular problem in five complex steps. Sati quietly told him that it could be solved in only two simple steps. The instructor was irritated at the brash child and ordered him to come to the board and make a clown of himself so they could have a good laugh. Instead, and to the

amazement of his teacher, Sati quickly scribbled out his two-part so-
lution. Sati was so gifted that he frequently matriculated through two
full school grades each school year. When he graduated with highest
honors from his secondary school, Sati was the youngest graduate
ever in the entire Ottoman Empire. When he was only thirteen, Sati
was accepted into Istanbul's Royal Shahany School, one of the Empire's most exclusive schools, where he received his B.A. in political
science in only a few years. By this time, his fame as an intellectual
had spread all the way to the Sultan's throne. As soon as he graduated,
he was appointed governor of Bayna in Yugoslavia, and while fulfilling
his duties as governor he also presided over the educational system
there.

Sati's time away from Istanbul and close to Europe was the most
enlightening and inspiring phase of his educational life. He traveled
into neighboring European countries and haunted their bookstores.
He frequented the libraries of Rome and Paris and took part in many
educational conferences. He befriended top European educators and
absorbed their theories. Sati's greatest interest was studying the na-
tionalistic traits of other people, so that as Arab nationalists they
would be prepared to form governments and institutions worthy of
their people.

In 1908 Sati returned to Istanbul a twenty-eight-year-old man,
wise to the ways of the world but saddened to witness the closing
days of the Ottoman Empire. During the final years of the Ottomans,
just as Jafar worked to create a stable rule, Sati helped to vastly
improve the educational system. He was so successful in his official
position that, after the fall of the Empire, President Mustafa Kemal
Ataturk, founder of modern Turkey, was known to say repeatedly,
"My only desire is to rule Turkey with the same excellence that Sati
Al-Husri administered his schools!"

Sati's experiences with his numerous stepmothers when he was a
child had closed his mind to the idea of early marriage. All his focus

was on his work; his only social pleasure was listening to opera and symphonies. But his profession as an educator brought him to love, though the route was circuitous. Sati was head of the Yeni Mektebi (the New Schools) in Istanbul, where he experienced great difficulty finding instructors fluent in English, French and German. One day, one of his closest friends, Jalal Hussain, mentioned that his only sister Jamila was highly educated. Although Jamila was exceedingly wealthy, she had grown jaded and disheartened with her life of useless luxury. Jalal believed his sister would be an ideal teacher to work in the new school system for his progressive-thinking friend, Sati Al-Husri.

Sati fell in love with Jamila Hussain Pasha during their first meeting, and until she agreed to marry him, all his energies were turned toward courting this extraordinary woman. Sati's marriage to a beautiful Turkish woman whose father was the Minister of the Navy and whose mother was a sultana, or princess, in the Sultan's royal court surprised everyone who knew him.

Jamila Hussain Pasha was the only daughter in a family of six children and was the favorite of her father, Hussain Husni Porsun, who was from Kosovo, which was ruled by the Ottomans. He became an admiral in the Ottoman Navy and his distinguished career led him to the high-ranking position of Minister of the Navy over the entire Ottoman fleet. Jamila's mother, Melek, was Ottoman, and as a first cousin of the Sultan on her mother's side, was a member of the ruling family. Melek was a famous beauty with skin so white that it was guarded carefully from the rays of the sun, and green eyes so brilliant that it was said they flashed bright lights when she was angry. Melek was so exceedingly wealthy that her riches made her arrogant. During a terrible famine, she insisted that her six white carriage horses receive excellent grooming and the finest foods, even as Ottoman citizens were falling dead in the streets from starvation. She even pranced those horses through the famished crowds begging at the palace walls. She was known to burn money, because she enjoyed the astonishment on the faces of observers, and her home was so massive, with more than seventy bedrooms, that after her death it was converted into an enormous hotel.

Jamila was fortunate because her father was not only an educated man, but was kind and interested in having his daughter complete her education as his sons had. But in the Ottoman world, the education of females was so rare that he arranged to send Jamila to the United States to study. When this extraordinary news spread through the palace, the Sultan heard about the matter and summoned Hussain into his offices and told him that he did not believe in educating women. The Sultan said that all one had to do was take a look at Hussain's own wife Melek to know that independence in a woman brought nothing but grief to the men in the family.

Hussain didn't know what to say, because he knew that the Sultan and Melek matched each other with evil, and he had been given the remarkable information that upon awakening each morning, the first question the Sultan posed was, "What outrageous act did cousin Melek commit during the night?"

But after the Sultan expressed his desire that Jamila not leave the country to seek an education, Hussain could not go against his wishes, for that would have been a death sentence. So Hussain secretly hired tutors, and his lovely Jamila was schooled in her home. She became highly educated and fluent in many languages, and knew as much as any man about sociology, physiology and psychology. Mayada knew this was the major force in the love that Sati felt for Jamila, because he was a man of such intellectual brilliance that an uneducated woman would have been unable even to gain his attention, and certainly could not win his undying love and affection.

Jamila could easily see that Sati Al-Husri was a man unlike others, and she returned his respect and love. The couple were married and went on to have two children: a daughter, Mayada's mother Salwa, and a son, Mayada's uncle, Khaldun.

As the only daughter, Jamila inherited her mother's possessions, which she passed on to her daughter, Salwa, who passed those treasured items on to her own daughters. Mayada inherited some valuable heirlooms and still possessed the "Decoration of Perfection" presented to Melek by the Sultan. This proclamation, consisting of a document with the seal of the Sultan, was written in gold and said that on the occasion of Melek's eighteenth birthday she would be bestowed with various districts of land. The document came with a sash and medal made of diamonds, pearls, rubies, sapphires and emeralds. Mayada had inherited one of the large diamonds and the document, but she was forced to sell the diamond in 1996 when she was living through the sanctions in Iraq and desperate to feed her children. But she kept the rare Ottoman document and hoped to pass it on to her own daughter, Fay.

The crumbling of the Ottoman Empire led to such a sudden break with tradition that many of the old ways lay in ruin, but this also paved the way for new ideas fostered by men such as Sati Al-Husri. He was so brilliant that kings sought his opinions and appointed him to positions of power.

Mayada's memories of her grandfather Sati were interrupted by the sound of a woman weeping. It took Mayada several minutes to adjust to the fluorescent light overhead, but as she rubbed her eyes and looked for the source of the weeping, she saw that the one grieving was the younger of the two women who had been incarcerated earlier in the day.

By this time other shadow women had gathered around the young woman, Aliya. She was so grieved that nothing they did or said brought her the slightest comfort. When Aliya began to wail, Samara took her face in her hands and whispered with authority, "You *must* control yourself, dear heart. The guards will follow your wails like bloodhounds follow the scent of a rabbit." She added, "Do you want them to take you away for some midnight sport?"

Mayada shivered at Samara's words, but they worked to dry Aliya's tears.

When Mayada had returned to the cell a few hours earlier, she had been too distraught about her own situation to notice much about the two new shadow women. But now she studied Aliya curiously. Aliya had arrived with enough supplies to last through a lengthy siege. She had blankets and pillows and extra clothes and copies of the Holy Quran and other Islamic prayer books, and even a supply of decent food, which was rarely seen inside the prison walls of Baladiyat.

Mayada had believed that no woman in the cell could be more beautiful than Samara, but Aliya was tall and slender with a lovely face. Her most striking feature was her unusually large and expressive black eyes.

Aliya settled on the floor with one leg crossed over the other, Iraqi style, and the other shadow women sat beside her. Mayada joined them, but she was not accustomed to floor sitting, because her mother had insisted that only an ill-bred servant would sit in such a way. She had taught her daughters to sit on chairs or sofas with their legs held in a proper manner.

So it didn't surprise Mayada that within a short time, her legs began to grow numb and she began to shift one way or another. Aliya looked at her with interest and asked, "You are new here?"

Mayada replied, "Not so new. I arrived the day before you came."

Aliya bowed her head. "I have been in detention for over two years," she said. "I have been warned that I can expect a fifteen-year sentence."

Mayada now understood Aliya's enormous sadness, for she was agonized by the idea of being held in Baladiyat for just another day and night. She decided that if she were notified that she would be incarcerated for fifteen years, she would end her life by chewing through her own flesh and digging her teeth into her veins, even though to commit suicide is considered a great sin in Islam.

Aliya spoke in a sweet, low voice. "I am from the Southern Governorate of Basra. My husband was a trained engineer but remained job-less for years. After the birth of our first child he became so fraught with worry that he left Basra and traveled to Jordan to look for work. He was unable to find anything in his profession and when he did find employment as a baker we considered it a miracle.

"After two years he had saved enough money to rent a room in Amman, and once he had furnished the room with a bed, a table, two chairs, a small refrigerator and hot plate, he sent for me and our little daughter Suzan. He said he had missed us so much that it was affect-ing his baking. He confessed that he had burned more than a dozen loaves while mourning the fact that his child was growing older with-out her father to guide her. He was certain that his depression would soon cause him to burn down the bakery, so he contacted my brother, a general in the Iraqi Army. I know it is unusual for a Shiite to be a general, but he was never offered big commands or given salary in-creases, like a Sunni.

"My husband asked my brother to prepare our documents. And he did. My brother is a generous man, and he also provided 700,000 Iraqi dinars [$350.00] for our passport tax and then gave me 100,000 dinars [$50.00] for the trip. My brother even agreed to travel with me as my required *Mahram*."

After the war deaths of so many husbands and fathers, and the economic weakening inside Iraq connected to the sanctions, some Iraqi women had slipped across the border to Jordan to work as pros-titutes to earn money to feed their hungry children. When Saddam discovered Iraqi women were dishonoring the country by selling their bodies, he ordered that all women must travel with a *Mahram*, who could be her husband or any male relative to whom a Muslim woman cannot be married, such as her father, brother, uncle, nephew, step-father, father-in-law or son-in-law.

Aliya continued her story. "At the Iraqi customs in Traibeel, our passports were taken away to be stamped and soon I was asked to step aside with my daughter and my brother. Pandemonium broke out when two secret policemen began to beat my brother with their fists. He fainted from shock when one of the men lunged at him with an electrical prod. My three-year-old daughter began to screech in fear. Other travelers began to shout and shift away from us. Finally, to restore order in the customs office, the guards removed us to a small office. They were screaming and shouting, demanding to know where I got my passport. I was struck mute with terror but, thanks be to Allah, my brother had revived by this time and he assured the men that he had requested a reputable passport bureau in Basra to issue the passport. When he went to collect the passport, nothing had been amiss.

"That horrible man with the electrical prod shouted that I was traveling with a stolen passport. He was so furious that he shocked both me and my brother.

"The men did not believe our innocence and transported the three of us to Al-Ramadi Detention Centre. We were locked up for three weeks. No one came to question us or torture us. It appeared that we had been forgotten. Finally my brother was released without explanation, but he could do or say nothing to make a difference in my case, since I was the passport holder. I was detained for six months in that first prison. My daughter was imprisoned with me. My poor baby was taken with me into the interrogation room. She was forced to watch while I was beaten." Aliya's face filled with sorrow at the memory. "The most difficult thing I've ever done in my life was to muffle my screams while I was being tortured. They beat me, but I bit my tongue until it bled. I wanted to spare my child the terror of hearing her mother screech. One of the more vicious guards once tied my baby to a table, taunting me with the threat of torturing Suzan. I was tied to a chair so I could do nothing but watch as they lashed little Suzan. My baby shrieked until her belly button flipped inside out, and when they saw what had happened, they howled with laughter.

"I had never seen a baby's belly button flip like that. I asked for a doctor but of course, they said no. So I wrapped my head scarf around her stomach. I thought her belly button might flip back inside, but it didn't. But the worst came later: During one of the torture sessions, two of the men threatened to rape me *and* Suzan. Thank God, they didn't rape my baby."

Aliya paused and gestured in the direction of another shadow woman who was sitting alone in the corner and said, "Rasha was there with me during the worst of it."

Mayada and the other shadow women turned to look at Rasha.

Mayada thought it strange that this particular shadow woman appeared to have no concern for Aliya's situation.

Aliya waited for Rasha to confirm her story but Rasha did nothing but glare at Aliya before turning her attention to her prayer rug and giving it a thorough shake, refusing to provide Aliya with the confirmation she so desired.

Aliya sighed and told them, "Poor Rasha is as innocent as I am. We were strangers throughout our lives. We are now linked in a way we could never have imagined." Aliya then turned to Rasha. "Can I tell your story as well, Rasha?"

Rasha refused to speak, but she grunted, and Aliya took the bitter sound as assent.

Aliya continued. "One day I was sitting in my cell holding little Suzan in my arms when the cell door was opened with a great force. I cringed, believing that I was going to be taken away for further beatings. Instead, a woman who had been tortured almost to death was thrown to the floor. Her face was raw with deep cuts, and her skull had been cracked. Blood oozed out of a hole in her head that appeared to have been made by an electric drill. Three of her fingernails had been ripped out, and so many cigarettes had been put out on her legs that the stench of burnt flesh soon filled the cell. The woman was Rasha.

"Everyone in the cell tended to her in an attempt to save her life.

She nearly died two or three times, until finally one of the women convinced the guards to take her to the hospital. She was brought back to the cell the following day but was barely coherent, and it took our most creative nursing skills to nurture her back to life.

"After three days, Rasha regained consciousness. From the moment she opened her eyes, our misery increased.

"You see, the mystery of my passport confiscated at Traibeel was that the passport was in fact Rasha's passport. Rasha reported losing her passport the year before. She had been jailed from that day, and the secret police, believing they were about to break up an important spy ring, intended to force one of us to turn evidence against the other."

Aliya shook her head with sorrow. "The interrogations became even more brutal than before. Every day, each of us was grilled separately. Then we were interrogated together. Our torturers yanked out Rasha's fingernails while demanding she tell them who she had sold her passport to. Then they would crush lit cigarettes on my bare legs, insisting that I admit to being in a spy ring with Rasha. Since nothing they claimed was true, neither of us knew a name to give them. Our claims of innocence only evoked more anger and torture."

To demonstrate how she had suffered, Aliya pulled the fabric of her dress down to her elbow and lifted her skirt to her knees. Several of the shadow women gasped. Aliya's arms and legs were covered in deep, raw wounds. The worst scars, however, criss-crossed her abdomen and thighs and buttocks, she told them.

Mayada realized fearfully that Aliya's torturers had stripped her in order to humiliate her while inflicting pain, and she wondered if Aliya had been raped, but she didn't ask that question, for no Muslim woman would ever admit that she had been dishonored in such a manner.

Aliya said, "For some reason Rasha and I have been moved from one prison to another. The worst prison was in my hometown, Basra. To be so close to home and unable to *go* home was the greatest torture of all. I knew that my family was only a few streets away from the prison where I languished." Tears streamed down Aliya's face but she continued talking. "While we were imprisoned in Basra, there was a small uprising when the population called for the downfall of Saddam. The government immediately claimed that those people had committed mutiny and captured thousands of people, ordering troops to pull down their houses and imprison the inhabitants. Entire families were tossed into prison. Men, women and children were suddenly packed together into cells meant for half the number. People began to die of overcrowding and starvation and disease. I had to watch more than a dozen children slowly dehydrate and die in my own cell. I tried to protect Suzan by keeping her tiny face covered with my abaaya, but it is impossible to keep a child of that age quiet and content enough to remain in her mother's arms all day and all night. So she caught a terrible infection. One day she started coughing. Then mucus dripped from her nose. Her eyes crusted tight with dried matter. Before long, my baby was whining nonstop. She developed a harsh cough and soon she stopped responding to my voice. I thought she was going to die at any moment.

"Despite my daughter's illness, I was still taken out for torture. Other kind women in the cell volunteered to watch Suzan. For the first time, I didn't feel the torturer's whip. I just wanted them to whip me quick and get it over with so I could go back to my child. I ran in a torture room once and cried out, 'Whip me, whip me fast!' which startled the torturers. In fact, it was the only time a man laid down his whip and told me to go back to the cell. I was possessed. All I could think about was my daughter.

"Praise Allah Suzan survived. The following year, our lives improved slightly when my brother met a man who knew one of Saddam's bodyguards. That man got my brother information about where we were being detained. After three months of paying bribes, my brother was allowed to visit me." She made a sweeping gesture with her hand at her pile of things. "He brought me clothes and prayer rugs and blankets and special food. He even received authorization to take little Suzan out of the prison, and now my child is living with my brother and his wife. Although I'll never forget how my darling baby screamed when my brother lifted my child from my arms and walked away, it is a great blessing to me that she is safe."

Aliya began weeping and Samara patted her back as she completed Aliya's story for her. "Our Aliya is an educated woman, a biochemist. She's even been awarded several certificates. Prohibited from teaching in pubic schools because she was not a member of the Baath Party, she taught privately."

Aliya then began to wail in earnest, "My husband is an engineer. He is working as a baker. I am a teacher. And now I am rotting in prison. My daughter will be a grown woman when I get out of here. And I have never done anything against the government."

Every eye in the cell overflowed with tears of sympathy for Aliya.

Through the wall, they heard Ahmed, the pious young Wahabi convert, begin his nightly prayers. Suddenly, his prayers turned into screams.

Mayada was so nervous by this time that she leapt to her feet and clutched Samara's arm, crying out, "They are going to kill him! They are going to kill him!"

Samara replied in a low voice, "No. But what they are going to do to him is even worse, particularly for a devout Muslim."

Mayada didn't understand until she heard them dragging Ahmed into the hallway, where they stopped in front of their cell door. The guards then took turns raping Ahmed. Mayada was horrified. The brutal rape went on for more than an hour, until Mayada heard one of the guards laugh like a hyena as he told Ahmed, "Relax. You are now the wife of three men and you must please us all."

4

Saddam Hussein

With her head still throbbing from Ahmed's screams, Mayada sat silently and watched as one by one, the shadow women melted away from Aliya's side. Aliya sat quietly on the floor despite Samara's appeal to organize her bedding and supplies, which cluttered the small cell. Aliya stared so intently at her hands, clutched tightly and curled in her lap, that Mayada wondered if Aliya was thinking of her daughter and how she would never again have the opportunity to hold and protect her child, because Suzan would likely be a wife and mother herself before Aliya was released from Baladiyat.

For a brief moment, Mayada envied Rasha's detachment, knowing that as she embraced the stories of the other shadow women, the weight of their sorrows combined with her own.

But even as those thoughts were working through her mind, Mayada knew she could never pull back from those shadow women, for she had quickly developed a true affection for each of them. Just then, Samara surprised Mayada with a small pail of water to wash her face and hands. Mayada felt her black mood lift slightly. Although she knew that prisoners were not allowed sharp objects, she had discovered that Samara was a miracle worker, and she asked Samara if there was any way of finding a hand mirror.

Samara glanced at the other shadow women, then nodded before turning and rummaging through the belongings she had packed away in the folds of a rough military blanket. Samara gave a mumble of satisfaction and proudly turned with a small broken mirror in her hand, which she waved enthusiastically. Samara whispered, "Up until a week ago there was a beautiful young woman held here. One of the guards took a special interest in her. He slipped her this mirror with the promise she would not share it with her cellmates. When that guard was transferred to Basra, he issued orders for her transfer, as well. She left me this mirror."

Mayada considered the steep price that poor woman was paying for the guard's special interest, but pushed the thought out of her mind. She knew that rape was a form of torture against both males and females in Iraqi prisons, but the most attractive women were raped repeatedly by many different men. For the first time in her life, Mayada was pleased not to be a great beauty.

With a sad sigh she took the mirror from Samara's hand and looked at her image in the mirror. She winced in surprise. In disbelief she turned the mirror over several times, first looking at the leaded back and then at the mirrored front before building her courage to gaze at her reflection a second time. Yes, the stranger in the mirror was indeed the oldest daughter of Nizar and Salwa and the mother of Fay and Ali.

She touched her face with her fingertips. She marveled that only twenty-four hours had passed since her arrest, but her skin had loosened and now hung in small folds. Lines she had never seen before circled her hazel eyes.

While thus involved, Mayada overheard one of the shadow women exclaim that even dogs in Iraq were treated better than prisoners, and she heard her own voice involuntarily call out, "Undoubtedly some dogs are treated better than us, but not our President's Doberman, Mukhtar!"

Some shadow women were busy arranging their personal items while others were braiding their hair or arranging their head scarves, but with Mayada's words, every woman but Aliya discontinued what she was doing and turned in Mayada's direction.

With a merry lilt to her voice, Samara looked at her. "Mayada, what nonsense are you speaking?"

With disbelief ringing in her voice, Roula, the most religious shadow woman in cell 52, asked, "A dog named Mukhtar?"

Roula's skepticism was credible because Mukhtar means "the chosen one," and is only one of the many names God called Prophet Muhammad in the Quran. To name a dog Mukhtar is the greatest insult to Islam's great prophet.

Without considering the consequences of discussing Saddam Hussein, Mayada began to tell the shadow women what she knew. "Yes," she told them, "it is true. During the early days when Saddam still felt warmly toward the mother of his children, he had given Sajida a Doberman pinscher named Mukhtar. And Saddam personally selected the unseemly name. I even met the dog after Saddam had given it a death sentence." Mayada continued, "Believe me, you would rather double your sentence in this prison than suffer as that poor dog suffered!"

Samara cautioned, "Watch what you say. If they are listening," and she tilted her head toward the metal door, "they will cut out your tongue and leave you to bleed to death. There would be nothing we could do."

Every Iraqi knew that to criticize President Saddam or a member of his family brought an automatic sentence of tongue cutting before death, so Mayada understood Samara's point. She moved away from the door and toward the rear wall of the cell. Once there, she settled back on the floor and lowered her voice to a whisper. The shadow

women were curious to hear her story and began to gather in a circle
for the second time that morning.

She continued to speak in a low voice. "This happened in 1979,
during the early days of Saddam's rule. Sajida and Saddam did not yet
hate each other, and with his new political position, he worried about
her security and the safety of their children. Saddam bought Sajida a
Doberman puppy, named it Mukhtar, only Allah knows why, and had
it well trained so that it would attack when given the simple command, 'Mukhtar, go!' One day Sajida was swimming, and when she
came out of the pool and reached for her towel, the dog was standing
by the edge of the pool watching her. Sajida is a cruel woman who
mistreats her house servants, so she is not the type to care about the
feelings of animals. She didn't want the dog around and without
thinking, she flicked her towel at it and said, 'Mukhtar, go.'

"Sajida later admitted to her doctor, a physician who tended to
my family during the same time he cared for Saddam's family, that her
words of attack confused the dog and that Mukhtar had looked all
around and, seeing no one available to tackle, attacked her. Sajida
quickly rolled up her towel and stuffed it in the dog's mouth, but by
then the security guards heard her screams and came and pulled
Mukhtar away. So she was not injured in any manner."

A young and unmarried shadow woman by the name of Sara gave
a little cry and placed her hand over her mouth.

Mayada smiled at the young woman before telling the rest of the
bizarre story. "When Saddam was informed of the incident he was so
furious at the dog that he held a little mock trial. I was told that he sat
behind his desk with the dog facing him while the dog was held tight
on a chain by one of his guards. Saddam was the judge and jury and
he sentenced Mukhtar to die by hunger and thirst, even though the
dog had performed flawlessly as trained. Before the dog was taken out
of the room to be put to death, Saddam took an electric prod and
shocked the dog three or four times for good measure.

"Yet the worst part was that Saddam not only wanted the dog

dead, but he said that the crime of attacking a member of the ruling family demanded prolonged torment prior to death, and so he sentenced Mukhtar to suffering as long as possible. Saddam instructed his security guards to chain the dog to a metal pole that was hammered in the ground beside the pool. Those guards later reported that Saddam said it would be comic for the dog to die of thirst while chained within a foot of a pool filled with water.

"That poor dog was chained so securely to the pole that its neck was almost flat against the pole, so it couldn't sit or lie down. And there it remained, day after day in the hot sun, while Saddam observed and laughed at the dog's pitiful howls. Once or twice a day Saddam or his oldest son, Uday, who every Iraqi knows is even more cruel than his father, would shock the dog with the electric prod.

"Everyone in that merciless household had a heart of stone other than the youngest daughter, Hala, but that dog's sufferings were so severe that even Sajida was upset about the sight. But of course, no one had the nerve to protest to Saddam on the dog's behalf."

Mayada finished the sad story by telling them that, "When the physician returned to the palace to check on Sajida for another medical problem, he saw Mukhtar dying in that pitiful way and asked one of the guards what was going on. When he was told that Saddam had sentenced the dog to die, the doctor built up his courage and went back into the house and told Saddam that he needed a watchdog for security and asked if he might have that dog. For some reason Saddam was in an indifferent mood at that specific moment, so he shrugged and told the doctor to take him. The doctor went to Mukhtar and had one of the guards help cut the chain choking the poor animal. The doctor told me that in the course of his profession he had witnessed the most horrific suffering, yet he had to fight back tears when he saw the condition of Mukhtar. As a result of the dog's efforts to pull free, the chain had burrowed into his flesh. The doctor said he thought the dog was already dead, but he scooped a little of the pool water in his hands and let it drip over the dog's face and saw a flicker of an eyelid. He lifted Mukhtar in his arms and carried him to his car and drove to his home, where he nursed the Doberman back to full health.

"A year or so later when I visited that doctor's house in Mosul, I was overjoyed to see the dog happy. The doctor proudly told me that the Doberman, now given a more fitting name, was a marvelous family pet." Mayada laughed. "I even have the dog's photograph, sitting in the living room with family members."

The shadow women sat in silence. Although every woman there was suffering at the hands of Saddam's own security forces, each had always held hope that should Saddam learn the details of their personal stories, he would intervene and have them released. But now with this new information, they understood for the first time that their President was clearly deranged and that perhaps he was the cause of all the brutality taking place in Baladiyat and every other prison in Iraq.

A petite shadow woman with jet black hair and blue eyes, a woman by the name of Eman, spoke to Mayada for the first time that day. While she was too frightened to ask a question about Saddam, she wanted to know the name of the doctor who had saved Mukhtar.

"I had best not say. He is still one of Saddam's physicians."

Eman nodded in understanding. Every Iraqi not employed in the vast Iraqi security apparatus took care to protect others in the only way they knew, by keeping them anonymous.

Their circle was interrupted by the sounds of a man screeching. He was pleading for mercy as he was dragged through the hallway. As he passed by their cell door he temporarily escaped his jailer's clutches. They heard him tumble against the metal door, and in a panic, he frantically banged on the door with his fists, begging to be let into their cell as though he believed it was a possible avenue of escape. But the guards jumped him and it was clear from the sounds that balled fists were hitting the man on his face and body. After a multitude of curses and hits, the weeping prisoner was taken away.

Mayada's eyes met Samara's eyes for a short time before she asked why there was so much torture this morning, since she had told her they did not torture in the mornings.

Samara's face flushed red and she shrugged and held her delicate white hands in the air. "There are times when they make an exception."

Mayada felt a rush of affection, for she now knew that Samara had lied to calm her fears. Samara added, "But it is true that they do the greater part of their torturing at night."

Roula murmured that Samara was telling the truth.

Everyone sat quietly and listened to the screams as they slowly faded away, before an older shadow woman wearing thick eyeglasses said, "I never considered Sajida's cruelty, before now. I felt sorry for her when Saddam took Samara Shabendar for his younger wife, and I decided then that I liked Sajida."

Samara sighed. "Iman, now we know you wasted your sympathy."

Iman nodded in agreement. "I had an image in my mind that was unreal."

Mayada wanted the entire world to know the complete truth about Saddam's family. "She is even more stupid than she is cruel, and she can be thankful that Saddam didn't divorce her," Mayada whispered. "Saddam hates her and she hates Saddam. The only thing they have in common is their children, and although they are still legally married, they rarely see each other."

Samara asked, "Truly?"

"What I am telling you is true."

"Tell us the whole truth of this woman," Iman implored.

One of the younger shadow women named Muna breathlessly asked, "Have you met Saddam?"

Mayada didn't answer but Samara laughed lowly, then cupped her hands and whispered. "Of course she has!"

Even Aliya had begun listening by this time, and she quietly joined the circle. She looked at Mayada and asked, "Will you tell us about him?"

Mayada nodded yes without hesitation. Yes, she would talk. Everything had altered for her over the past twenty-four hours, and she had moved past her usual precaution of refusing to reveal what she knew about Saddam and his family or his inner circle of officials. She had changed so radically since the morning of her arrest that her only regret was that her audience was too small. If she could will it to be true, her listening audience would begin to multiply until the entire world could hear what she knew about Saddam Hussein.

"Just speak with a low voice," Samara urged once again.

"I will tell you everything, from the beginning." Then she smiled at Samara. "And I will whisper."

Samara was understandably nervous about the topic. "We *must* be prepared, so if the door opens, I will act as though I am discussing my favorite foods, and," she gestured toward an older shadow woman with blond hair that Mayada did not yet know, "Anwar, you argue with me that I do not know the meaning of good food. The rest of you, start chattering about this or that so that nothing we are saying is understood." She looked at Mayada and smiled widely. "These men believe we are nothing but a bunch of stupid women."

Anwar laughingly agreed to her role in the deception, and then everyone looked expectantly at Mayada and asked her to go on.

Mayada told them that her mother met Saddam in 1969, only a year after the unpopular Baath military coup in which Ahmed Hassan Al-Bakir became President. She reminded them that the Baathist Party was not accepted by Iraqi intellectuals, and that her parents had never joined the party. In reality, when the Baath Party seized power, there was political confusion in Iraq, and many former government officials were waiting for the true faces of these new rulers to be revealed before deciding whether to remain in Iraq or flee to a neighboring Arab country.

"My parents had been invited to a foreign embassy for a small party, and because it was summer, a dinner buffet was served in the garden. My father, Nizar, was having a discussion with one of the foreign ambassadors in attendance, and my mother was filling her plate while chatting with the wife of the Lebanese ambassador. It was a routine social function, with female guests talking about the upcoming social season and male guests discussing politics, although everyone was more wary than usual since word had spread throughout Baghdad that the Baath leaders were averse to any criticism. My father told me that the Baathists didn't have any patience for friendly political bickering, which as you know is an innocent form of entertainment common in the Arab world—men have been known to sit for hours in a coffee shop while enjoying hearty arguments about the current ruling party.

"Round tables covered with white tablecloths decorated with floral arrangements were scattered throughout the garden. The Lebanese lady suggested to my mother that they find a place to sit, and when they saw a table with two available seats, they walked to take their place. Two men were already seated at the table, and both were eating. Mother later described one of the two men, who she said was young and handsome. He was eating very slowly and had excellent table manners. She took note only because most Iraqi men have atrocious eating habits, and this young man's manners set him apart.

"Mother said that the young man looked up and smiled and said hello without introducing himself. She later remembered that the young man's eyes were deep black and enormously round and that they were shining with uncommon brightness that reminded her for some reason of an animal's eyes.

"Mother spent her time talking with the Lebanese woman, and then after a while the Kuwaiti ambassador's wife passed by the table, pinched her on the arm and leaned down to whisper, 'I didn't know you knew him. Call me tomorrow and tell me everything.'

"Puzzled, not knowing who the Kuwaiti woman was talking about, Mother said nothing and resumed eating. A few minutes later, the large-eyed young man approached her and asked, 'How are you, Ustatha [Professor] Salwa?' "

"Mother replied that she was fine, and asked him how he was. 'Well, it's a heavy burden,' he remarked cryptically.

"Mother said she had no idea what burden he was laboring under, but assumed his comment had to do with the problems of a big family or a family business. Then he made a few comments that she thought little of, for she had heard similar remarks about her father from every Iraqi. 'I am a great admirer of Sati Al-Husri,' he told her. 'I used to go to your father, Sati, every other Friday when I was a poor law student in Cairo. I asked him many questions, but that great man never once turned me away or tired of answering my questions.' Mother thanked him before pushing aside her sadness—her father, Sati, had died the year before, only four months after the Baath Party came into power. His absence had left a hole in her heart. She wanted to ask the young man his name, but thinking that would be rude since he assumed she knew him, she said nothing. His words about her father were flowing by now. 'I have always said that Sati Al-Husri could have been the wealthiest man in the Middle East if he had charged only a few coins for each of the textbooks he authored. But instead of charging a fee for his books, he won the hearts of millions.'" It was a well-known fact that Sati's books were used in every Arab school and that he had refused author's royalties, proclaiming that knowledge was like the air and should be free, so he gave permission for every school to print and use as many of his books as they needed without charge. While he accepted royalties from books sold through traditional outlets such as bookstores, he never once accepted royalties for his books that were used in teaching.

"Mother was becoming embarrassed by this time, and since she thought this man was having problems with his business, she decided that my father might be able to help him, and finally invited the young man to bring his wife by the villa. She offered my father's help with his difficulties.

"Mother said that the young man's eyes immediately lit with merriment, before he lowered his lids and smiled. Later, when she discovered that she had been speaking with Saddam Hussein, the man known as Mr. Deputy, she realized that that was the moment he first understood that she did not recognize the man who held the second highest office in the country."

Several of the shadow women tittered, hardly able to imagine the dazzling lives that Mayada's family had lived, and unable to conceive of a mother so confident that she had dismissed the Baathist upstarts as a gang that would be out of power so quickly that she didn't even need to bother to note the physical appearance of the powerful Vice President.

Of course, in the beginning, Saddam had preferred to be unknown, and had avoided the glare of publicity. The Baath Party first grabbed power in 1963, but came and went so quickly that when they returned in 1968, most people did not take them seriously, fully believing that their second brush with power would be as brief as their first.

But *everyone* underestimated Saddam Hussein.

Even though Saddam was only thirty-one at the time of the second Baathist takeover, he had learned from the mistakes of 1963, and he was clever enough to remain in the background until the future of the party was assured. Every Iraqi now knows that he built his power base in the party through the intelligence service. From the beginning, the Mukhabarat—the government's terror and intimidation organization—had reported to Saddam, but although he was the sole architect of terror and would personally take the lives of many Iraqis, he made a concerted effort to present himself as a refined gentleman with polished manners.

Mayada told them that her own first meeting with Saddam came at the saddest juncture of her life, so she had intentionally pushed every memory of that meeting out of her mind until now.

"My father died of colon cancer in 1974, and before the funeral we received a telephone call from Saddam, who was still Vice President. He offered his condolences, and said he hoped to attend the Fattiha [men's mourning]."

When a family is in mourning in Iraq, the doors to their houses remain unlocked for seven days. People come and go without ringing or knocking, and sometime later that day someone from the presidential palace entered Mayada's mother's home and delivered an envelope from Saddam.

"When Mother looked inside the envelope, she saw that the envelope was filled with 3,000 Iraqi dinars [$10,900]. That could have bought a house, but thankfully we already owned our home. Mother insisted that we call Saddam to offer our thanks but I reminded her that in Iraq one does not react that way to an act of kindness. Although Iraqis do not acknowledge gifts until later, and they do so by returning a favor rather than by verbal thanks, Mother was adamant that it would be appalling manners not to thank the Iraqi Vice President for his good turn. She said she didn't care what an Iraqi might or might not do. My mother took her own father Sati's beliefs about Arab Nationalism to heart, and always claimed she was not Iraqi, or Syrian, or Lebanese, but that she was an Arab, plain and simple. She would behave with good manners even if I would not.

"Since my mother had no sons, it was up to me as the oldest daughter to represent the family. I didn't want to make that call. From the beginning of my life I had been influenced by my father. He disliked the Baathist regime, so I disliked them. Even though many of my school friends were members of the party, I never joined. As we all know, the Baathists made everyone who registered at a university join the party, but the children and grandchildren of Sati Al-Husri were given an automatic exemption from that rule. Although we were not Baathist, we were given priority status in many things. I did not want to talk to Saddam Hussein, a man my father distrusted.

"But my mother was not a person easy to refuse, and so I had to do her bidding. I was only eighteen, but I called the Vice President on his direct telephone line. I noticed that his voice was nasal but that he was extremely polite. I wanted to get off the phone as quickly as possible, so I thanked him for his kind gesture and then waited for him to say goodbye. He told me that he was very sorry but that he would not be able to make the Fattiha, and he asked the family to forgive him for that. He was so humble during that call that he won me over." She confessed to the shadow women, "I'm ashamed to say that when I hung up the telephone, I was a supporter of Saddam Hussein."

Samara nodded in understanding along with several of the other shadow women. In the beginning of his reign, many Iraqis supported Saddam Hussein. He came into power with ambitious ideas to improve the country, and quickly began to make changes that soon benefited most Iraqis. He had been influenced by Sati's belief in education for every Iraqi, and he launched a large-scale building program of schools in every village for young Iraqis and tutors for older citizens. Then he focused on health care, building hospitals and medical clinics. Within a few years he opened every profession to women, creating an atmosphere of equal opportunity for women in Iraq unknown anywhere else in the Middle East. For a short time, it appeared that good things were coming to Iraq. And, of course, Saddam had been so guarded about his plans to build an internal security organization that ordinary citizens didn't have any idea what kind of security nightmare was on the horizon.

"My mother was considered one of the most fashionable women in Iraq, and she traveled to Paris frequently for the designers' shows, where she would select her fall or spring clothing collection. Saddam knew about this, so shortly after meeting Mother at the dinner party, she received a men's clothing catalog from the palace, along with a note from Saddam asking her to please look through the catalog and note any appropriate day wear for a man in his position.

"Everyone who knew him understood that he was a man who loved clothes—he changed designer suits five times a day. Mother told me that she sympathized with a village boy who was previously deprived but now found himself in a position to buy a house of fashion, if he so desired. So, she turned to the pages and items he had indicated he liked and was astonished to see that he fancied the velvet jackets worn by roulette tenders in gambling houses and casinos, where the jackets have no pockets for obvious reasons. My mother had been in the company of world leaders for her entire life, so she had no qualms about telling Saddam that his selections were unsuitable and to *never, never* purchase a velvet suit without pockets. Anyhow, after writing him a note about the tasteless velvet suits, she looked through the catalog and made a number of better selections and had the family driver return the catalog to the palace. Later when Saddam was televised at one government function or another, Mother and I saw him wearing a variety of the choices she had made."

The shadow women were stunned and urged Mayada on.

"Later, in 1980, Mother was the head of a committee that was compiling a special display book about Iraq. The book was a very expensive production with full-color photos, and when it was finished, Saddam, who had overthrown Bakir in 1979 and appointed himself President, received a special, hand-delivered copy from Mother's office. He was very taken with that book and asked Mother to come by his office and bring her two daughters with her. By this time Abdiya was newly married and living in Tunis, so I went alone with Mother.

"We were escorted into Saddam's offices the moment we arrived at the palace. The war with Iran had not yet started so Saddam was wearing civilian clothes. He had on a white suit with a black shirt and white tie, and Mother nudged my side with her arm. I almost burst out laughing when I looked into her face and saw that she was giving me a cross-eyed grimace because the President of Iraq looked like a junior version of the mobster Al Capone in that suit. Mother later told me that Saddam Hussein was one man who shouldn't be *allowed* to select his own clothes. But that soon ceased to be a problem, because he discarded civilian clothes altogether when the war with Iran erupted. He was never seen out of his military uniform, and Mother once said that that was the only good benefit of a terrible war.

"In June 1981, I had a weekend column at the *Al-Jumhuriya* newspaper called 'Itlalat' ['Overviews'] and I had written an article about the concept of time—comparing it to the time of Allah, which is unlimited—and I touched on the Einstein theory and the backward effect of time, and how much I wished there were forty-eight hours in the day instead of the current twenty-four.

"Everyone at the paper praised the article, and then I received an unexpected telephone call from Mother saying that I must hurry home. Someone from the palace had called and would be calling again soon. I hung up with a sense of dread. I was frightened that my article might have displeased the President, who had become increasingly testy after the start of war, so I was uneasy. Within minutes of returning home, the telephone rang and the caller was a man by the name of Amjed. He was polite, identifying himself as Saddam's private secretary. He went on to say that President Saddam wanted to see me at 5:00 in the afternoon the following day. I was told to come to the Al-Qasr Al-Jumhouri, or the Republican Palace at Karadda on the Tigris.

"I was becoming increasingly anxious and didn't believe I could bear a full night wondering why I was being summoned by Saddam, so I bluntly asked the secretary if anything was wrong. Amjed chuckled and said, 'No, no, you should say, is something right, dear sister, because you are being commended by the President for your work.'

"His words put my mind at ease so I called my editor at the paper, Sahib Hussain Al-Samawi, and told him what was happening. Of course, he was thrilled, and said that the minute I left the palace I was to come by his office and report on everything that happened.

"I was married at the time but everything was going wrong with Salam. But he was pleased about the situation and told me that he would ask for a pass from his military camp to take me to meet with the President. His military commander gave him permission to take off the entire day because of the event. So at 11:30 the following morning, he came to the house, took a bath and changed clothes, and assured me that he would return at 4:00 that afternoon to take me to the palace.

"My marriage was troubled because Salam had several girlfriends, and when he did not return by 4:30, I knew that he had lied once again. I had to rush to find a taxi to take me to the palace because Mother, believing that I could rely on Salam, had used the family car and driver to take her to an afternoon function.

"I arrived at the palace disheveled and breathless five minutes before my appointment, although I managed to pull myself together. I was escorted by a junior secretary from one large room to another until I finally arrived in a vast living room, which was filled with many other Iraqis waiting to meet with Saddam. Despite the war with Iran, there was an abundance of everything at the palace. Palace guests were served juice and offered various brands of soft drinks, which were served in tall crystal glasses worth more than most Iraqis made in a week. After a few minutes, everyone was ushered into a second large room, which was set up for dining with a buffet table with every conceivable kind of food displayed. There was even a huge mound of the most expensive Beluga caviar in the center of the table, but most of the people present were poor Iraqis and had never seen Beluga caviar and refused to eat those tiny shiny black fish eggs, even after I assured them it was an edible food that was terribly expensive and considered to be a delicacy throughout the world. There was a second side table laden with sweets and every kind of fruit—pineapples, mangoes and cherries.

"I was too nervous to eat, but everyone else was eating with enthusiasm. A lady with brightly colored orange hair edged in my direction. She made an attempt to befriend me, telling me that she was eager to meet with Saddam and had written him a letter about a lost inheritance, and that she was sure she was going to have success in getting her birthright back. She hinted that she had a romantic crush on the President, and that made me wary, so I slowly moved to the opposite side of the room where I initiated a conversation with an older lady. But that poor woman was so nervous that she could barely whisper her name, and her hands were trembling so hard that she dropped two glasses of juice on the Persian carpet. So I moved away from her as well.

"After finishing our dinner the group was escorted back to the living room, where tea was served. We sat and waited, and just as I was thinking that we had been forgotten, a man dressed in military fatigues entered the room and called out my name. When I walked out of the room, I thought I felt envious eyes upon my back.

"I was taken to another living room, smaller but more posh than the large one. Soon I heard a huge commotion and military men were running and shouting and I understood that Saddam had arrived at the palace. In about an hour a second military man came into the room and requested that I follow him. I was exhausted by this time but did as I was told. I was taken to yet another room, which had a large wooden desk in the center with a number of blue upholstered chairs with gold-leaf designs on the wood.

"The second military man shook my hand and congratulated me, then gave me instructions on how to conduct myself when I met the President. He was frighteningly firm when he said that I was not to speak first, nor was I to extend my hand to shake Saddam's hand but to respond accordingly if he offered first.

"I was surprised, because Saddam had been so approachable and humble the last time I had met him. I told myself that the new face of Saddam was emerging."

Samara laughed and whispered, "Perhaps that was his real face and his old face had been the fake."

Mayada nodded in agreement before finishing her story. "Two tall, wooden doors were opened by a military usher. Saddam was sitting behind a desk in yet another room. He was wearing large-rimmed glasses that I had never seen before, and he was dressed in his military clothes, but his personal appearance was much the same as it had been the last time I had seen him. He was a dark man with very curly hair and a heavy masculine jaw, and still had that small, light-green tattoo on the tip of his nose, the one he had removed a few years later.

"Saddam then surprised me with a smile and extended his hand, which I shook according to the instructions I had received. He asked, 'How is our creative writer?' I replied in the proper Iraqi manner, saying that as long as he was well and strong, all Iraqis were well and prosperous. He then asked me how everyone was at the newspaper, and I reported that they had all asked me to convey their love and respect to him.

"He smiled broadly before saying, 'I read your time account in the paper and it was excellent. You are a fitting granddaughter for Sati Al-Husri. He would be pleased.' He then tapped me lightly on my shoulder and said, 'I want you to promise me that no matter what, this pen of yours will go on writing on behalf of our great revolution. Write what your integrity sees fit and you are on the right road.'

"I thanked him for his kind words, and he then asked me if I owned an automobile. I replied that I did, so then he asked me if I was pleased with my home. I said I was and he seemed amused. He said, 'You are Salwa's daughter. You don't need anything or anyone,' which I thought was an odd comment, but after considering his words and the manner in which he said them, I understood that he was giving me a compliment, because my grandfather Sati had raised his daughter to be a strong woman with opinions and insisted that she seek a noteworthy education, which gave her independence, and having those qualities combined in an Arab woman is a rarity in Iraq.

"Saddam then buzzed someone from his telephone and a photographer came into the room and took several pictures. Saddam surprised me when he kissed me on my forehead and told me to continue making the great Sati Al-Husri proud. Then, at the last moment he told me, 'Just thinking about your grandfather, Sati Al-Husri, and what he stood for, makes me proud to be an Arab.' Then he shook my hand for a final time and walked me to the door.

"When I walked into the next room, the man named Amjed, who had been my original contact regarding this meeting with Saddam, presented me with an envelope and two leather boxes. He said that a car was waiting to take me wherever I wished to go. I told him to take me to the *Al-Jumhuriya* offices, where I went to meet my boss, Sahib Hussein Al-Samawi, as I had promised him.

"Sahib was ecstatic about the meeting and Saddam's praise, and he began to make plans to print my article in the paper for a second time the following day. There was even a side editorial about Saddam's interest in Mayada Al-Askari's work and his admiration for that particular piece.

"When I arrived home I opened the envelope, and once again, there was exactly 3,000 Iraqi dinars. Inside the two leather boxes were two watches. One was an expensive Patek Phillipe with diamonds on white gold and the name Saddam written inside the watch, and the second one was an Omega gold watch with Saddam's picture on the face. I played a small joke on my mother. When she came home I had one watch on each wrist. Mother choked with laughter. I wore one watch for a few weeks, but soon put them both away in a drawer because I couldn't bear to see Saddam's face, or his name, every few minutes.

"A few days later a palace representative came to the newspaper and presented me with a leather-bound folder with a gold-leaf border. Inside were two pictures of Saddam with me. Sahib framed one for the newspaper offices and sat it on his desk, and Mother framed the second one and placed it on a bookcase in the sitting room."

Mayada paused and stared at the faces of the shadow women. The women were staring back at her, wanting to hear more stories. Samara said that she must not stop—that she had to tell them every detail of every meeting with Saddam.

Mayada laughed and said that her voice would not last much longer, but that she would share the most important points of two or three more meetings.

"In 1982," she continued, "I had written an essay for *Fonoun* magazine titled 'This Beautiful Silence,' which had to do with war but was primarily a romantic account of a woman telling a man that she didn't need words to express her feelings for him, because their love was like great poetry. Muhammed Al-Jazaeri, who was the editor-in-chief of the magazine where the article appeared, had telephoned me the day the piece was printed. He was excited to tell me that the Minister of Information, Latiff Nusaif Jassim, was going to present me with a letter, a large sum of money and a television set. I was to appear at the Ministry the following morning at ten o'clock."

"That night was sleepless," Mayada said. "I was startled that the romantic piece had caught the interest of Saddam."

"Why were you surprised?" Iman asked. "All Iraqis know that Saddam is a romantic man."

"That is true," Aliya claimed. "My brother the general knows one of his guards, and he says that Saddam is devoted to stories centered around the love of beautiful women for a brave warrior. He must have seen himself in the article."

"Well, maybe," Mayada agreed. "In any case, the following morning I presented myself at ten o'clock. The Minister of Information was exceptionally pleasant and said, 'Your writings never fail in making Abu Uday [father of Uday, meaning Saddam] our great leader, may Allah preserve him, happy with your writings.' Minister Jassim reported that he was conveying the President's exact words and that the President asked him to tell me, 'It is like a breath of fresh air to read her writings while [he is] in the middle of his national duty (meaning the war with Iran).' The President was sorry that he was unable to present me with the award himself, because he was away at the front commanding Iraq's heroes."

Mayada did not share the rest of the story, which had a painful ending for her. That article was published the second time the follow-ing week with a reference to Saddam's award, or *takreem* as it is called in Iraq. She was introduced as the writer and her photograph was printed, and as a result she received bags of letters from soldiers at the front. One letter that she had never forgotten came from an anony-mous soldier. He confided that he had always looked for her articles but that he would never do it again, because now he knew that she was "one of them"—meaning Saddam's followers—and was writing only what they told her to write. She was deeply wounded by the let-ter because she knew that she had never been told what to write by anyone. Mayada did not write political commentary, which always had to follow the party line—she simply wrote what she felt about life and love, and it just so happened that Saddam had been drawn to her writings.

She told the shadow women, "My third *takreem* was presented in 1983, after I returned from a lengthy government trip to Sudan and wrote a piece called 'Vertical Rays of Sun,' referring to the Sudan's in-tense heat, and in the piece I discussed the country's poverty. Being in that country reminded me how much I loved Iraq.

"Once again I received word from the Ministry of Information that I was going to receive a *takreem* from the President, and that I should appear at the palace at 4:45 the following afternoon.

"Although it was late November it was still warm. When I arrived I was astonished to see that the palace grounds were teeming with crowds of men and women and children, and I thought for a minute that the palace was holding a fair or some other entertainment for the public. After a second look, however, I saw that there was no gaiety in the crowd—everyone looked miserable. The women were dressed in black to mourn their martyred sons or husbands who had died at the front. I thought that the palace looked as shabby as the poor Iraqis squatting on the lawn, and then I remembered that all the proceeds from the sale of oil were going toward the war effort, so that should not have been a surprise.

"I suddenly realized that the crowd was there to collect money. I knew from news stories that every widowed woman, or every family that lost a son, received 5,000 Iraqi dinars [$15,500] for their sacrifice. These payments were considered a *Diyya,* or compensation for death. I knew the routine. Saddam would receive all the people there, five at a time. Each person would hand Saddam a letter, explaining where the father or son had been killed. Saddam would read the letter and then write instructions on it, saying how much money each person should be given. The mourner would then take the letter to the palace accounting office, where the money would be paid.

"Although the government made the payments in the beginning, the money ran out before too long. There were just too many dead soldiers. I was told later that the Saudi and Kuwaiti governments were the ones issuing the funds for payment. Iran had become the neighborhood bully, and the Al-Sabah family of Kuwait and the Al-Sa'ud family of Saudi Arabia were rewarding Iraqis for keeping Iran off their own backs.

"When I went into the palace, the secretary ushered me into Hussain Kamil's office, a man who was a junior officer at the time but who would one day marry Saddam's oldest daughter, Raghad, and consequently become one of Saddam's most trusted assassins. But after all those good things came Kamil's way, it all ended when Uday, Saddam's oldest son, became jealous of the enormous sums of money that Kamil was skimming from various government projects. Uday became his brother-in-law's devoted enemy. Knowing that Uday, who everyone knew was insane, would eventually murder him, Kamil fled to Jordan and humiliated Saddam with his disloyalty when he began to inform Iraq's enemies of everything he knew about Iraq's weapons program. When Saddam deceived him into returning to Iraq by assuring his safety and even holding his hand on the Quran and swearing that he would never harm the father of his grandchildren, Kamil foolishly returned and, of course, was murdered within a few days.

"But on the day that I met him, Kamil had not yet come into

favor—or gone out of favor." She began to laugh and covered her mouth with her hand. "I admit that I felt an instant loathing for Hussain. It had nothing to do with the fact he was an unattractive man of small stature with a long crooked nose that overshadowed a big bushy mustache. I was truly repulsed after looking into his eyes. That man had eyes that were filled with contempt for everyone around him, including me.

"However, he industriously attended to his duty. I was there with a poet and a musician, all invited there to accept cultural awards.

"Both of them were unusual. The musician was a tall, dark man whose eyes flashed with happiness. He had written a very popular patriotic song that was quite catchy, and Saddam had commanded that it be played at all the military posts. The verses were, 'Oh land, your soil is my Kafour' [the substance that Muslims sprinkle around a dead person's cloth before they are buried]. Do you remember that song?" Several shadow women began to nod and Samara bobbed her head as she hummed a few notes.

"The poet was the musician's physical opposite, a small, skinny man with yellowed skin. He had written a poem celebrating Saddam's greatness, a poem that expressed the love Iraqis felt for their President.

"Soon the three of us were led into another room. I was called to see Saddam before the poet and the musician. When I left those two, they were so giddy about their first meeting with Saddam that the musician had jumped to his feet and sung his song, while the poet had begun to chant his verses."

Samara burst out laughing, and Mayada laughed, too.

"I was relieved to leave them both behind. However, I could still hear their voices ringing all the way to the end of the long hallway."

Each of the shadow women joined in the laughing.

Mayada gathered herself and continued, "This meeting was different from all previous meetings. When I saw Saddam, he seemed preoccupied. I understood the reason for his ill temper. During those days, the war with Iran was not going well. Saddam had underestimated

Khomeini. I still cringe when I remember that Khomeini used young children as minesweepers. How would Iraq defeat such an adversary?

"Saddam complimented me on my writing and said he was pleased I was so free-thinking. He said he expected nothing less of Sati Al-Husri's granddaughter. He began to speak in a rush when he told me that regardless of what others thought, he wanted diversity when it came to writers. He said that that was what I was giving the people. He told me that I was pleasing him and that the last thing he wanted was journalism wearing a uniform. I'll never forget him saying that the Iraqi people needed to think of other things besides war. He added that the love of a loyal woman was every man's dream.

"Well, I was so stunned at his 'free' talk that I could barely answer him. He then smiled and said, 'Let's have a photograph.'

"I felt that he was in a huge rush to push through his appointments, so I told him that I was already the proud owner of a photograph with His Excellency. I really didn't want to take too much of his time, considering the war.

"When I said that, he laughed for the first time. He said, 'So let's make an album, and if you keep writing with such talent, an album is in your future.'

"After our picture was taken, he asked me if I needed anything in particular, that he wanted to present me with a special gift. He was in such a fine mood that I blurted out what I really wanted. I told him that I longed to take my baby Fay and travel to London to visit my mother. She was recovering from surgery. He asked me if I wanted to take Salam with us, but I replied that my husband was fighting on the front and I wouldn't think of taking him away from that important duty. Then, just like that"—she snapped her fingers—"Saddam told me that my wish was granted. I have never been so surprised. As we all know, Iraqis are prohibited from leaving Iraq during wartime, unless it is for government business. I stood there speechless while he called in his secretary and issued orders for airline tickets for me and my baby. We were going to London. Then Saddam surprised me even further when he issued a second order that I should be given 5,250 Iraqi dinars [$16,275] for the trip. I'll never forget the look on the secretary's face. I was not a member of the inner circle, so he was stunned that I was receiving this exception.

"Although my style of writing appealed to Saddam, I knew that my connection to Sati was a major reason I was so privileged. As I departed the palace I thought about how the respect and admiration won by my grandfather, Jido Sati, from every Iraqi, including Saddam Hussein, was now affecting my own life in such a positive manner. I thanked my Jido Sati and hope he heard me.

"From that time, I heard that Saddam followed my writings. In 1984, the Iraqi News Agency in London called Mother when she and I were visiting England, informing her that her daughter's writings had been pointed out by President Saddam Hussein as the best writings for 1983. I was surprised that the writings that most intrigued Saddam were several articles I had written about fortune-telling. Those were the most desperate days of the war, and fortune-telling was becoming very popular in Iraq. Iraqis were looking for solutions in many unorthodox directions. I had also written a paper dealing with parapsychology. This was part of a program for Saddam's eyes only, which was conducted for the General Publication Surveillance Directorate, which was listed under the Ministry of Information but was in reality functioning as a solo department.

"One day I received a telephone call from the palace with a message that Saddam wanted to question me about that research. I went to the palace hoping he would be in high spirits. But he was still in a low mood because of the Iranian war. Saddam got to business in a hurry. He told me that he was highly interested in something called ESP, or extrasensory perception, and he wanted me to do some special research for him on out-of-body experiences. He then confided that the Russians were doing excellent work in that field.

"I worked as hard as I could on the research and presented it to the committee. But I heard nothing about it from Saddam. I forgot about it. Then in 1986, I received a message from the Journalists Federation. They told me that President Saddam Hussein had been so impressed by that particular research that he had presented me with two pieces of land. Those plots were in a location called Saydiya in Baghdad. And that was the last of my private encounters with Saddam."

Not wanting the morning of storytelling to end, Samara said, "What about Saddam's wife? You promised you would tell us more about her."

Mayada nodded and agreed, but before she could tell those stories, one of the guards burst through the door. That man had an evil grin on his face, and when he called out Samara's name she burst out crying because she knew that she was being taken away to be tortured.

After Samara left the room, the women were no longer in the mood for gossip. Mayada pushed herself from the floor and sat quietly on her bunk as the other shadow women slowly returned to their own bedding. They all sat and waited, because they knew that when Samara returned she would need their support. The knowledge of what was happening to Samara was so depressing that Mayada could do nothing but despair. A few hours later the cell door opened and Samara was thrown back into the room, where she stumbled and fell into a heap on the floor. Her small cries brought all of the women to their feet, and everyone gathered around her broken body. In one quick glance Mayada saw that Samara was bleeding out of her nose and her ears, and that her arms were covered with cigarette burns.

Tears began to roll down Mayada's face as she stooped and helped lift Samara to her feet. For some reason the face of her gentle father flashed through her mind. Her father had taught her to be soft, saying that if she did not quarrel, no one on earth would be able to quarrel with her, but standing there looking at Samara, she knew with a great certainty that her father had been wrong.

5

Saddam's Wife, "The Lady" Sajida

Eager to help Samara, two or three shadow women tried to lift her up, but they lost their grip and Samara slid back to the floor. Mayada, too, reached out toward Samara, but to Mayada's surprise, her vision blurred and Samara's arm seemed first to grow tiny and distant, then to swell large and immediate. Shaken, Mayada propped herself against the prison wall and stood quietly. Although she could feel the coolness of the thick concrete on her face and body, the darkness encircling her was almost total, and the shadow women appeared as misty figures, like spiraling smoke that would speedily disperse.

Mayada's range of vision shrank further and she turned to the wall for comfort. The concrete was cracked, and Mayada noticed for the first time indentations in the wall, thin grooves made by fingernails. She pulled back in alarm. The claw marks, she knew, belonged to other terrified Iraqis frantic to escape the hell that their life had unexpectedly become. Mayada reached to place her own hands in the grooved cement and discovered, to her horror, that her fingers were a perfect fit. Mayada wanted to scream and run away but there was nowhere to run. She was a prisoner in a tiny cell with other women. She collapsed against the wall and struggled to regain her composure.

Although she could do nothing, she could hear the other women struggling to help Samara.

Thoughts of a day now long distant began to crowd out the ugly present. It was 1982, and Dr. Fadil had stopped by Mayada's home for a brief visit, returning two books he had borrowed from her mother's extensive library. Soon after he left, Mayada heard the front doorbell ring. Her mother was sitting in the back garden reading a book, so Mayada rose to open the door. She saw with some surprise that their visitor was Um Sami, the mother of a neighboring family.

Although the two families lived near each other, they were not close; earlier contact between the families had been limited to a brief meeting followed by polite nodding in passing. Recently, however, Mayada and her mother had found occasion to discuss Um Sami, because when they first met her, she was overweight, but in a matter of weeks her fat had melted and she was now reed thin. Most noticeably, Um Sami was seen more than once pacing her garden while she ripped at her hair and pulled at her clothes, clear signals that she was in a state of mourning. In fact, only a week before her unexpected appearance at Mayada's family's doorstep, Mayada had approached her to ask if a relative had passed away. But Um Sami had gestured for her to go away, and she complied.

Now she hoped to discover the source of the poor woman's tears.

Um Sami lingered on the doorstep a moment before feverishly asking, "Was that Dr. Fadil I saw? Head of the secret police?"

Mayada nodded, knowing that every Iraqi would recognize Dr. Fadil, because his picture was often in the paper or on the news. Something terrible must have happened to her or her family, Mayada mused. "Yes. That was Dr. Fadil," she confirmed.

Um Sami threw herself onto Mayada, exclaiming, "I must know the fate of my sons. I have twin boys, Omar and Hassan. They are both only fourteen. They went to the market for a new football, and they never returned."

Mayada gently led Um Sami into their sitting room. "Come, sit," she urged.

Um Sami continued to wail. "We have searched Baghdad. We have gone to hospitals. Police stations. Graveyards. We found nothing. Nothing. Nothing! My beautiful sons have disappeared."

Mayada hurried to pour Um Sami a glass of water, then sat to face her distraught neighbor. Mayada's gaze wandered across the woman's face; she took in her neighbor's sloping shoulders and her hands, which trembled uncontrollably.

Um Sami sipped and carefully placed the glass on the round table to her side. She cleared her throat before continuing with her story. "This morning my husband received an anonymous phone call. The caller was a man who claimed to be a former prisoner of the secret police. He was in a cell with our sons. He said our boys had given him our telephone number. From what he could recall of their story, they had been walking down the street when two men jumped them and began to kick and slap them, claiming they were staring at them. They were members of the Mukhabarat." She turned her face to Mayada in bewilderment. "Staring? Since when is staring a crime?"

Mayada clutched her hands together. "Go on."

Um Sami begin to slap her own face and cry out. "My sons are still babies. Still students. They have never gotten into trouble."

Mayada felt a touch of nausea as she recalled seeing Omar and Hassan playing football in the street. Both boys were polite and attractive, always smiling. The twins never failed to halt their game when they heard Mayada start her car to pull into the street. Those children were in prison? For the "crime" of staring? That was an offense that she would bet was not on the books.

Now she murmured, "What can I do?"

Um Sami had a wavering, uncertain look about her when she touched Mayada's cheek with her hand. "I know Dr. Fadil can help. Please, call him for me. Ask him to help me find my boys." With one long, pale finger she began to mechanically thump her chin. "I know they are in prison. That caller described them perfectly. Tall, slim boys with brown hair. Each with a small brown mole on his cheek. How many twins are there with that description in Baghdad?" Her voice went soft, then insistent again. "The caller said they were being tortured. *Tortured!* I must find my sons." With that, Um Sami began slapping at her face once more until Mayada grabbed her hands and held them tightly between her own.

Mayada knew that the most prudent course was to do nothing, but it was impossible for her to ignore Um Sami's grief. The poor woman was so miserable that Mayada recklessly promised, "I will contact Dr. Fadil. Tomorrow. I will ask him to find out where your sons are. If they are in jail, and if he can find them, he will have them released."

Um Sami jumped to her feet and began to kiss Mayada repeatedly on both cheeks. "I knew you would help me."

At that moment, both women's attention was drawn to the noise of a television that had been left on. The evening news had begun. On the television screen, a male figure smiled as images of soldiers and exploding fireworks swirled behind his shoulder. He began to sing a song about Saddam, a tune that was played before every newscast:

> "*Oh Saddam, our victories;*
> *Oh Saddam, our beloved:*
> *You carry the nation's dawn*
> *Between your eyes.*
> *Oh Saddam, everything is good*
> *With you.*
> *Allah! Allah! We are happy;*
> *Because Saddam lights our days.*"

The image of Saddam Hussein flashed on the screen. He was shown first patting the heads of dark-curled schoolgirls in billowy white dresses. Then he was depicted striding onto a balcony to wave at his chanting supporters clamoring approvingly below. The newscaster's image reappeared, and he continued to praise Saddam's greatness.

Mayada and Um Sami stared at Saddam's image on the television screen, and then at each other. Neither woman said what they were thinking, yet Mayada sensed that Um Sami thought Saddam was evil.

Over the years, Iraqis had suffered a cycle of hope and despair from countless coups and attempted coups, leading ordinary citizens to lose touch with their government. In 1968, when the Baath Party seized power from the government in power at the time, Iraqis hoped that the new party would not simply prove to be one tyrant replacing another. And at first, Saddam had charmed and endeared himself to his people. But now, the veil that obscured Saddam from scrutiny was fluttering, and people were catching glimpses of the tyrant beneath.

Um Sami made an attempt to smile, but she could only manage a grimace as she stumbled to the door, repeating, "I told my husband, I knew you would help me. I knew you would help me."

The following morning Mayada woke early. She dressed and went in to work an hour sooner than usual, so she could call Dr. Fadil at his offices and explain the problem.

At first friendly, Dr. Fadil quickly became irritated, and with a cold, indifferent voice said, "Mayada, I prefer that you mind your own business."

Mayada persisted, telling him, "I cannot in this case. Um Sami is going mad with grief. These boys are only fourteen years old. I saw their innocence with my own eyes. I know you have the power to help them. Please."

Dr. Fadil was silent. Mayada could picture him chewing the inside of his cheek while he mulled over what to do. Finally he spoke. "Have Um Sami appear at the police headquarters at Park Al-Sadoon. Tell her to be there at ten o'clock tomorrow morning." He then added, "Mayada, please don't make a habit of this. Perhaps these boys are murderers or smugglers. All boys are innocent in the eyes of their mothers, you know."

Mayada hung up the phone without answering and left work so she could rush to tell Um Sami the wonderful news: Dr. Fadil was going to help her find her sons.

A few days passed while Mayada waited for good news about the boys. When Dr. Fadil briefly dropped by to ask Salwa a few questions about one of Sati's books, Mayada asked him about the charge of "staring." But Dr. Fadil had a chill in his voice when he asked Mayada, "Do you believe criminals speak the truth?" He added quickly, "I prefer not to discuss business away from my office." Dr. Fadil then asked for Mayada's mother and turned his back to examine a set of Sati's books, stacked nearby on a table. His indifferent manner discouraged any further questions.

Mayada was so disappointed in his lack of humanity that she left the room as quickly as proper decorum allowed.

But later, alone in her bedroom, she permitted herself to imagine the happy moment when Um Sami would appear at her door with her sons. Once again Omar and Hassan would play football in the streets, and she would wave at them on her way to work. Mayada was so energized at the thought that the twins would be saved that she decided to bake a cake and present it to the boys on their homecoming, so they could enjoy a small party with their playmates.

Hearing nothing after several days, and impatient to see the boys safe at home with their parents, she finally visited the neighbors' house. Um Sami came to the door and, catching sight of Mayada's expectant face, gestured with a finger poised over her lips that it was not safe for the two to speak inside the house, and motioned for Mayada to follow her into the garden.

As Mayada followed Um Sami, she noted that the poor woman was letting herself go badly. Her clothes were horribly wrinkled, as though they had been slept in. Her hair was in disarray, and her shoes were old and badly scuffed.

Mayada sighed and turned her attention to the garden. It was springtime and the trees and bushes were in full bloom. The welcome aroma filled the air. Mayada brushed the white flowers hanging from a low tree branch with her hand and watched as the petals drifted to the ground, dappling the narrow, winding path.

When they reached the garden's back corner, Um Sami looked anxiously around before she whispered to Mayada, "In addition to the twins, I have two other sons. They are married and live in their own homes. They've been threatened if I speak to anyone—even to you, someone who knows Dr. Fadil."

In tense silence, Mayada stood alongside Um Sami, wishing now that she had not sought news. Mayada forced herself to stand in place, when her greatest desire was instead to run to the sanctuary of her bedroom. She wished nothing greater than to settle into a familiar spot with a beloved book, to forget the cruelty of the world in which she lived. But Mayada moistened her lips with her tongue and steeled herself to listen.

"I went to the reception area, just as instructed," began Um Sami. "Hundreds of people waited outside the gate, but our names were on a list so we were allowed inside. The guards treated us with grudging respect. Dr. Fadil had intervened in our case. We were led into a square room. At the end of the room, a large door led to a huge cooler, big enough to hold dozens of bodies. I was in shock, because I went to Park Al-Sadoon believing I would find my sons in a cell and bring them home with me. But my stomach began to twist and turn as we were handed a list of names that hung on a wall beside the cooler. We were told to examine the list for our boys' names. We searched every name, but they were not listed. We were taken to another room where a terrible stench held me back, but I covered my mouth with my abaaya and forced myself to go in. Inside were a great many bodies, but I saw my sons at once. Just as they were bonded in life, they were together in death. They were there in that ghastly place, side by side in a sitting position." Her lips quivered as she burst into a torrent of speech. "My beautiful sons had been horribly tortured. Blackened blood covered their face and hands and feet. There were visible burn marks.

"I screamed, but a guard shoved me backward cruelly and ordered, 'You! No shouting!' So I was forced to stuff my abaaya in my mouth to silence my grief.

"While my husband identified our sons, I couldn't help but look around the room. Was this the place in which my poor sons had breathed their last? I saw things no mother should ever see. I saw one young man whose chest bore the searing print of an electric iron. I saw a second young man whose chest spilled open, having been dissected from his neck to his stomach. I saw a third young man whose legs had been hacked away. I saw a fourth young man whose eyes had been squeezed out of their sockets. His eyeballs lay on his slack face.

"They told us that we were lucky! *Lucky!* Can you imagine? They said that a special order had come down so we could take our sons' bodies. Dr. Fadil gave that order. Those men refused to tell us why our boys were arrested in the first place, although I could not restrain myself and asked if *staring* was now a death sentence. I was told to shut up, and we were ordered to bury our two children in silence, and to refrain from talking about the manner of their deaths."

In a sort of fitful spasm Um Sami clutched Mayada. "Without your help, I would still be searching. I thank you for that." After turning around and studying the shadows in the garden, as though she believed a member of the Mukhabarat might lurk behind a scented tree, Um Sami said to Mayada with vehemence, "Leave Iraq if you can. If my innocent sons were taken, no one is safe."

Mayada stretched out her arms and hugged Um Sami, then left her without a word. Mayada was so struck by the image of the boys' deaths that the white-blossomed trees in the garden that had lifted her spirits now oppressed her. The lovely trees now seemed to be forbidding pillars, whose heavy leaves crowded to block the cleansing rays of sunlight. The air she breathed was thinned by grief, and she hurried along the path that now seemed to lead away from the gloomiest place on earth.

Mayada had been so aggrieved by Um Sami's sad tale that she did not speak to anyone about what she'd heard, not even to her mother, with whom she usually shared everything.

Soon afterward, Um Sami and her husband sold their house and left the neighborhood. Their absence had made it possible for Mayada to successfully repress the memories of that day, until they returned this moment in the cold cell.

Other memories followed the first, and images previously disconnected came together to form a clear pattern of innocent imprisonment and death.

It was 1970, and Mayada's classmate, Sahar Sirri, was weeping. Mayada's friend was from a prominent Iraqi family and her father, General Mithat al-Haj Sirri, was a commanding officer in the Iraqi army. He was a popular commander, and Saddam, who was the true ruler of Iraq despite Bakri's presidential title, had decided he was a threat, so Saddam had him arrested and tortured. Sahar's father appeared on national television, confessing that he was a spy for Israel, a lie everyone recognized. But he had been hung by his hands and beaten for days, then injected with a variety of drugs. After confessing, he was hanged. Mayada's friend Sahar no longer had a father. From that point on, Sahar's entire family was persecuted, banned from travel and, on occasion, arrested and interrogated. Even Sahar was occasionally interrogated and returned to school with eyes red from weeping.

A coworker at the newspaper had once confided to Mayada that Saddam's security forces were awarded cash bonuses for arresting Iraqis, and that they were given promotions within the party if they displayed extra zeal during torture sessions. After receiving cash for making arrests, those same men extorted money from the families of the prisoners, with the pledge that their loved ones would receive lenient treatment. Poor Iraqi families sold their homes and automobiles and bankrupted themselves in the hope that they could save a loved one. The coworker told Mayada about a family who had sold their home and automobiles to save their innocent son from a fifteen-year prison sentence. Instead, he had received an eight-year sentence.

Now Mayada examined the faces of the women who shared the crowded, filthy cell they all called home. From the first day of her confinement, Mayada had been most shocked by the joy with which the prison guards terrorized innocent women. Could desire for money and advancement alone explain the devoted cruelty of the torturers? It was too much to think about. Mayada's head turned as she followed the sound of voices. The shadow women were all speaking at once, each suggesting what they might do to help Samara.

Mayada peered over the shoulders of a shadow woman and at Samara's silhouette. Samara's legs were twisted sideways and bunched toward her chest. Mayada inched closer and studied Samara's face. Her eyes were closed, and her thin yet swollen face frowned in pain. Her mouth opened, gasping for breath. Mayada realized that Samara would probably die in Baladiyat, ringed by women who had known nothing of her life until a few months before. And awed by Samara's goodness, she wondered how *anyone* could deliberately mutilate this sweet, beautiful woman whose heart overflowed with kindness.

Every shadow woman remained crowded around Samara. To- gether, all hands reached to gently grasp the wounded woman by her back and shoulders and waist. The women slowly lifted Samara, mov- ing her toward the scant comfort of her bedding. Her feet and legs dragged on the floor behind her. Samara whimpered softly as the women tenderly lowered her into her bunk.

A woman named Dr. Sabah, whom Mayada knew little about other than that she had a Ph.D. in engineering, rushed to the cell's lone sink to dampen the fabric of her long blue skirt. She returned to moisten Samara's forehead and lips with the wet clothing. The woman's gentle voice was at odds with the animation flashing in her eyes. "*Habibti* [my love], try to think, do you think there's any internal damage?"

Poor Samara wept without answering.

Wanting to help but unsure what she might do, Mayada walked forward and brushed Samara's cheek with her hand. She ached to ease her friend's despair and pain. "Samara," she whispered, "Samara."

Dr. Sabah glanced at Mayada and shook her head in sorrow. She whispered, "This dear girl has been tortured too many times—more than all of us put together."

Dr. Sabah held Samara's head between her hands and raised her voice. She brushed saliva from Samara's lips and chin. "Samara, can you hear me?"

The sweet-faced young woman named Muna patted Samara's hand. "Tell us what we can do, habibti. Just tell us, sweetheart—we want to help you."

Mayada stood quietly, her heart breaking. The dismal truth was that every prisoner in Baladiyat was physically tortured at one time or another. Mayada trembled, knowing that her time with the ceiling hooks and foot paddles and electricity would come soon. But she could do nothing about that now, so Mayada turned her thoughts back to Samara and to the shadow women near her. As individuals, these women were defenseless against the cruel men running Baladiyat, but together, they emerged as a great comforting force, whose concerted love and care proved so powerful that they could coax one another back from the black door that led to death.

Samara moaned softly and pulled her hand away from Muna. She placed the hand atop her stomach and chest as she murmured, "The thickset guard who wears the heavy boots kicked me. I felt something give way inside me."

Dr. Sabah and Muna exchanged an anxious look. "I know him," Muna muttered. "That one is a beast."

Mayada knew enough about medical care to realize that while they could soothe external injuries by massaging sore joints, or ease cigarette burns with cool water, they were powerless to minister to internal damage.

Mayada whispered, "Shouldn't we call the guards? They can take her to the hospital." Mayada remembered the sympathetic Dr. Hameed from her first night in Baladiyat. She knew the kind doctor would help Samara, if he could.

Dr. Sabah's eyes closed as she shook her head. "Not yet. We call them only if we believe someone is a few steps from death. If we made a habit of calling them after every torture, they would beat us all."

Mayada nodded in understanding—thus far, she had not witnessed even the dimmest spark of patience in a single guard here. Dr. Sabah and Muna loosened Samara's clothes to look for signs of physical damage. Mayada stood quietly and watched.

Samara moaned and Mayada peered at her fair skin and disheveled hair, then searched into the woman's eyes, now dark and still. Mayada experienced the woman's pain as clearly as if it had been her own body that had endured the cigarette burns and stomach kicks and electrical shocks. While she looked into Samara's anguished face, pieces of a long-forgotten poem written by the Englishman Thomas Gray floated forward out of Mayada's educated past:

> *To each his sufferings, all are men,*
> *Condemned alike to groan,*
> *The tender for another's pain,*
> *The unfeeling for his own.*
> *Why should they know their fate,*
> *Since sorrow never comes too late,*
> *And happiness too swiftly flies?*

She noticed Dr. Sabah turning her black, deep-set eyes in her direction. Mayada's mind went blank. She wondered what she had done to draw such probing scrutiny from Dr. Sabah.

Muna smiled at Mayada's look of astonishment. "You were quoting poetry," she told Mayada, "speaking certain lines in English and others in Arabic. But what I heard was haunting. Who wrote it?"

"I can't even remember speaking," Mayada admitted in a puzzled tone, convinced that the lack of oxygen in the small cell was impairing her capacity to think clearly. She smiled faintly. "This stale air is affecting my brain. Events are vanishing in an unexplained manner."

"I believe that you traveled back in time." Muna shrugged as sadness gathered on her face. "You said that happiness flies away too swiftly. Happiness is a state that I can no longer remember."

Samara groaned and whispered hoarsely, "This time I thought they had killed me."

Mayada turned to ask one of the women to bring a glass of water.

Several women moved as one—Aliya grabbed a cup while Iman reached for the water pitcher.

Mayada held the tiny cup to Samara's lips. "Drink."

Samara's hand trembled against the cup as she drank. "Thank you, dear sister."

Relieved that Samara was now speaking, the shadow women gathered closely once again.

Dr. Sabah announced, "I have checked you closely. I do not see anything life-threatening. But we shall keep a close watch." She touched Samara's shoulder. "You frightened us. Now you will remain in bed for a few days."

"If they allow it," Samara whispered. "They are becoming more enthusiastic." She looked at Mayada and nodded. "I heard the talk of poetry." She paused and then said, "I know a poem, as well."

Mayada leaned toward Samara. "Save your strength."

"While I cannot walk, I can speak." With a smile she closed her eyes and whispered, "At the last prison, a poem was etched in the wall. Some poor, suffering, nameless woman died there. Wishing to keep some small part of her alive, I memorized her poem. I say this poem to myself, every day."

"Tell us later," Dr. Sabah encouraged.

"No. Let me tell you now, please."

Mayada glanced at Dr. Sabah.

Dr. Sabah nodded. "All right. But do not tire yourself."

Samara's face and body twitched and she haltingly shared the verses she had so carefully memorized:

> *"They took me away from my home*
> *They slapped me when I cried out for my children*
> *They imprisoned me*
> *They accused me of crimes I had never committed*
> *They interrogated me with their harsh accusations*
> *They tortured me with their cruel hands*
> *They stubbed out cigarettes on my flesh*
> *They cut out my tongue*
> *They raped me*
> *They cut off my breasts*
> *I wept alone, in pain and in fear*
> *They sentenced me to die*
> *They staked me to the wall*
> *I begged for mercy*
> *They shot me between my eyes*
> *They dumped my body in a shallow grave*
> *They buried me without a shroud*
> *After my death, they discovered I was innocent."*

As she stood as one with the other shadow women, Mayada told herself that she was living a great moment in her life and that she would never forget a single word from Samara's lips. Every flutter of Samara's movements would be a part of her until the day she died.

She cried quietly and soon all the shadow women were crying together.

Mayada looked around and her words broke the sadness binding them all. "We are comrades-in-tears," she said. Several shadow women chuckled wistfully.

Samara reached up to touch Mayada's arm with her hand. "What about Saddam's wife, you promised you would tell us more."

"Another time," Mayada suggested. She was no longer in the mood for storytelling, especially about Saddam Hussein.

"The waiting, the fear, the silence in this place, it creates never-ending tedium. Mayada, your stories are like a trunk filled with rare and interesting photographs," Dr. Sabah said as she smiled.

Samara was determined. "Dr. Sabah is right. Our lives are so tedious. And now, my skin is on fire. If you share your stories, it will turn my mind to other things."

Mayada agreed only because she could not refuse Samara anything.

The shadow women began to settle in various corners of the small cell. The shadow woman named Wafae fingered her homemade prayer beads while others looked at Mayada expectantly.

Mayada tugged on a blanket she had been given and folded it into a square. She tossed the impromptu seat onto the floor in front of Samara's bunk, using it as a pillow of sorts; she would never become accustomed to sitting on a cement floor, but Mayada sat on the blanket and crossed her legs. Her voice was edged with a dreamy quality as she began to speak.

"My mother would never have met Saddam's wife if my parents had fled in 1968. Everyone was surprised that my parents remained in Baghdad after the Baath Party seized power that year. Since they recalled how Baathists had targeted the intelligentsia during the party's short-lived 1963 rule, all of our Al-Askari and Al-Husri relatives fled to safety in 1968, when for a second time the Baathists returned to power. But my father's battle with cancer kept us tied to Baghdad. He was receiving medical treatments. After his death in 1974, relatives encouraged Mother to move out of the country, but she didn't. I believe Mother was in great shock after my father's death, and she insisted it wasn't then the time to make important decisions. At the time she was a director in the Ministry of Information. She loved our home. She had good friends in the country. My sister and I were in school in Baghdad. And Mother always felt confident she could live peacefully in Iraq, despite the fact that Baath officials did not look favorably on the intelligentsia. Mother heard from more than one Baath official that Saddam was so enamored of Sati that Sati's daughter and granddaughters would always be safe under his rule. So she remained, hoping for the best. And she managed to have a good life, particularly during those early years.

"I stayed with her until time came for me to attend college. I followed my father's wishes and traveled to Lebanon to attend the American University of Beirut. So I was not in Baghdad when my mother initially met Saddam's first wife, Sajida, the mother of Saddam's five children.

"We learned later that Saddam had encouraged Sajida to befriend Mother, to seek her advice on social issues. That's why Mother received so many invitations to attend functions at the palace. But she was usually too occupied to bother." Mayada chuckled quietly. "Thankfully, that was before the time when to refuse such an invitation would be cause for torture and imprisonment." As Mayada glanced around the room in which she now found herself recounting her mother's social successes, her voice reverberated with emotion. "One whiff of our little cell, and Salwa Al-Husri would drop dead.

"Anyhow, Mother had visited me in Beirut after receiving yet another invitation from the palace. Sajida had invited her to meet with a group of ambassadors' wives. Mother said that the invitation fell on a day that she was free, so she accepted.

"I was curious about Saddam's wife and asked Mother to remember every detail." Mayada smiled without realizing it. "No two women could have been more different than my mother and Sajida Khayrallah Tilfah. Their meeting was ill-fated from the start.

"As you know, Mother had led an unusual life for an Arab woman. She held a Ph.D. in political science. She even attended Oxford University in England for further studies. Her grandmother was a sultana, or princess, in the Ottoman royal family. Her father, Sati, was one of the most celebrated men in the Arab world, a man who valued knowledge and education above all things. Jido Sati owned homes in many Arab lands, so he and his family traveled constantly. From the time she was a child sitting on her father's knee, my mother was comfortable chatting away with kings and premiers. She was so favored by King Ghazi, son of King Faisal I, that he kept a photograph of her on his desk, beside his own son's picture.

"Saddam's wife Sajida was the daughter of a peasant, Khayrallah Tilfah. She was raised in her father's home on the western bank of the Tigris, in a lower-class Tikriti district. She had little education compared to my mother, and she knew nothing of the world outside Baghdad and Tikrit. Sajida was married at an early age to her father's nephew, Saddam Hussein. She quickly had five children by Saddam. When he seized power, she was woefully ill-equipped for her new position as wife of the President of Iraq."

Mayada pulled on the blanket and covered her bare ankles.

"Mother told me later that she detested Sajida Tilfah. It didn't surprise me when she said their dislike was mutual.

"I asked Mother what Sajida looked like in person. Although I had seen a few pictures of Sajida, I think it's difficult to tell a person's true appearance in official photographs. Mother said her first impression was that she looked like a clown. Her face was covered in thick white makeup. At first glance, Mother said, she thought someone had thrown flour on the woman's face. Sajida was an olive-skinned woman who could have been attractive, but she aspired instead to be light-skinned. And Sajida's dark hair had been dyed repeatedly, until it was brittle and a bright yellow color.

"Mother said she felt sorry for Sajida for about five minutes, but after she heard the woman shouting abuse at her servants, her sympathy evaporated.

"After the luncheon, Sajida told Mother that she wished to purchase some silver antique pieces and that her husband Saddam had told her Salwa would recognize the best quality work. He encouraged Sajida to invite my mother to go along with her to the shops. Thinking that this was a woman who needed social guidance, Mother agreed to accompany her. Mother said she was soon sorry she agreed. The moment the two women were alone together, Sajida tugged on Mother's fur coat and demanded to know if it was real fur. Then Sajida grabbed her hand and fingered Mother's emerald ring. She had the nerve to ask if it was imitation. Mother sputtered in stifled exasperation. My mother is not a woman who would wear fake fur or imitation jewelry, so she was offended and angry. She tried to think of a believable reason to end their planned shopping, but she knew she was trapped. So she went into the antique store with Sajida, although she said she was ashamed to be in the company of such an uncouth woman. Mother said she didn't know why she was invited, because the silly woman didn't ask her advice but instead rushed through the store, grabbing every garish item available. Then she humiliated my mother further by leaving without paying, telling the worried shopkeeper that someone from the palace would arrive shortly to handle the finances.

"Mother said she learned later that every shop in Baghdad dreaded Sajida's arrival at their store. In fact, if a shopkeeper was given notice that Sajida was on the way, most pulled down their doors, locked up and claimed a family emergency. It was a well-known fact that even with all her riches, which were basically stolen from the Iraqi people, Sajida never paid the full price. Some shop owners were known to go out of business after her visits. But who could they complain to? They would be killed for suggesting that Saddam's wife was nothing but a common thief.

"Mother said that after they stepped back into the car to return to the palace, Sajida began to speak loudly and tell her about a problem she was having with an Iraqi woman named Sara, from an old aristocratic Christian family in Iraq. Sara had earlier moved to Paris, and

Sajida had been staying with her every time she visited Paris. Sajida said that she had asked Sara for a 'simple favor' for her sister, the woman married to Saddam's half brother, Barzan Al-Tikriti. Sajida's sister was going to Paris for six days. While there, she needed some assistance, Sajida said. Sajida's sister wanted her eyelashes lengthened one inch, and she wanted her hips narrowed by five inches. The sister also wanted to visit De Beers to purchase some flawless diamonds at a good price.

"Sajida didn't believe Sara when Sara told Sajida she had never heard of a way to lengthen eyelashes. And, Sara told her, the only way to remove five inches from anyone's hip line was through surgery, which would take a lot longer than six days for recovery. Lastly, Sara explained to Sajida that De Beers was a supply company and did not sell directly to individuals. Sajida thought Sara was lying, that the Paris-based Iraqi woman just didn't want to help her. Sajida knew that a person living in France could have anything they wanted. All they needed was enough money. And her sister had the riches of Iraq backing her, Sajida explained to my mother needlessly.

"Sajida told Mother she was going to trick Sara into visiting Iraq. Then she would have her thrown into prison.

"Mother was dumbstruck. Like Sati, she believed that stupid people were dangerous. Mother said she mumbled something in response to Sajida's story, saying she had no idea what modern medicine might accomplish, so she was not the appropriate person to ask. Her answer obviously angered Sajida, who moved to the corner of the automobile and refused to speak.

"Mother knew Sara, so she immediately phoned her and warned her not to visit Iraq," Mayada told the rapt women in her cell.

Dr. Sabah muttered, "Oh, my. I had no idea Sajida was so unpleasant."

"Indeed, she is," Mayada explained. Other memories about Sajida followed the first. "She really is a thief," Mayada emphasized. "Do any of you remember what happened in 1983, when Saddam said that every Iraqi family had to donate gold to support the Iraqi army in the war with Iran?"

Mayada saw several of the women nodding. An older woman cried out softly. "I had nothing made of gold. My husband was on the front and there was no way to get enough money to buy a gold trinket to give, so I was forced to sell my cooking stove. From that time on, I cooked over a wood fire outside."

With her words, a shadow of pain fell across Mayada's heart. She knew that the donations had been a sham and that most of the gold never got to its proposed destination.

"Let me tell you a true story about that proclamation. About a government minister's wife who was a close friend of our family. Her name was Dr. Lamya, the wife of Dr. Sadoun Hammadi. He was the Prime Minister for a short time in 1991, but was soon dismissed because he was too honest to succeed in Saddam's corrupt government. Anyhow, Dr. Lamya was not a greedy woman. She actually owned only one set of expensive jewels—a beautiful gold and sapphire collection, which included a necklace, earrings, bracelet and ring. It was a wedding gift from her husband, but her husband forced her to donate it to the cause. She claimed that she wept for a week after being forced to part with those jewels.

"Well, a year passed and Dr. Lamya was invited to a function that Sajida was attending. She couldn't believe her eyes when Sajida walked into the room wearing *her* set of beautiful jewels. The very same jewels that she had donated to the cause of Iraq's young men at war were draped around Sajida's neck and wrist. She was so startled she couldn't move. In her disbelief, she just stood and stared. Sajida noticed her intent look. She grew annoyed and sent one of her security men to shout at her. He ordered Dr. Lamya to take her eyes away from 'The Lady,' as Sajida insisted on being called."

"Some lady," Dr. Sabah said harshly.

"Well, now knowing that her sacrifice had meant nothing, Dr. Lamya rushed home to complain to her husband. Dr. Hammadi told her to keep quiet, saying that a complaint wouldn't get her jewels back, but it *would* land them both in prison. He then stated what everyone else knew, that Sajida Tilfah had such greedy eyes that they would not be satisfied until they were filled with dirt.

"That's not all. Sajida's gluttony for possessions is so insatiable that she gave orders for all the jewels stolen from Kuwaitis during the Gulf War to be delivered to her palace. Trucks packed with jewels were transported directly to her hands. All those Kuwaiti royals can find their precious jewels in Sajida's palace.

"There was one funny story I'll never forget. Palace servants reported that Sajida had even gotten into an argument with her second son, Qusay, over those Kuwaiti treasures. Qusay admired one diamond set in particular, and when he told his mother he was going to present the jewels to his wife, Sajida ordered him to get out of her home. Sajida wanted everything for herself."

Mayada smiled widely. "Some of her servants later claimed that the sight of Sajida scurrying through the palace with bowls spilling over with jewels was one of the most ridiculous sights they had ever seen. That greedy woman hid set after set of expensive jewelry throughout the palace, and she warned the servants that she would have their tongues cut out if they dared share her hiding places with any of her children."

Iman made a grunting sound deep in her throat. "I am disgusted! We Iraqis were starving and there she was, dripping diamonds and pearls!" Iman dipped into a deep curtsy and began to pantomime a fine lady fanning herself. No longer would Iman be a blind supporter of Saddam's wife, Sajida.

Low laughter erupted in the cell.

So many reminiscences etched in Mayada's memory now came forward. "I could take her thieving easier than her cruelty," Mayada confided. "She is unbelievably spiteful to her servants."

The religious Roula turned her gaze to Mayada. "That's not a surprise. Greed seems to attach itself to cruelty."

Mayada agreed. "I am haunted by one particular story. About a poor Christian girl named Rosa. She was related to Hala's nanny." Mayada explained, "Hala, as you know, is Sajida and Saddam's youngest child, a daughter. Hala is the only one of Saddam and Sajida's children who was born without a black heart. She is known to slip behind her mother's back and try to assist those poor unfortunate souls who draw her mother's angry attention. Hala truly cares about Iraqis, unlike the rest of the family. She's been known to take money from her parents and distribute it to the poor. Anyhow, Rosa's relative thought she would be a good companion for Hala, who she said often seemed lonely in the palace. While Hala was at school, Rosa was assigned a few housekeeping duties in the palace. One day she was told to go into Sajida's bedroom suite and vacuum the floor. In the middle of her chore, she heard something metal clink inside the vacuum tube, so she turned the machine off and looked inside the bag. To her surprise, she found a magnificent diamond ring among the dust.

"Rosa took the ring to the head housekeeper and turned it in. The housekeeper took it to Sajida, who said she was so happy that she was going to give Rosa the ring as a reward. It would be a useful lesson to the rest of the household, which she claimed was filled with thieves.

"Rosa was overjoyed at her good luck. She rushed home after work and gave the ring to her parents. Her parents went to the goldsmith shop and sold it. The family took the money and went to the food market and selected special foodstuffs, then paid some overdue bills and even purchased some decent clothes and a few pieces of cheap furniture for the house. With the rest of the money from the sale of the ring, they also paid for repairs to their house, which was in poor condition.

"Well, a few weeks later Sajida summoned Rosa and asked her about that ring. Sajida said she had thought that it was a glass ring, and that was why she had given it to Rosa. But she had since discovered that it was a rare, white-blue diamond, and she angrily ordered Rosa to return the ring at once.

"Rosa almost fainted. She stammered and told her mistress that no one in her family had need of such a ring and that they had sold the ring that very first day.

"Sajida began to scream and curse, threatening to have Rosa's home torn to the ground if the ring wasn't returned the following day.

"Rosa ran home and told her parents about the awful turn of events. They went to the goldsmith to try and get the ring back. That man told him a lady had bought the ring the same day. She paid cash and left no name or address.

"Poor Rosa faced Sajida the following day and confessed that the ring was gone for good. And her family, she insisted, had no way of replacing it with a ring of similar value.

"Sajida jumped to her feet and hit and kicked and cursed the girl. Sajida has forgotten the destitution of her youth and has no concept of the poverty of her Iraqi servants, so she didn't believe that the family had sold the ring to buy food or clothes. She accused Rosa of keeping the ring for herself. So she summoned her guards. Sajida was still pacing and cursing. Then she pulled on Rosa's long black hair, her loveliest feature, and ordered her guards to shave Rosa's head. The poor girl grew hysterical.

"Then, because Rosa protested and fought the guards who were shearing her hair, Sajida ordered the guards to beat Rosa with a whip. The guards did what they were told and whipped Rosa's back until blisters opened. Sajida had by this time worked herself into a full-blown fit, and commanded one of her maids to bring a domestic iron. They plugged the iron into an electrical outlet, and Sajida had guards hold Rosa's hands down on the floor. Sajida ordered one of the guards to iron Rosa's hands. Rosa's screams angered Sajida even further, so she told the guards to press the iron harder onto Rosa's hands and fingers. The poor girl's hands were horribly burned. Sajida laughed and told Rosa that she might as well bring the ring back now: Her hands and fingers were so badly disfigured she surely would be ashamed to wear a beautiful cocktail ring.

"Rosa was then thrown out of the palace. She wandered the streets with burnt hands and a shaved head and a blistered back, until a kind-hearted taxi driver delivered her to her home."

Mayada's eyes grew misty and she looked at the shadow women, one by one. "And, that, my dear cellmates, explains the true heart of the woman who wants to be called 'The Lady.' "

Never had their cell been so quiet. While many Iraqi men embraced the cruel tactics now plaguing the country, rarely did the cellmates hear of a woman so pitiless that she could cause physical harm.

Everyone looked at Dr. Sabah when she coughed and cleared her throat. Her feelings showed first in her dark eyes and then on her thin lips.

Dr. Sabah pulled her cloak over her shoulders and tied it in a big knot in the front. She said, "I want to tell you about my life. I grew up poor. But unlike Sajida, I've never forgotten it. My father was a simple worker in a cigarette factory on the outskirts of Baghdad. My mother was an illiterate housewife. I watched them labor until they grew old early. I wanted to avoid the backbreaking work that crippled my parents, so instead of working hard with my body, I worked hard with my brain. Every year I was at the head of my class, and I chose a career in engineering. Like many Iraqis, I was harassed until I joined the Baath Party, but my heart was not in their teachings. I mouthed the words I knew I needed to say to avert their suspicions and concentrated on my work.

"I worked harder than any man at the Ministry of Construction and Works. I was told by my supervisor that even Saddam had heard of my determination and skill. In 1979, Saddam sent orders that I was going to be appointed the next Director General of the General Establishment of Constructional Projects. I thought my future was made.

I had moved to the top levels of a field usually reserved for men, and in only a few short years.

"But not long after my advancement to Director General, everything crumbled. I was ordered to attend a meeting in the party headquarters. One of our comrades was pointed out as a plotter against Saddam. I knew him well. He was a former college classmate and now a colleague. I also knew his wife, and had held his babies in my arms. I knew that he was not a plotter. But I was told that as the Director General, I had to take part in executing my friend.

"Well, I couldn't move a muscle." With a half smile, Dr. Sabah looked around the room. "I refused to take into my hand the gun I was offered. What did I do? I vomited. Everywhere. I vomited on my shoes and on the shoes of the party official telling me I had to execute my friend. He would say, 'Kill him!' And I would vomit. He would scream, 'Take this gun!' And I would vomit. Finally I fled the building and ran all the way home, more than thirty streets away. I called in sick the next day and the day after that. On the third day, I had a visit from two men wearing dark sunglasses. They were polite. They shook hands with me and then told me they were from the Mukhabarat. They said they understood I had disobeyed orders. They understood I had vomited rather than execute a criminal who threatened the very stability of Iraq. I stood there like a frightened rabbit. I was unable to speak. I couldn't move. But I did notice one funny thing. Both those tough men stood well away. I suppose they thought I might vomit on their shiny black shoes. They grew tired of waiting for me to speak. Finally one of them said that my vomiting had been reported to Saddam. Our esteemed leader said to tell me that he fully understood why I had vomited. I had vomited because I was a woman. They told me that vacation time was over, and I had to go with them back to work. I imagined they would take me to prison, but the two men insisted Saddam had told them not to arrest me, and instead to give me one more chance.

"On the way back to my offices, one of the men looked at me

with a smirk and asked, 'How is your younger brother, Ahmed? Is he in good health?' The man said he hoped that a good future was waiting for Ahmed.

"I knew right then that my entire family was in danger. How I wanted to go back to my simple life, but I couldn't. I didn't know what to do to change things, so I went back to work. But never again did I enjoy one minute of one day. I kept waiting for another order to kill this person or that person. Happily, everything went smoothly for a long time. I married a lovely man. I had two wonderful sons and one beautiful daughter. I was not asked to kill anyone else. Then everything fell to pieces again, in 1992. I had a different problem this time. With all of Iraq suffering under the sanctions, Saddam called a big meeting about the money shortages. He was building one palace after another, but he told us that as directors, we must devise ways to raise money to pay *all* the expenses of our construction ministry. Saddam said that as of that day, all funds were cut. No more money would be made available from the government to pay employee salaries, operating expenses or for the building projects. We, the directors, had to come up with a plan to make money to support the government.

"After the meeting, several of us were allowed to thank Saddam for the opportunity to help the country. When I walked up to him he laughed for the first time that day. He asked if I had suffered any recent vomiting attacks. Everyone around laughed with him, even me. I told him no, and I thanked him for asking."

Dr. Sabah then looked positively fierce. "I thought to myself: Let them laugh! I was the only one there without blood on my hands. Well, I left that meeting in a fog of worry. I knew if I didn't find a way to meet expenses, I had a lot more to lose than my job. I had a husband and children I loved. I had brothers and sisters I loved. Those siblings had children. For several days I walked around in a trance, wondering how I was going to find enough money to finance an entire department.

"One day on a job site I had an idea. I looked around and saw a great deal of wood and cement and screws and nails. I went back to the office and called in Abu Kanaan, my subordinate, and laid out my plan.

"This was my plan. The agency I ran was created solely for construction projects. We gave out contracts to various companies. These contractors were independent and from the private sector. One company would provide the equipment, another would provide the wood, another the cement and so on. I decided that I would start a new policy. Each contractor that worked on the project would be required to leave behind all unused items. One by one, each contractor would not suffer so terribly. But altogether their forfeited items would be valuable. Because of the sanctions, there were shortages all over Iraq, so I knew I could get the maximum price for everything. We would auction everything off. Then we would take the proceeds of those auctions to pay salaries and other expenses.

"The more I thought about it, the more I was convinced the brilliant idea would save us.

"We presented our recommendations directly to Saddam. He studied our projected figures and appeared to be impressed. He said we could go ahead with the plan. Our agency carried on with that plan for several years and we succeeded in covering our department expenses.

"Five months ago, I was paid another visit by two men in dark sunglasses. They came to my office. I was terrified that they were going to order me to shoot somebody. I asked to call my husband and children. They forbade it. They said they needed me for only an hour or two. There were a few questions I needed to clear up. They brought me directly to this place. They blindfolded me when I got out of the automobile. Then they led me up some steps. I couldn't see, but I knew I was in for a terrible time when an intense odor of urine overwhelmed me. They removed the blindfold and I found I was standing opposite a man who immediately slapped my face and barked, 'Welcome, thief!'

"When I was interrogated, I was told I was arrested for using my position to 'steal' goods and equipment from the private sector. My 'crime' was called a conspiracy to undermine the state's economy. This, despite the fact I never kept a single dinar for myself. Every dinar from every auction was put back into the Ministry coffers."

Her forehead creased into a frown. "My torturers are hinting that I will be given a prison sentence of twenty-five years. I don't think my husband and children know where I am, although I was told that they were informed that I am a thief."

Dr. Sabah sighed and looked at the wall.

Mayada stared at Dr. Sabah, at a loss for words. She felt tears returning to her eyes. *Twenty-five years!* Dr. Sabah would never survive a twenty-five-year sentence. She was fifty years old.

Mayada pulled the folded blanket from under her and held it to her face, getting tufts of the thick blanket in her mouth. She choked back a cough. She stifled a sneeze. She pushed the crumpled blanket back under her legs.

She longed to reassure Dr. Sabah in some kindly way, but didn't know what to say. She started speaking without really knowing what she might say. "We will have our revenge, though we might not know it," Mayada mused aloud. "Saddam is frantically swimming in ideas to further his lasting reputation. His only pastime now is to puff up and polish his accomplishments. Because he adores himself, he believes he is adored by others. He wants only one thing, which is to live forever in Arab lore as a great hero. But that will never happen.

"I remember something Jido Sati told me once. He said that history never sleeps. When future historians write about Saddam Hussein, pages and pages will be written about his failures. But historians will scour the records in vain to find *one good thing* to say about his achievements. What can they write? Only that Saddam Hussein built a lot of palaces. An empty legacy of stones."

Mayada looked around. The shadow women seemed to be listening, but she couldn't tell for sure. She sighed, got up, rolled the blanket and stood in a corner of the room. She stood there quietly as, one by one, she studied the faces of the shadow women. Their tiny cell was a world of worry unto itself, with every woman frantic for her family, mothers despairing at the emotional blow of not seeing their growing children.

The sweet-faced Muna was weeping quietly.

Dr. Sabah's lips were turned down. Her entire countenance appeared pulled downward by the weight of her sorrows.

Aliya's face was so red that it looked aglow.

While Mayada scanned one expressive face after the other, it was clear to her that deep sorrow was lodged in every shadow woman's heart. This was prison life, Mayada decided: tears and fears and sorrow.

She turned her gaze back to Samara. The lovely Shiite woman was silent, but held a desolate look that spoke volumes. Did Samara believe that good fortune had abandoned her forever? Would she, Mayada, be an unwilling witness to a terrible tragedy? Would the beautiful Samara be tortured to death? Would Samara, like the author of the anonymous poem, go to the grave before her time?

Mayada's thoughts reached out to probe the people responsible for this mindless torture and pain. Although Saddam Hussein was the man who fashioned modern Iraq into a hell on earth, there was yet a second man responsible for many Iraqi tears. A man she would never forget.

Mayada stared at the ceiling, remembering one of the most physically exquisite men she had met. An image of his handsome face floated before her eyes. She recalled how a playful smile often dimpled his mouth. He was so handsome, it was rumored that many women fell in love with him at first sight. At the time Mayada first met him, her husband Salam had already destroyed any chance of love in their marriage. Mayada's heart was empty and she was vulnerable. But thankfully, the handsome man's true character was soon revealed, so she never entertained a thought of seeking his romantic affection. She had quickly discovered that his beautiful face concealed a rotten soul.

In time, Mayada discovered this man, Ali Hassan al-Majid, known as Chemical Ali, was one of the most brutal men in Iraq.

6

Chemical Ali and the Veil

Mayada first met Ali Hassan al-Majid, first cousin to Saddam Hussein, in April 1984. Little was known at that time of the man who had recently been placed atop the nation's secret police, after Dr. Fadil was elevated to the head of intelligence.

That April bloomed soft and lovely. The dazzling splendor of spring in Iraq had peaked. Bushes and trees nodded heavily with multicolored blossoms, and the air was saturated with their heady scents. The springtime days were warm and sunny; the nights were cool and comfortable. Baghdadis knew that once the long summer season descended upon their city, polite society would withdraw indoors to escape the wilting heat. So in spring, Iraqi society crammed its social calendars with garden parties.

Several nights each week, Salwa's manicured garden was the setting for dazzling evening buffets. Before each evening's guests arrived, Salwa's servants would move sofas and chairs from inside the house to spots outside beneath the towering date palms, welcoming visitors who would arrive just after sunset, when the aquamarine sky mellowed to pink.

The swish of gentle swaying trees and the clatter of night insects would fill the air, and Salwa and Mayada would entertain some of the most intriguing people in Baghdad. Mayada was fashionably trim in those days, and she loved to display her figure in chic designs bought by her mother in Paris, Rome or London. Mayada could not know that this was the last summer that she would be considered one of Baghdad's trendiest women. Dusky Iraqi beauties, their dark hair pulled back with colorful flowers, strolled Salwa's garden in stylish fashions from abroad that often pushed the limit of Middle East propriety, while elegant men smoked cigars, tipped small beakers of liquor, and whispered misgivings about the current war, confident that their opinions went unrecorded in the sanctity of Salwa Al-Husri's garden.

Despite these pleasant moments, a gathering darkness had settled over Iraq. A ghastly war with their Persian Iranian neighbors had raged for four long years, surprising Iraqis accustomed to wars no more than a month long. But as the Iraqis reminded themselves, they had little experience fighting other Muslims. Iraqi wars were generally fought against Israelis, and everyone knew that wars with the Jews didn't last very long.

Iraqis had good reason to imagine that the current conflict with Iran would be similarly short-lived. Soon after the war's 1980 start, the Arab League had tapped a "Committee of Good Endeavors," composed of Arab officials, and sent the committee to Iran to seek peace. Iraqis believed the committee would quickly return to Baghdad with an agreement.

Mayada, however, had misgivings about the committee's journey, thanks to a window on world opinion that few Iraqis shared. Most foreign publications were forbidden in Iraq, but Mayada's mother had recently returned from a trip abroad with her suitcases crammed with prohibited items, including news magazines. No one at Iraq's border dared search the bags of Salwa Al-Husri, family friend of Dr. Fadil. And when Salwa unpacked her luggage, she passed around foreign newspapers and magazines, some of which analyzed the current situation between Iran and Iraq. Mayada read them all, asking friends to translate the foreign languages she could not read.

One smuggled magazine was the well-regarded German news-weekly *Der Spiegel*. One cartoon in *Der Spiegel* made Mayada reflect on the daunting task that faced the Iraqi military. The cartoon depicted Saddam in military fatigues kicking Khomeini, and was captioned, "Okay, so you got your boot inside. Now how are you going to get it out?"

The specter of Khomeini's obstinate personality, backed by millions of Iranians willing to die for their leader, dampened Mayada's spirits. With three times Iraq's population, Iran could absorb three casualties for each Iraqi casualty. And Iran was led by a man who was every bit as mulish as Saddam Hussein. The numbers did not bode well for Iraq.

In October 1980, two months into the war, Mayada and some fellow journalists sat in *Al-Jumhuriya's* fourth-floor offices, overlooking Baghdad. Without confessing to her colleagues about the European magazines she had read, Mayada opined that the current conflict might prove to be a lengthy, difficult one. Her friends ridiculed her naïveté and, permitting their laughter to silence her doubts, Mayada set aside her reservations to join the conversation, which was considering the possibility of a ten-day countdown to the conquest of the Iranians. The gathered reporters even began to sketch a victory celebration. Defeat was so unthinkable that it was simply never explored.

But then a massive number of Iraqi corpses began to filter back from the front. The streets of Baghdad were suddenly filled with flapping black funeral banners, each emblazoned with a soldier's name and death site, along with a verse from the Quran, "Martyrs never die," and a slogan from Saddam, "Martyrs are more generous than all of us." The number of black banners swelled daily, and soon everyone recognized that the Iraqi army was hemorrhaging soldiers.

In the beginning, Saddam gave each martyr's family a plot of land, 5,000 Iraqi dinars ($15,500) and a current-model Toyota. A catchy children's tune soon acquired new lyrics to reflect the times, as Iraqis expressed their scorn for the war's daunting toll:

> *Now my father will return from the front*
> *Nailed to his coffin.*
> *My mother will marry another man,*
> *But I will ride a new Toyota.*

Although Mayada suffered enormously through the terrifying air raids, petrified for her one-year-old baby, Fay, she was strangely removed from the day-to-day conflict itself. Unlike most Iraqis, she didn't have a brother or a father or an uncle or a cousin fighting at the front. All of Mayada's male relatives were either dead or living in exile. And her husband Salam was in no immediate danger, because he was stationed at a base close to the city. In fact, Salam was so privileged that he was allowed home every other day.

Mayada even enjoyed a successful career as a feature writer at *Alef Ba* magazine in Baghdad. Her professional situation was an unlikely one, since a media career was generally open only to Baath Party members, but shortly after Al-Bakir and Saddam seized power, they made it clear that the Salwa Al-Husri family was so loyal to Arab Nationalism that they did not have to join the Baath Party to prove it. Mayada had graduated from high school and had studied at a university abroad without joining the Baath Party. Mayada's sister Abdiya enjoyed the same exception, although a bully from the university had once tried to force her to join the party. After Abdiya calmly replied, "I will be sure to ask Saddam about your invitation and get back to you," the subject was forever dropped.

After Dr. Fadil befriended Mayada's family in 1979, other unexpected perks for an Iraqi outside the Baath Party began to fall Mayada's way. She was appointed a reporter and a feature writer for several publications. She was invited to become a member of the Journalists

Federation and the Writers Union. She worked in the Arab Labor Organization for eight years, and, unlike every other Iraqi in the organization—and thanks to her family history and Dr. Fadil's influence—she was never forced to work with intelligence officials, a job that would have forced her to spy on colleagues, friends and even family. She even knew a man in the Arab Labor Organization who had turned his own wife in for ridiculing Uday, Saddam's eldest son. That unfortunate woman was now serving a long prison sentence. And through it all, no one approached her to join the Baath Party.

Despite her political insulation, Mayada's common sense warned her not to test the waters of political journalism. Instead, she chose to write about her love of Iraq, which was genuine, and to pen stories that focused on love and romance. Such efforts matched her writerly aspirations, and she knew only too well that opinionated reports too often created political problems for the author. Now that she was a mother, she had to value her personal safety.

But one Thursday morning in April 1984, Mayada's happy estrangement from political journalism abruptly ended. Kamil Al-Sharqi, her editor-in-chief at *Alef Ba*, called Mayada into his spacious office and told her, "This is a difficult time, Mayada. All Iraqis must sacrifice. We have many reporters at the front, and our feature writers must now accept extra duties."

Mayada nodded in agreement, unsure of where the conversation was leading.

"You have been chosen to write a piece about Saddam and Iraqi security policy during this war with Iran. You must seek an interview with Ali Hassan al-Majid. While you interview him about Saddam and security, try to find out some personal details about the man, too. The Iraqi public is curious about this mysterious cousin of our great President and General, Saddam Hussein."

Mayada rolled her head back in surprise at his unexpected request. Although she had received a number of writing awards from

Saddam, she was not a member of his inner circle. Did Kamil believe she could dial the palace and ask the President to make his cousin grant her an interview? If so, Kamil was mistaken.

She remained silent, trying to recall what little she had heard about Ali Hassan al-Majid. Dr. Fadil had recently been promoted to Head of the Intelligence Service. When he had described his promotion to Mayada and her mother, Dr. Fadil had mentioned in passing that Saddam's first cousin, Ali Hassan al-Majid, was taking over Dr. Fadil's old post as Director General of the Iraqi Secret Police, better known as the Amin Al-Amma. The position made Ali al-Majid an extremely powerful man. Ali was also one of the most prominent members of the Baath Party. Despite his new eminence, however, Mayada had heard from senior reporters that Saddam's cousin had little use for the media and refused all requests for interviews, in an effort to maintain a low public profile.

Mayada pursed her lips before asking Kamil, "I understand he does not give interviews. How will I convince him?"

Kamil shrugged and smiled. "You will figure it out, I am certain."

"I'm not so sure," Mayada admitted.

Kamil stood up from behind his desk and walked around to escort Mayada from the room. "You will get your interview. Just put your mind to it!"

Although pleased to be taken seriously, Mayada left Kamil's office with foreboding. She was entering new territory. But she could hardly refuse such an assignment and still expect to advance in her career. Yet given that Ali Hassan al-Majid hated the press and declined all interviews, Mayada hardly knew where to begin. Further, Ali was a powerful cousin of Saddam Hussein and a busy man during this time of war. What would make him agree to an interview with *her*, a feature writer of what many people would consider soft, womanly journalism?

Mayada spent the afternoon calling many influential friends who might have contacts with Ali Hassan al-Majid. After being turned down by more than ten friends, each of whom assured Mayada she was wasting her time pursuing a man who did not give interviews, she decided to go home. Perhaps her mother would have some ideas.

Later that evening after she put Fay to bed, Mayada sat down to dinner with her mother. After the cook had served the food and returned to the kitchen, Mayada explained her delicate problem.

Salwa listened carefully, then breezily volunteered her advice. "Mayada, ask Dr. Fadil to intervene on your behalf. He called earlier and said that he plans to drop by on his way home." Seeing Mayada's look of skepticism, Salwa confidently assured her daughter, "He will help you. I am certain of it."

Mayada was not convinced. She had overheard Dr. Fadil insulting Ali Hassan al-Majid more than once, leaving little doubt that he soundly disliked the man. Dr. Fadil insisted Ali al-Majid was an uneducated brute, like most of Saddam's relatives. And although Dr. Fadil's new post as head of the entire intelligence service placed him in the bureaucracy above Ali al-Majid, Saddam's cousin was nearer and dearer to the powerful President's heart, which would give Ali the emotional edge in any political conflict with Dr. Fadil. Surely Dr. Fadil recognized that reality, and that would explain Dr. Fadil's dislike for al-Majid. So why would he contact a man he hated? Just to help her?

While waiting for Dr. Fadil's visit, Mayada took a pen and paper and wrote down everything she had heard about Ali Hassan al-Majid.

From the few photographs she had seen, he was an attractive man who appeared to be in his late thirties or early forties. He was born in Tikrit, the first son of Saddam Hussein's uncle, the brother of Saddam's deceased father. Like Saddam, Ali's family belonged to the Sunni Muslim al-Bejat clan, part of the al-bu Nasir tribe, which was the dominant tribe in the Tikrit district. Like all Iraqis of that day, tribal loyalty played an encompassing role in his early life, and he forged lifelong relationships with clan members, including Saddam.

From his earliest days, Ali al-Majid was a fervid supporter of the Baath Party, but unlike Saddam, his status was strictly low-level. Before the 1968 revolution, in fact, Ali was a lance-corporal who functioned as a simple army motorcycle messenger. But as his cousin Saddam solidified his power, Ali's influence skyrocketed.

Ali had earlier demonstrated a head for courting power when he married the daughter of Ahmed Hassan Al-Bakir, Iraq's President after the 1968 revolution. But when Saddam pushed Ali's father-in-law Al-Bakir aside to seize the presidency in 1979, Ali remained loyal to his tribe and to his cousin Saddam, rather than to his wife's father. In Iraqi tribal society, Ali's decision was no surprise. If forced to choose, a man would always retain loyalty to his tribe rather than to his wife's family.

After Saddam's seizure of the presidency, Ali advanced quickly in the Baathist hierarchy and became one of Saddam's most trusted officers. He was a Baath Party veteran and a high-ranking member of the Revolution Command Council. With the Iran-Iraq war in progress, Ali was now one of Saddam's closest military advisors.

When Dr. Fadil arrived, Mayada's mother quickly forced the topic out into the open. She poured Dr. Fadil a drink and gushed over his latest book before saying, "Mayada has a special favor to ask of you."

Mayada studied his reaction. Dr. Fadil didn't look very pleased. Since he had first come into their lives as an admirer of Sati, Mayada had asked Dr. Fadil more than once to help neighbors and friends with security problems. On most occasions, he had proved pleasantly helpful. But after her awkward appeal two years earlier for assistance in helping Um Sami locate her twin sons, Dr. Fadil had grown wary of Mayada's requests.

Dr. Fadil cupped his drink in his hand. "Of course," he said to Salwa and her daughter. "I will do anything I can for you, Mayada. You are a proud daughter of Iraq."

She spoke in a rush. "Kamil has given me a difficult assignment. I am supposed to contact Ali Hassan al-Majid and secure an interview. Kamil wants the magazine to do a piece on Iraqi security policy. And on Saddam. Lastly, while I'm at it, I have been told to find the 'real' man behind the military officer. Thus far, no one can help me. He's very elusive."

Dr. Fadil winced. *"Ali Hassan al-Majid?* Why should the Iraqi people care about him?" Dr. Fadil pretended to spit. "I spit on him!"

Mayada drew back in alarm. She glanced at her mother.

Salwa watched Dr. Fadil's outburst with a half-smile on her face. She sipped her coffee and then spoke. "Dr. Fadil, do not worry if you cannot do this. It seems that no one can convince this al-Majid to agree to an interview, anyhow. I'm certain he would turn you down, as he has everyone else. He has become far too powerful to bother with those he feels are beneath him."

At Salwa's words, an unfamiliarly frightening expression flickered in Dr. Fadil's eyes. He sat with his mouth open for a brief moment before he pushed his chair back and jumped to his feet. He even tipped his drink over in the process. His face was flushed a deep red. "Do you really believe he would *dare* to refuse me? Never!" Dr. Fadil fumed for a few minutes, then looked down at Mayada and said with certainty, "You will get your interview. Do not worry." He then rushed from the room, shouting over his shoulder, "I will call you tomorrow with the time and place for your interview!"

Once the door was slammed behind him, Mayada's mother began to laugh and clap her hands lightly.

"There is a little lesson for you, daughter. No Arab man can bear hearing that another man is believed to be more powerful. The man will do whatever is necessary to prove otherwise."

Salwa leaned forward and lovingly pinched Mayada's cheek between her fingers. "Listen to my words. You will get your interview." She brushed the front of her dress with her hands while yawning. "Now. I am tired. I believe I will retire early this evening and read for a while. There is a new magazine article recently released about your Jido Sati. I want to see if the writer got his facts correct."

Watching her mother gracefully walk from the room, Mayada felt a flash of admiration. Her mother *never* failed to get what she wanted.

While she was lying in bed the following morning, anxious about the day and the task before her, her telephone rang. The caller was Dr. Fadil.

His voice was businesslike, almost abrupt. "Mayada. Ali Hassan al-Majid will be pleased to see you. Go to my old offices. That is where he spends his days. Be there Monday morning at nine sharp. Let me know how it goes." Dr. Fadil hung up the phone before Mayada had a chance to thank him.

Dr. Fadil had come through for her once again. She leapt from her bed with new energy. She couldn't wait to see Kamil's face when she informed him that she had secured an interview with the elusive Ali al-Majid. The article would be a triumph for the magazine.

Although pleased, Kamil failed to show the expected surprise when she told him the good news. Instead, he invited her into his office to prepare questions for the interview. It was early April, and Saddam's birthday was April 28. Kamil wanted to run the first article about the President, and if Ali al-Majid saw fit to make a few personal comments about himself, that would be icing on the cake.

Kamil ended their meeting by telling her, "Mayada, it is difficult to give you advice on this interview. No one knows this man. This is his first interview. Follow your instincts, and see where the interview takes you."

The following Monday, Mayada arrived at Dr. Fadil's old offices. She was anxious and wished for a moment that she was there to see Dr. Fadil rather than his intimidating successor. Her hands shook with nervousness. She didn't know what to expect.

She was escorted into his office, and was surprised to see that Ali al-Majid had changed nothing of the decor. The ceiling was still discotheque tacky, the game tables still stood expectantly, and Dr. Fadil's old furniture was still in the same position. She glanced down and saw that the brown carpet that Dr. Fadil had long trod still covered the floor. Then Mayada lifted her gaze to the back of the large office.

Ali Hassan al-Majid stood behind his desk.

He was tall and slim with broad shoulders. His eyes were large and expressive, colored the blackest black. His nose was small, but well-proportioned for his face. His complexion was smooth and fair.

A perfectly manicured mustache shaded his lips, which were spread in a smile that displayed dazzlingly white, even teeth. With a military bearing, he walked around the desk and toward Mayada. He towered over her, and the look in his eyes was a little too intent. He gestured toward a chair that faced his desk. "Welcome to my office. Please, sit and be comfortable."

Mayada broke her stillness and settled into the chair, then busied herself rummaging in her bag for her pen and a notepad. With her reporter's tools in hand, she rushed through her questions without thinking, jotting down Ali's answers and failing to follow up, trying only to bring this dangerous interview to a rapid end.

Ali al-Majid looked at Mayada quizzically as she made a fool of herself.

"So, you are the granddaughter of the great Sati Al-Husri?"

Mayada peered up from her notepad to see him examining her with squinted eyes while rubbing his chin with his hand.

"Yes," she replied. "Sati Al-Husri was my mother's father."

"By God, Saddam says your grandfather was one of the greatest Arabs. He said Sati Al-Husri was a rare man, a scholar with nerves of steel. Is it true that he refused to allow the British to steal all our treasures?"

Mayada's apprehensions relaxed just a bit. "Well, he didn't greet them with a dagger in his hand. Jido Sati was rational but brilliant. So he outwitted them, instead."

Ali al-Majid looked at her and considered her answer.

"Tell me about that," he insisted.

With this talk of Sati, Mayada suddenly felt so comfortable that she teased the powerful man. "I am here to interview you, not the other way around."

"Then—tell me *one* story of how a man defeats his enemies without using his physical strength."

Mayada held back her laughter, watching Ali al-Majid flex his muscles like a strong man at a circus.

He looked at her with a teasing smile. "Go ahead. I am ordering you. Tell me one story about your grandfather," he bargained, "and I will tell you everything you want to know about me."

This interview was going better than she had ever hoped. Kamil was going to be ecstatic.

Mayada thumbed her pen against her pad. "All right. I will," she agreed. She leaned back into her chair. "When I was a child, I spent many hours with my Jido Sati, and I remember the day he told me this particular story. So I know every word is true.

"When modern Iraq was first formed, King Faisal depended upon my grandfather for many things. He was the Director General of Education. He was the Dean of the College of Law. And he was the antiquities consultant to King Faisal, despite the fact that the British High Commission in Iraq, Sir Percy Cox, had appointed Gertrude Bell, an Englishwoman, as honorary Director of Antiquities. After Miss Bell's death, however, Sati assumed full ownership of the post.

"As you probably know, Gertrude Bell was an extraordinary woman. She was a writer, an adventurer, a close friend to Lawrence of Arabia and even an advisor to kings. She was a very powerful representative of the British government. Few could stand up to her strong personality, and her government generally backed her bold initiatives. She even played a role in selecting Faisal as the first king.

"And Miss Bell took her honorary appointment seriously. Only a year or so after Iraq was recognized as a nation, Miss Bell walked into Sati's office waving a document, saying that she wanted him to get the Cabinet's approval for a new law. She told him she already had an expedition digging at the Ur site. She wanted this new law passed, a law that would change the method of handling the treasures uncovered.

"My grandfather was the most honest man who ever lived, and when he took that document home to review the project, he was horrified to see that she was proposing a new law based on the treaty signed between the Allied Forces in Turkey—a law that would allow the outcome of the digging to be left to the digger. In other words, she would be allowed to take many of Iraq's treasures to England. Then my grandfather studied the old Ottoman law, the law that had always applied to the area, and he discovered that all antiquities dug up would belong to the government—the digger could only take replicas, or casts. Foreign expeditions were not allowed to take *any* antique objects out of the country.

"The next day, Gertrude Bell returned to Jido Sati's offices for the signed document, but she didn't get the answer she was expecting. My grandfather shared his research with her, and told her he was sorry, but he could not ask Parliament to sign the new law she was proposing, that the law would be harmful to Iraq."

Mayada chuckled. "Jido Sati said he had never seen a woman get so furious, so fast. He said her face turned bright red, and she breathed so fast and heavy that it sounded like she was blowing a horn. He thought she might shout at him. However, he stood with a calm face. Miss Bell finally mustered her British cool and simmered down; she grew very calm and talked of other matters. Jido Sati said he knew she was considering how she might sidestep him. He was right. Three days later, he was advised by the British that responsibility of digging at archaeological sites had been given to the Ministry of Transport and General Works. The man who headed that post was rather weak, and he readily crumbled to Bell's demands.

"My grandfather said that they had to compromise for a while, and that he believed that Iraq had lost a lot of antiquities because of Miss Bell's law, but he got his law passed later and saved many other antiquities for the Iraqis. Gertrude Bell was much displeased with my grandfather, to say the least."

Ali al-Majid looked gladdened at Mayada's story. "Go on," he said, "tell me more."

"There was another incident shortly afterward, an even more interesting one about Iraq's ancient Golden Harp. A British representative sought an appointment with King Faisal to advise him that King George V of England would soon celebrate a birthday. That man strongly suggested that King Faisal should present the Golden Harp of the Sumerians to the British King.

"That advice put King Faisal in an awkward predicament, because the British seemed determined to get the harp, the rarest harp in the world. Faisal made an excuse to the envoy and insisted, 'Later, later.' The King then called in Jido Sati and asked his opinion of how they might prevent such a catastrophe. Sati assured King Faisal that he would handle the matter and would divert British anger onto his own head. Sati went straight to the British and advised them that his King was in no position to give away the Golden Harp of the Sumerians, much as he might want to honor King George, that there was a law that forbade such a transfer. Sati told the British envoy he could point the man to a storehouse of antiquities for which replicas already sat in Iraqi museums, and Sati would be happy to help the man select an appropriate replica for the King's birthday.

"The British were flummoxed because they pride themselves on being a law-abiding country. So they had to settle for a replica rather than a one-of-a-kind golden harp.

"King Faisal always teased Sati after that and told him the harp had been saved by Sati's strong heart and personality. King Faisal insisted that Sati was the only man in the entire country who could have saved the harp patrimony for the Iraqi people. Without Sati, he said, greedy British fingers would have strummed that instrument for years to come.

"My grandfather was hated by the British after that. They were not satisfied until they exiled him from the country, which they did years later, when they used a popular uprising as an excuse to put Sati on the list of undesirables."

Ali al-Majid seemed suddenly bored with talk of antiquities. His smile faded and he demanded of Mayada in a loud voice, "Let me see that ring." He stared at Mayada's finger, encircled with a sapphire and diamond cluster ring recently given to her by her mother.

Mayada noticed that when Ali spoke in a loud tone, he employed a nasal voice not unlike Saddam's. She was so taken aback by his request that she slipped the ring from her finger and handed it to him.

Mayada watched as he studied the ring carefully. He turned it over in his hands and looked at the stones from the underside.

"By God, are these stones real?"

She stiffened. "Of course they are real. My mother purchased it at Tiffany's. In celebration of the birth of my baby, Fay."

Ali gestured now at Mayada's dress. "Where did you get your outfit?"

"My mother bought this dress in Paris."

The man's physical beauty diminished in Mayada's eyes with every word he spoke.

Ali smiled, then tilted his head down to the side in a charming, sort of boyish manner. "By God, do you dye your hair?"

Mayada's earlier nervousness was lifting, as Ali al-Majid stared at her artlessly. Perhaps he was one of the most powerful men in the country, but this man was nothing but an uneducated village boy. He was devoid of social graces, unable to hide his brazen curiosity. Perhaps Saddam Hussein didn't *allow* Ali al-Majid to give press interviews, she thought. Unlike the man in front of her, Saddam had made every attempt to increase his knowledge of the world. He had attended law school in Cairo, taught himself to eat properly and to dress like a gentleman—anything to distance himself from his rustic past. Ali was a different story. She was certain that Saddam must be embarrassed for Baghdad society to know that such a man was his first cousin.

Ali al-Majid smiled gleefully, seemingly happy to be unleashed from his self-imposed—or Saddam-imposed—silence. He answered every question on Mayada's list and then insisted she take his private telephone number. He urged her to call him after Saddam's birthday celebration so he could give her a much lengthier interview about his personal history. "I will tell you about my entire life," he promised with an engaging smile.

When Mayada left Ali Hassan al-Majid's offices, she went straight to the magazine offices. Kamil met her at the door and escorted her into his private office. He was surprised and pleased when she read him her notes. "He opened up to you," he described with a broad smile. "I hoped he would."

Mayada gave Kamil the best news yet. "He promised me a broader interview. He says he will give me every detail of his personal life."

Kamil laughed with her. "This is a huge success. No one has ever gotten this man to speak on the record!" He then scurried to make arrangements to remove a story scheduled for the magazine's next issue, so Mayada's piece about Saddam could be inserted instead. A week later, Mayada's story ran. The article was the talk of Baghdad, because it was the first time that Ali Hassan al-Majid had spoken out.

And Ali Hassan al-Majid delivered on his promise to give Mayada information about his own life, so that she could write a piece about him. When Mayada telephoned his office after Saddam's birthday celebration, she was graciously invited to return. When she arrived, she was once again struck by the man's gorgeous exterior, though his beauty no longer stirred magic in her.

Ali al-Majid seemed overly pleased to see Mayada, announcing that he had cleared his schedule for their meeting. He shouted for someone to bring her tea and cookies and, before she could respond, he abruptly ordered her to sit. "Today, I will do all the talking!"

Ali seemed as excited as a child. And so Mayada sat and listened.

Ali braced himself against the edge of his desk and looked impatiently at her while Mayada organized her pad, pen and tape recorder. The moment she was ready, the story of his life gushed from his lips, those of a man who apparently had longed for an attentive audience for his entire life.

He loudly announced, "This is the life of Ali Hassan al-Majid Al-Tikriti, the proud son of Hassan Majeed Al-Tikriti." I have three brothers who stand beside me, Abid Hassan, Hashim Hassan and Suleiman Hassan." He flashed a huge smile before continuing.

Mayada was mesmerized by this man-child, feeling a hundred years older than this, the head of Iraq's secret police.

"Because of our great leader, Saddam—may God preserve and bless him—everyone knows that I was born in the poor rural area of Tikrit. I had to skip school when I was a child, because my brothers and I took turns tending the sheep. I had to walk long distances to find places to graze, but I was alert to wolves and not one ever ate a single sheep when I was on guard. Not one! By God, my brothers could not match my diligence. But those vicious wolves would slink around the edges of the herd and I would toss stones and rush at them with my hands spread like this."

He imitated those long-ago movements with his hands in the air and got into a crouched stance that she had to admit looked rather fierce. But Mayada was not afraid, and she laughed. He laughed back freely.

"By God, those sheep-guarding days shaped me into an alert soldier, someone who never takes his eye off the enemy.

"We were so poor that I didn't know there were such things as movie houses until I was a grown man. So I didn't get into the habit of going to the cinema, and I have seen only one movie in my entire life, a religious film about the Prophet Joseph." He shrugged. "It was all right, but I had rather look at newspapers and magazines.

"I have high blood sugar that turned into diabetes, and I have to inject myself with insulin every day." He startled Mayada when he rushed to a cabinet against the wall and pulled a thin needle and a tiny medicine bottle from a drawer. He then ran back in front of her and gave himself a shot in the arm.

He laughed when she winced, but she told him that her reaction was from surprise rather than a fear of needles. "Before my father died of cancer I learned to give him his shots, for pain. When the nurse left our house each afternoon, I had the responsibility to inject him. I was also trained to give IV injections."

Ali al-Majid seemed genuinely touched by her father's ordeal and looked at Mayada with sympathy. He told her he was sorry, that to lose a father would be the worst thing for a young girl. He loved his own daughter more than his own life, he told Mayada, but he would tell her about that later. Then Ali returned to the subject of his diabetes.

"It's a pity for me that I have diabetes because I love sweets more than any other food. Sometimes I eat lots of sweets and simply hope for the best. My favorite sweet is a trifle cake with jelly—custard and fruits in layers. I also like chocolates." He walked around to reach under his desk and pressed a buzzer. When a servant entered the room, Ali told him, "Go and get a box of each brand of my favorite chocolates."

Mayada protested, because she had watched her weight all her adult life and couldn't imagine eating chocolates freely. But Ali al-Majid was not a man who listened. Moments later, boxes of Mars bars, Kit Kats and Smarties covered her lap and, since Ali seemed thrilled to give her a little gift, Mayada accepted the boxes, thinking she would offer the chocolates at her office later.

"I want you to come to a wedding in four days. My brother is marrying Dr. Fadil Al-Barrak's sister-in-law."

"I have heard," Mayada mumbled, still surprised that two men who admitted such dislike for each other agreed to permit their families to join in such an intimate way. To avoid a discussion of Dr. Fadil, Mayada changed the slant of the conversation. "How old is the bride?" she asked.

"Sixteen."

"That is too young," she protested, thinking of her own daughter, who would be sixteen in only fifteen years. Mayada would never allow her darling Fay to become a child bride. The Arab custom of young brides was primitive, she thought.

Ali al-Majid laughed. "Sixteen is the perfect age for a girl to marry. My brother is a lucky man. He can mold her exactly as he wants her to be."

Mayada said nothing to this remark, but she was struck again by an inner happiness that she had been born into an educated family, where females were valued as highly as males.

Ali al-Majid plucked a small red rubber ball from the top of his desk and kneaded it between his fingers as he raised the topic Mayada had hoped to avoid. "How do you know Dr. Fadil Al-Barrak?"

"In 1979, he approached my mother and asked to borrow my grandfather Sati's books and papers," Mayada explained. "He was writing a book and wanted them for research. After that he became a generous friend of our family. The friendship came about because of Sati, of course," she added quickly.

Ali wobbled his body from head to toe in disgust. He threw the ball against the wall and watched it bounce around the room. "I do not like Fadil."

"Why? I can think of nothing bad to say about him."

Her words won her a frown from Ali, who proved eager to explain his dislike.

"When I took over the secret police, I got a complaint about him from a group of gypsies. Fadil had ordered them to abandon a piece a land they were living on. It was in the suburbs of Baghdad. I summoned the head gypsy to my office and discovered that he was the brother of Hamdiya Salih, a well-known gypsy singer." He looked at Mayada and smiled. "I like the gypsies. They are human beings, after all. Anyhow, those poor people had nowhere else to live. So I telephoned Fadil and ordered him to send one of his high-ranking officers to deliver this gypsy back to Fadil's new office at Intelligence." Ali laughed loudly. "I ordered Fadil to apologize and to give the land back. I think he had built a big house on it by then and he had to give that up." Ali could not stop himself from laughing at the memory of Dr. Fadil's humiliation.

So *now* she understood the reason that Dr. Fadil hated Ali Hassan al-Majid. Due to Ali's close family relationship with Saddam, Dr. Fadil was forced to obey Ali's commands, despite the fact that Dr. Fadil held a higher office. Mayada still felt uneasy, not wishing to disparage Dr. Fadil in any manner, so she remembered one of her mother's tactics and flattered the man. "That was kind and generous of you."

He looked at her intently. "I am like that, you know. I am the kindest man. The kindest!"

Ali al-Majid slid back onto his desktop and began to swing both feet. "Let me tell you another story. A woman came to me saying that her only son had been executed because he was an Islamic activist. She had nowhere to turn. Her husband was dead. Her son was dead. She had no brothers. That poor woman was old, almost blind. So I ordered that she be given a house and a monthly income of 100 dinars a month [$330]. Just because her son had done wrong didn't mean we should punish her."

He looked at Mayada and smiled brightly. "What do you think of that?"

Mayada nodded and agreed. "I am glad you helped her. I hate cruelty. I really do." Yet she wondered why the woman's son had to be killed in the first place. Being overly religious now guaranteed a death sentence in Iraq, and that frightening fact saddened and angered her.

Ali puckered his lips before asking, "Do you only write for the magazine?

"No. I have other projects. I am writing a book of short stories."

He became excited. "By God, I have two or three perfect stories for your book." He began talking rapidly and breathlessly. "Listen to me! This is a military story. A few weeks back one of our soldiers escaped from his unit and hid in the marshes of Umara. To survive, he drank the water of the marshes and ate the fish he caught. Then one day there was a large offensive carried out by the Iranians against the Iraqi units close to the area, and this young soldier forgot he was a deserter. So he fought alongside in another unit and ended up being a hero who captured five Iranians. Then he remembered that he was a deserter and that he was with the wrong unit. He admitted his status to the head officer of that unit, and he was given the death penalty. Well, he was lucky that I heard this story before he was shot. I contacted the President and told him about this hero who had suffered one cowardly moment. Saddam the leader, may Allah preserve him, told me to save that soldier's life and bring him to the palace. I did, and guess what? The soldier received the Wissam Al-Shajaa [Medal of Bravery] from Saddam the leader, may Allah preserve him, and even got a cash bonus. Put that story in your book.

"And here's another." He actually jumped from the desk and stamped his feet on the floor.

Rather than tell the story, Ali's voice changed and he seemed to sing a ballad to the world about his great kindnesses. "A few weeks ago I was on my way to the office and my Mawkib [cars filled with bodyguards that surround his car] was overtaken by a fast-moving automobile. When the driver pulled beside me and recognized me, he stopped his car. My bodyguards surrounded his automobile and told him to step out. Well, by God, that poor man looked so frightened that he couldn't stand up straight and he collapsed on the pavement. I stepped out of my car and tried to calm him down. Finally I told him to ride with me. I saw him trembling when he stepped to my automobile, but I talked to him and took him to my office where I had my staff serve him tea and cookies. I joked with him and finally he realized I was not going to order him to prison for passing up my car." He looked at her, puzzled. "I don't understand why people are afraid of me. I protect Iraqis from our enemies. Why is that so bad?"

She wasn't brave enough to mention that there might be a valid reason for Iraqi fears, considering the punishments meted out from the secret police, so she just nodded and said nothing, although the story of Um Sami's boys kept running through her mind. She longed to tell Ali al-Majid that tragic tale, but couldn't find the courage. Mayada remained extraordinarily calm, considering the situation. She decided Ali reminded her of a girl she had known in school who exhausted every classmate until they began to avoid her. She wondered if Ali's physician had ever suggested he take sedatives.

His euphoria was building to an alarming pitch. "I told you that I used to be very poor, but now I am well-to-do and I like it. Of course, your family was prosperous from generations back, so you have no idea what it is like to go hungry or barefoot, or to not have the books you want to read or slip into the designer dresses you like to wear. You were born lucky, by God. But while I suffered in my youth, now I ride in cars that I could only dream about before. And I live in a house that is like a museum to me. Saddam the leader, may Allah preserve him, comes to visit me often, and he has an eye for beauty. Each time he visits, he orders me, 'Ali, add an aquarium! Ali, change the shape of your pool! Ali, knock down that wall!' It's a big joke with my elder and beloved cousin, Saddam, that I will never have the house he believes suitable for me. He told me once that I should have gone to school and become an architect, so I could carry out his suggestions to his satisfaction." Ali al-Majid smiled happily. "Our President just wants me to have all the good things we never had in Tikrit. He is a good cousin."

He cleared his throat. "What next? What next? Oh, my children. My eldest son is Omar. I have a second son named Hassan. Then my wife got pregnant a third time. I had a feeling I was going to have a daughter. I was excited and decided that if it was a girl, I was going to give her a special gift, an original name. So I called her Hibba, which means 'bestowed.' I did not believe any other Iraqi—or even any other Arab—had ever thought to give their daughter such a beautiful name. Then one day I was driving with my entourage. Sitting next to me, my bodyguard spotted an ice cream store by the name of Hibba. I was so surprised that we stopped the cars. I got out and found that the owner was shaking with nerves. I urged him to calm down, that I was only there for an ice cream. When he served my ice cream, I asked him where he got the name Hibba. He told me that Hibba was the name of his eldest daughter, and that he had named the shop after her. I was so shocked. I discovered that day that Hibba was a well-known name, and that many daughters of many proud men carried the name." He sheepishly added, "And I thought I was the first man to think of that name."

Ali appeared to be thinking back, trying to remember other stories. His ruminations turned again to the fear he inspired in others. "I don't understand why so many people are frightened of me." He looked at her with a sly smile. "Are you frightened of me, Mayada?"

For the first time she was afraid. She whispered, "Should I be?"

A gleeful flicker appeared for a moment before he said, "Never! You are the granddaughter of a great man. All of Iraq cherishes you, just as your Jido Sati cherished you."

When he went to pour himself a glass of water, she slipped a peek at her watch and saw that he had talked nonstop for three hours. Thankfully, his telephone rang and he answered it. He whispered a few words into the receiver, then told Mayada that he had another appointment. But he insisted that she return the following morning, that he had many, many other interesting stories that must be included in her articles and books.

Mayada had mixed feelings. On the one hand, she couldn't believe her good fortune. She had done nothing to win this man's trust, a man who had previously refused to even speak to the press, yet he poured out his heart to her, urging her to print his personal life stories in her magazine and in her book. On the other hand, this uncouth man who imagined himself to be quite extraordinary could keep a writer busy for many years.

Mayada's mother had the most likely explanation for Ali al-Majid's bizarre behavior. She suggested that Saddam had encouraged his cousin Ali to open up to Mayada. Otherwise, the man wouldn't dare spill every personal story of his life in such a fashion. Ever since he was a penniless student in Cairo, Saddam had been captivated by the reputation and gentle conduct of Sati Al-Husri. Saddam knew the great man never turned away even the poorest student who chose to

ask him questions to further the student's knowledge. Saddam's fasci-
nation for Sati had been automatically transferred to Sati's daughter
and granddaughters.

For three days Mayada listened quietly, nodded politely, and took
down everything Ali al-Majid said. There were times she would be
writing and would look up to see that Ali al-Majid's eyes were fas-
tened on her face. She would peer attentively at him, but she soon
realized he was not really seeing her, but seeing himself in the pages
of a book. Ali's manic behavior was exhausting and depressing, and
Mayada was relieved to present her completed material to Kamil, who
excitedly assured her that indeed, she had enough material for several
articles, as well as a book.

From that time, Mayada's career advanced. Rumor spread that she
could get interviews with even the most elusive government officials.
This success filled the emptiness of her loveless marriage, and there
were times when Mayada felt wonderfully happy, as though everything good still lay ahead of her.

A few months later, the head of Ali al-Majid's office, a man named
Dr. Saad, called Mayada at home to tell her, "There is a democratic
exercise tomorrow. Ali al-Majid wants you to be the reporter to
cover it."

Of course she agreed. Mayada believed the report would be a
great scoop for her. Immediately, she called Kamil to tell him the
good news. She would not be coming to work tomorrow; instead, she
would be at Ali al-Majid's office.

When Mayada retired that evening, she was thrilled and excited,
believing that her career was heading in an important direction.

She had never been to such an event, so she showed up at Dr.
Fadil's old headquarters at 8:45 the following morning.

It was a beautiful summer day in Baghdad. Mayada wore a crisp
new white sailor dress with blue ties, which her mother had bought
for her in London. She had sprayed her wrists and ears with the scent
of Fashion De Leonard. She felt carefree and on top of the world.

The secret-police complex was huge, but Mayada was led to the appropriate meeting room by one of Ali's assistants. The event was slated for the headquarters' gymnasium. There was an indoor swimming pool and a large stage, which bore a long table and many chairs. Two microphones stood onstage, one at each end. Neat rows of chairs faced the stage.

Mayada was led to the front row. She took her seat. She was the first person to arrive, so she sat and waited and watched as others filed into the room. For some reason, she hummed the Mamas and the Papas' famous hit "Monday, Monday."

Soon the gym was filled, and the crowd fell into a hush when Ali al-Majid strode in, surrounded by his bodyguards. A large group of other high-ranking government officials trooped in right behind.

Ali glanced through the room and saw Mayada sitting in the front row. He gave her a nod and a smile, then stood in front of one of the microphones. He delivered a brief lecture, telling the audience that matters in the security offices would now be handled differently. Big changes had been made since he had taken over from Dr. Fadil. Ali explained it would be a total democracy, with complete support from his cousin, the leader Saddam Hussein, may Allah preserve him.

Everyone smiled and clapped just a little too readily.

After the applause ended, Ali al-Majid resumed his talk, saying he had saved the most important part of the exercise until last. For the first time that day, his face turned sad and stern. "Before I came into this office, wrongdoers in this nation simply disappeared. They would be given a prison sentence, or even executed, but the family would not be notified where they were or how much time they would have to serve for their crime . . . or even if they were alive. This was wrong. And by God, this is over, I can tell you that. From this time on, when a criminal is arrested, charged and sentenced, families will be notified. Perhaps the family will choose to disown these traitors, but that will be their choice."

Mayada looked around uneasily. Many people in the audience

were shifting uncomfortably. No one could believe the free way Ali al-Majid was speaking, apparently without concern that criticizing another department might create a problem. Such openness was taboo in Baathist Iraq, even by one of Saddam's relatives, and particularly in the setting of a public forum. Mayada decided that something important was about to happen. So she stopped writing, turned on her tape recorder, and listened carefully, as her heart pounded.

Ali al-Majid said, "I want the family of every criminal to know exactly what happened to their loved ones. By God, it is only right." He then looked to the back of the stage and called out a man's name. A tall slim man with a receding hairline and gentle-looking face approached the stage. He stood in front of the second microphone and said, "My only son was arrested six months ago. I do not know where he is. Here is his name." He walked toward Ali al-Majid and handed him a slip of paper. Ali studied the name for a moment, then wadded the slip in his fist before shuffling through two or three papers handed him by an assistant. Ali pulled a cassette tape out of a small box and said, "Yes. Your son was accused of high treason. He has been executed. The whereabouts of his grave is unknown. Here is a tape of his confession. Go home and listen to it so you won't grieve the death of this traitor."

The poor father fell back a step in astonishment. For the briefest time he restrained himself from breaking down, but he touched Ali's shoulder and cried out, "My son is dead? My son is dead?" Two assistants rushed on the stage and caught the man before he tumbled to the stage floor. As he was led away, Mayada saw his hands clutching the tape as though it was as precious as the body of his dead son.

Mayada could not move her eyes, which were fixed on one spot, Ali al-Majid's face. He was smiling an absurd smile, and he shouted with an air of conviction, "It is good for that father to know his son is a traitor. Yes! Perhaps it is some mistake he made as a father. Now he can watch how he raises his daughters."

Mayada lowered her eyes and stared at her feet.

She listened as, one by one, Ali al-Majid called out names of hopeful relatives, all attending this democratic exercise in the belief they had come to take a long-lost relative home to celebrate with their loved ones. She heard individual footsteps marching hopefully to the stage. Yet she knew that none would receive welcome news. To her mind, she was listening to a chain dragging across the stage, a chain of Iraqis, all linked by a terrible grief, all hearing the same sad fate about the person they loved.

Mayada sat like a stone lodged as securely as the stones of the Great Pyramid until someone tapped her on her shoulder, and a voice whispered in her ear, "Watch out, they are looking." Mayada lifted her head and stared blindly ahead, feigning interest in the painful scenes.

Mayada listened to the sounds of the anxious conversation among relatives of prisoners, now dead or sentenced, while keeping her eyes on Ali al-Majid. His energized expression revealed that he was enjoying himself immensely as he played a tape of a young man being tortured, his cries ringing out across the large auditorium. The dead youth's mother jumped and waved her arms about, as though believing she could stop her son's anguish. Her wild gyrations elicited laughter from the audience. When she fainted and dropped to the floor, her action merely heightened the laughter.

Mayada knew that everyone in the audience must be as sickened as she was, yet they feared Ali al-Majid and felt they must support his every move. Otherwise, they knew, their own future might include a long walk across a stage to listen to a tape of their loved one's moans.

She watched the sweet faces of two young women who heard that their father had received a twenty-year sentence for smuggling. They babbled to Ali al-Majid that their father had once been a teacher but had lost his job. His family was starving, and that was the only reason he had taken the tires.

Disregarding their grief, Ali looked happily at his audience and said, "By God, smuggling is smuggling, a big crime. But we are entering a new age when these people can learn the truth about their loved ones."

He threw a quick glance at Mayada in the audience and smiled and said, "By God, I am a kind man!" The audience clapped enthusiastically.

My God, would he never stop smiling? Mayada was terribly shaken; her whole body was trembling. She was in a state of absolute terror that this man even knew her.

Mayada looked down at her lap, thinking she could not bear to see another hopeful face dashed by disappointment. To distract herself, she sniffed the perfume on her wrist.

When Mayada looked up, she paled. A tall, bony man dressed in rags stood on the stage. His skin looked like burnt toast. His hair was melted to his scalp. With a gaping mouth devoid of every tooth and his fingers clotted with blood, the skeletal man stood next to Ali al-Majid.

Ali al-Majid looked at the man with pity and shook the man's bloody fingers warmly. Ali then gazed at the crowd, his large black eyes blazing like burning coals. He told the audience the man's name. He then called out a woman's name, explaining that she was the wife of the bony creature.

Mayada's uneasiness increased with every minute. Then a short, spare woman no more than thirty years old stumbled onstage to stand in front of the second microphone. She was wearing a black abaaya Iranian style, holding it under her chin. She stared at Ali al-Majid with fright and suspicion in her eyes.

Her frail husband kept looking at her, a look of anger mingled with disappointment.

Ali spoke to the man in a loud whisper. "You should have divorced this whore a long time ago. You knew she was Iranian. You should have broken one of her bones and looked inside. You would have discovered shit."

The man began to address the audience, drawing out his words with difficulty, speaking with unutterable sorrow in an unsteady voice. "See these hands?" He held them away from his body. "See how my fingernails were ripped from my fingers? For ten days, one a day, until every nail was gone. And my toes," he attempted to lift a foot but was too weak to balance on one leg, so he pointed instead. "I have no nails on my toes. Another ten days of one nail a day. Then I was taken to a small room and placed in a chair. My hands were tied to the chair. A man with a small pair of pliers came into the room and yanked out a tooth. He pulled my teeth, one by one, until every tooth was on the floor. After that I was taken by force and put into a large oven, big enough for two men. I was put into that oven and told I was going to be roasted to death and then fed to the dogs. But they left me only long enough to toast my skin and melt my hair." He patted his burnt head with his bloodied hands. He looked at his wife in sadness and could hardly bring out the words. "All of this because my wife became angry and wrote a letter to the secret police. She told them I was an Islamic Party member, who planned to assassinate officials in the government."

Mayada sat quietly, amazed at the idea of such pitiless revenge. Her own husband had disappointed her time and again, but she would never plot for his harm. She scanned the woman's face. A spark of anger built in Mayada. How could a woman do that to the father of her children?

The poor man burst into tears and could not be comforted, although Ali tried to soothe the man by telling him he would be well compensated for the torture brought on by a fake charge, that he had already signed the documents awarding him a substantial sum of money.

Then Ali flared when he turned to the woman, who by now was visibly shaking. "What did you do, whore, to your husband?"

The woman was too terrified to speak, although she opened and shut her mouth two or three times in succession.

Ali reported the circumstances of her crime. "This," he spit on the

floor for emphasis, "is an Iranian whore. She lives in Kerbala." He gestured toward the bony man. "She had three children with her husband. When he was called to the front to perform his patriotic duty,
defending our holy motherland against Iranian aggression, this whore
received men at their home. Even with three young children inside,
she turned her home into a bordello.

"Our Iraqi hero returned from the front and was told what had
been happening. He confronts this whore, and of course, she is a liar
as well, so she denies it. When he returns to the front, she writes an
anonymous letter, accusing him of being a traitor. He is arrested, interrogated and punished. Then we discover that she is an Iranian
whore and we bring her in. What do we discover? The whole sordid
story comes out. She has been lying the entire time. She wanted her
husband dead so she could continue her whoring habits."

Ali frowned menacingly at the woman and said, "Listen, whore.
Today you will be thrown into the no-man's-land between the Iraqi
army and the Iranian army. Your children will be thrown there with
you. The artillery shelling is so heavy that eventually you will all be
killed. And that will be a good thing for Iraq."

Ali al-Majid suddenly burst out laughing, just like a child. He
shouted, "I am a kind man. I am a good man. I seek justice for this
poor man." He continued to bray his strange laugh and gazed at the
audience with glittering eyes.

Mayada shivered. The audience tittered with Ali, before beginning
to clap. The applause slowly built into a loud commotion of approval.

Mayada struggled for breath while staring at the poor man whose
burned legs had finally given way. He had buckled to the floor. He
was now going to lose his children. She wanted to cry out to Ali al-
Majid not to do this thing. Yes, the woman should be punished with a
prison sentence, but the children were innocent.

But Ali al-Majid looked well-pleased with his verdict, and Mayada
knew she had no way of reversing his decision. She gripped the sides

of her chair, fighting an overwhelming desire to jump up and run as far away as her legs would take her.

Two men rushed onto the stage and took the struggling woman away. Two nurses came and led the injured husband to the back of the stage.

The six-hour-long nightmare ended at 3:00 in the afternoon, when Ali Hassan al-Majid thanked them all for coming, adding that he would have such events on a monthly basis. "By God, I am a fair man, and in my position as head of the secret police, I will notify Iraqis of the fate of their loved ones."

Mayada forced herself to smile, fighting through the crowd to the exit. Just as she reached the door, one of Ali's assistants ran toward her and reported that his boss requested that she remain behind to discuss the success of the democratic session.

Mayada had always lived honestly, but now she lied without pause. "Thank him for his kindness in inviting me. Tell him my baby daughter needs me. I will speak with him later."

And then she fled that auditorium as though she had been pulled out of it by force. Fleeing from Ali Hassan al-Majid, a man she now knew was mentally unbalanced, one moment ordering the death of an only son and the next moment awarding that same son's mother a life pension, Mayada drove her car as fast as the speed limit allowed. She rushed home and ripped her sailor dress over her head and jumped into the shower. Even standing under the warm water, cold shivers ran down her spine.

When she returned to her office the following morning, Mayada brushed past Kamil and went to request a meeting with Suhail Sami Nadir, a wonderfully sweet man who was in charge of the entire magazine. Mayada and Suhail were not personal friends, but she had always sensed that he liked her. She put her life into his hands by confiding her feelings about the events of the previous day.

Mayada told Suhail, "I cannot see that man again. Ever. I cannot write this piece about him. I am going to resign. I cannot be a reporter in Iraq any longer."

Suhail looked at Mayada closely. He agreed at once, as though he had already thought it over. He said, "Listen to me. If you want to withdraw, Mayada, I understand. But do it gradually. Once I had a similar experience. I refused to do a piece. And what happened to me? I spent three years imprisoned by the Mukhabarat. This piece can be published without your name. Then step by step, you may pull away from political pieces. It is best that way."

Mayada suddenly understood why Suhail always appeared so quiet and withdrawn. Now she remembered he had a limp, and an arm that hung at an angle. He held many memories in his body.

For a few months, Mayada received frequent telephone calls from Ali Hassan al-Majid's offices, advising her about one event after another that he urged her to cover. But as a mother, she had a believable excuse with her baby, who had the usual childhood fevers and colds and could not be left alone. Before long, calls from al-Majid's offices ceased. She hoped she had been forgotten.

But her life was cut in half on that day of the democratic exercise, creating two parts, both belonging to the same woman. It was on that day that she began to feel a mysterious call to change her life. Mayada, once a chic Baghdadi, dressing in the latest fashion, slowly evolved into a devout Muslim. She took comfort in wearing the veil. She drew consolation from veiling despite her mother's angry accusations that she was embracing their primitive past.

After the birth of her second child, Mayada divorced her husband. Soon her only joys came from her children, Fay and Ali, and from the pages of the Quran. Her life had changed forever.

But now a loud pounding on her cell door at Baladiyat brought Mayada back to the present. The door was flung open. Mayada jumped aside as two burly wardens burst into the cell.

"Out! Out! All of you!"

Mayada's maternal great-grandmother, Melek, who was a princess and the first
cousin of Ottoman Sultan Abdul Hameed, photographed with her diamond
tiara. She had a medal with diamonds the size of grapes. Mayada inherited six
of the diamonds and was forced to sell them during the sanctions. Mayada also
inherited the Shehname (a decree signed by the Sultan saying that Melek had
come of age and was now a sultana, and listing all the lands she received).
She still has this document.

Mustafa Al-Askari (Jafar's
father, Mayada's great-grandfather) in Baghdad:
Commander of the 4th
Ottoman Army.

Jafar Al-Askari in his Dervish
outfit when he traveled incognito
behind enemy lines into Cairo to purchase goods for his army.

Jafar Al-Askari in his military uniform.

1955: A five-day-old Mayada in Beirut, Lebanon. Here with her mother, Salwa;
her father, Nizar; and Scottie.

1957: Mayada, nearly two years old, playing seesaw with her doll in Baghdad.

1965: In Broummana, Lebanon. Sati Al-Husri; his daughter, Salwa; and his two granddaughters, Mayada and Abdiya.

1981: Mayada receiving her first writing award from Saddam Hussein.

1983: Mayada receiving her third writing award from Saddam Hussein.

1923: Sati Al-Husri
in his private library
in Baghdad.

1923: Sati's wife,
Jamila, in his library
in Baghdad.

1953: Salwa Al-Husri with her husband's uncle, Nouri Al Said, who was Iraq's Prime Minister for forty years and was murdered in a political coup in 1958, along with the Iraqi royal family. This photograph was taken at the Dorchester Hotel in London in November 1953. It was an "Arabian Nights" ball.

1993: Mayada's children, Fay and Ali, with their grandmother Salwa in Amman, Jordan.

Dr. Sabah moved quickly in the direction of Samara, stammering. "This woman cannot move. She has been injured."

"Out! Everyone!"

Knowing it was useless to expect mercy, Dr. Sabah and Muna reached for Samara and held her between them, Samara's feet barely touching the floor. The other shadow women quickly crowded to the door, and Mayada was pulled into the jostling crowd.

The head warden waited outside their cell. He was a tall, heavyset man with a powerful chest. He glared at them with his fierce face and shouted at the top of his voice. "Stand in line! Make a straight line!"

Mayada's entire body was shaking with fear.

"Make a straight line!" He looked at them, one by one. "Now! Walk to the end of the corridor. Now!"

The shadow women were so close that each woman was touching the woman in front and the woman in back, a train of terrified women.

Mayada was standing behind Roula, and Iman was standing behind Mayada.

"Straight ahead!"

They quickly arrived at the end of the corridor and were herded like sheep through the narrow door. As they entered the room, a collective gasp swept through the line. The strange room was a cave. The walls were pitted and dark. Buckets lined the floors, containers filled to the top with urine. Human excrement was piled high.

Samara called out, "This is where they execute the prisoners!"

A terrible roar of fear radiated from the shadow women.

Every mother began to call the names of her children. The shadow women without children began to call for their mothers.

More burly guards rushed through the open door, striking them with truncheons and wooden sticks, forcing them against the wall.

Several shadow women were shouting, "We are going to die!"

Mayada prepared herself for death. She prayed aloud, "Please

God forgive me for whatever bad deeds I might have done in my life. Please keep my two children safe. Please get them out of Iraq so they can live a decent life."

Wails and grief filled the air.

Out of the darkness Samara began to sing, her voice low and feeble. She sang to the tune of a sad old Iraqi lullaby, hundreds of years old, altering the words to fit the moment:

> *"I lost my mother,*
> *When I was only a child,*
> *But I remember how she held me,*
> *Loving me in her arms.*
> *Now I beg you,*
> *Walk softly on this soil.*
> *Perhaps they buried her in this place,*
> *So walk softly on this soil."*

Other voices began softly to hum, learning the new words as they went along. As the women continued singing, five additional guards stalked into the room. They held rifles at their sides.

The warden shouted, "Face the wall! Prepare to die!"

The shadow women moved together into a crowded circle, weeping and clinging to each other. Two of the oldest women fainted.

Three or four guards rushed at those women and began to pull their hair and strike them in their faces with balled fists. Their groans of pain mingled with the sounds of women's screams and men's laughter.

Mayada felt herself shutting down. It was God's will that these were her last moments on earth. She closed her eyes and covered her face with her hands. She prepared herself for the end, because she had no choice.

She heard the warden hoarsely call bitter and sarcastic words, "Pray to your God, if you will. But He will not hear you. I am your God today!"

The warden couldn't stop laughing. "I am your God!"

The men laughed with him.

Loud laughter echoed around and around the room.

The laughter was driving Mayada mad. She held her breath, waiting for the bullets to strike her body.

Then she heard a number of clicks.

The guards were preparing their weapons.

Sara cried out, "Mother! Mother!"

A guard batted her in the face.

Muna was sobbing and clinging to Mayada's neck. "I cannot die. I have a baby who needs his mother. I am too young to die!"

Mayada's mind was racing. Would she feel the bullets as they entered her body? Would she feel pain? Would she black out?

The men continued laughing.

The shadow women waited for death.

No gunshots rang out.

The shadow women waited longer.

Finally Mayada opened her eyes and cautiously turned her head without moving her body.

The men's guns were pointed to the floor.

The only thing raised in their direction was a camera.

The other women began opening their eyes to look at the guards.

"Turn around," the man with the camera ordered. "Face forward."

Mayada froze. Perhaps the cameraman was there to record their deaths by gunfire. She knew that the government often took photographs of executions. Would her execution be shown on television? Is that how her children would discover she was dead? Through a television show?

The warden shouted, "You are a mighty bunch, I must say." He spat on the ground in disgust at their fear and terror. "I praise Allah that I have a wife and sisters and daughters at home that do not even know how to buy groceries at the market," meaning that they were so pious they did not go out of the home. "And look at you, a bunch of filthy criminals. You are a disgrace to your families. And cowards, too."

He spat once again.

The warden informed them, "You are here to have your pictures taken." Then he began laughing so hard that he doubled over and slapped his thigh.

The rest of the guards laughed loudly. One guard began to imitate their fear. He hovered in a corner and mimicked Sara, yelling, "Mother! Mother!"

The guards laughed even louder.

Mayada suddenly realized what had happened. The guards at Baladiyat had grown bored and someone thought of a new sport to terrify the women.

Several of the women were still weeping. Mayada saw three of them lying unconscious on the floor.

Mayada was numb. She could barely move when ordered to stand in a certain place to pose for her prison picture.

After her photograph was made, she stumbled to a corner and huddled, watching as the other women had their pictures taken.

After an hour, the women were led back to their cell, but no one spoke.

Mayada lay in her bunk and turned her face to the wall and cried. For the first time, her weeping was a solace. She had not died tonight. Perhaps God was going to allow her to see her children again.

7

Torture

The feigned execution only whetted the men's appetite for cruelty that evening. Baladiyat's walls echoed with agonized wails throughout the long night.

The torture room lay only a few doors from cell 52, and Mayada could hear every sob. Years earlier, she had read Aleksandr Solzhenitsyn's novel *The Gulag Archipelago*, in which he said it was more painful to hear the torture of fellow prisoners than it was to be tortured. Now Mayada understood what he meant.

The long night crawled by. The prisoners listened as boots stomped up and down the concrete corridors. They listened to the beatings. They listened as the guards' words were quickly followed by the inmates' shrieks.

With each thunderous boot step, the shadow women feared the sound of a key unlocking their cell door.

At dawn Mayada heard the crier's musical call to prayer, "God is great, there are no other Gods, but God; and Mohammed was His Prophet. Come to prayer. Come to Prayer. God is great. There is no God, but God."

The women welcomed the morning. And the dawn's call to prayer brought the shadow women some hope. After the stillness of morning prayers, the stuffy cell bustled as twenty women readied for a new day. They straightened their dresses, twisted their long hair into knots and took turns at the toilet before sitting quietly to await breakfast. Mayada returned to her bunk after her morning prayers and sat in silence. She crossed her arms and patted each upper arm nervously as she peered at the women who shared her cell.

Samara was still too sore to move. So when breakfast arrived, Muna adopted Samara's usual role and distributed the bland food. Mayada accepted the single piece of bread and small cup of water offered to her. The small cell didn't enable all its prisoners to sit comfortably, so some shadow women chose to pad around the tiny room as they ate their breakfast of lentils, moldy bread and tepid water.

A few hours after breakfast was served, the cell door boomed with a sudden pounding. Guards banged on the portal as a key turned in the lock. The three men crowded into the doorway, stirring anxious commotion and whimpering among the twenty women.

The guard bellowed, "Jamila! We are waiting!"

Mayada's eyes turned toward the cluster of women sitting at the back of the cell. Jamila had been imprisoned at Baladiyat three months before Mayada, and only Samara had been more frequently tortured than she. In the confines of the small cell, Jamila could not be ignored; she writhed, continually contorting her shoulders up and down in a manner that seemed disturbingly purposeless.

Mayada saw Jamila on the floor among the other women in the cell, her face filled with fear. Her mouth hung open with half-eaten lentils and bread. After a moment's hesitation, the woman resumed chewing and swallowed.

"Jamila!" The guard shouted a second time. His heavy black eyebrows twitched as he glared from one woman to another.

Sighing heavily, Jamila stared at the guard. She was a forty-eight-year-old mother to many daughters and one son. The year before, her husband and son had been accused of being Islamic activists. When the secret police broke into their home in the middle of the night to arrest them, the police discovered that the two men of the house had escaped from Iraq into Turkey. The police had taken Jamila as hostage, insisting she would be held in her men's place until the husband and son returned to Iraq to face execution. Since Jamila's first day of imprisonment, she had wept almost continuously. She explained that her tears were for her beautiful girls, daughters who now lived without a father or mother. But thinking about her girls had not strengthened Jamila's resolve, and the woman had sunk into the blackest depression.

Like all the women, Mayada watched Jamila as the guard fumed in the doorway. Only the day before, Mayada had heard Jamila ask Muna to help layer clothes on her back with a thick pad, so that she might move more comfortably. When Jamila dropped her pajama top to accept the cloth, Mayada saw that her back was badly disfigured by deep purple scars, encrusted by freshly scabbed wounds. Mayada finally understood why Jamila continually writhed her shoulders, lowering them in one direction and then raising them in another. She explained that one moment her sores hurt and the next moment they itched.

Slowly, Jamila bent forward and laid her plate of lentils on the floor. She placed her piece of half-eaten bread atop the lentils. Carefully she pushed her glass of water to the wall. Then she stood up.

She was dressed in the same rose-colored pajamas that she had been wearing at the time of her arrest. After three months they were grimy with prison dirt, baggy in the seat and torn in several places. The waistband elastic was so slack that the pants constantly threatened to fall down, so Jamila kept the pants pulled high to her chest. Her pajama top now was gaping open, so she took a moment to button the top button and smoothed the front of her pajamas with her hands.

As presentable as she could be under the circumstances, Jamila looked at the guards. Her forehead was tightly stretched, and her dark eyes were sunk deep into her head. She took a small step forward. Then she took a step back. She stared at the three men, who glared back at her. She stumbled forward, then backward again, like an invisible cord was pulling her back and forth against her will.

One of the guards lost his patience. "You'll pay, by God! You'll pay!" he thundered.

Jamila walked mechanically toward the door on her bare feet, so frightened that she had forgotten to put on her slippers.

The shadow women looked on, sad and silent, as two of the guards caught Jamila by the arms and dragged her out of the cell.

The moment the cell door slammed, they heard a guard curse.

Poor Jamila uttered a single loud shriek.

At Samara's instructions, Muna, Dr. Sabah and Mayada began to prepare for Jamila's return. They laid a pad of blankets on the floor. They collected two or three small, clean cloths. They emptied the remains of water glasses into a small bowl and set it aside. They were as ready as they could be to nurse poor Jamila's new wounds.

Samara reminded them, "She bleeds heavily from her back. You can take one of my blankets, if necessary, to staunch the bleeding."

At that moment, they heard Jamila's voice screech. They heard her plead for mercy.

The shadow women silently exchanged long looks of sorrow.

Jamila wailed and cried continuously for nearly an hour.

Samara sighed. "Never have I heard such pitiful screeches."

Then, without warning, Jamila's screams abruptly ended.

The shadow women nervously awaited her return.

During long months of confinement, Wafae had cleverly twisted the threads dangling from an old and tattered blanket into a set of prayer beads. Now those well-worn beads were passed from hand to hand as every shadow woman prayed urgently for Jamila's safe return.

After several hours of waiting, Mayada grew agitated. She prayed. She wrung her hands. She prayed some more. Her heart began to throb violently. She looked to Samara for answers.

Finally Samara spoke, answering Mayada's unasked question. "Yes. You are right. Something is terribly wrong."

Later, a guard with a broad nose opened their cell door and asked, "Did prisoner Jamila leave any personal belongings behind?"

Everyone stared at the ugly guard but no one answered.

He screamed, "Where are her things?"

Muna stood and moved around the cell gathering Jamila's meager belongings.

Samara called out to the guard from her bunk, "Where is Jamila?"

Every one of the women stared hopefully at the man's face. He glared at Samara and refused to answer. As Muna handed him Jamila's belongings, a single worn slipper dropped to the floor. The guard bent his portly frame forward to snatch up the slipper and plucked the rest of Jamila's scanty belongings from Muna's hands. He left the cell without saying another word.

Samara's voice cracked when she murmured, "They have finally killed her. I knew this day would come."

"How do you think they killed her?" Muna wondered aloud.

"Many prisoners suffer heart attacks. I have known a number whose hearts stopped during a bad beating," Samara said softly.

As the shadow women mourned Jamila, the door to cell 52 burst open once again and two guards appeared.

The taller of the men was severe. He held a short whip in his hand.

All of the women turned toward him. He shouted, "Where is Mayada Nizar Jafar Mustafa Al-Askari?"

When she heard the guard shout her name, fear enveloped Mayada. Her eyes fixed onto the whip-wielding man's face. Her breathing grew squeezed and difficult.

The man slowly tapped the whip upon his leg and repeated Mayada's name, in a tone that aimed to turn the proud name into an insult. "Mayada Nizar Jafar Mustafa Al-Askari?"

Samara responded swiftly, "Is she being released?"

The guard's loathing for the women powered his reply. Disgust rolled across his face as he spat, "*No.* She is *not* being released." His rasping voice shouted Mayada's full name a third time.

Terror clamped tight into Mayada's heart. She looked around the room, wishing desperately she could vanish. Her body trembled slightly as she finally responded, "I am Mayada."

The guard glowered at her, his bushy eyebrows squeezed across his brow. "You! Out!" He gestured toward the door with his whip.

Mayada tried to push herself up from the floor, but a weakness she never knew before now coursed through her body. It sapped the strength of her shoulders, her arms, her hips and her legs. Fearing she would be unable to rise, and knowing every moment she delayed would only anger the guard, Mayada wrenched her body sideways in a desperate struggle to stand. Forcing her body to do what her mind forbade, Mayada pulled a muscle in her right side. She groaned softly.

"Help her," Samara ordered to no one in particular.

Muna and Dr. Sabah together rushed to pull Mayada up from the floor.

Standing now, Mayada's head and shoulders shuddered with tear-less sobs. Muna patted Mayada on the shoulder, and Dr. Sabah gave her hand a gentle squeeze.

As Mayada stumbled out through the cell door, she heard Samara gently call out, "We will be waiting for you, little dove."

Mayada trailed one guard into the hall while the second guard followed close behind. The men did not blindfold Mayada, and this gave her some hope. Her mind danced upon the possibility of discharge. Perhaps Samara was right, perhaps she *was* going to be released. The guard had said that such was not the case, but would he truly know anything of her case? Mayada's heart was flooded by the dazzling possibility of again seeing Fay and Ali. Perhaps Dr. Hadi Hameed, the young doctor from her first night, had telephoned her home. After his message, Fay would have likely called her grandmother in Amman. Salwa Al-Husri would have contacted every official in Saddam's government until someone ordered Mayada's release from prison. After all, Mayada knew from experience that her mother was the most tenacious woman in the Middle East, perhaps in the world. Salwa Al-Husri *never* failed to get what she wanted. Yes, Mayada mused, that's what has happened.

Confident now that her release lay at the end of her march between the two guards, Mayada turned to look into the face of the younger man who strode behind her. This youthful guard had not yet spoken, and Mayada asked him confidently, "Am I being discharged?"

No answer came from either guard, although the older man who marched in front of Mayada stopped in his tracks and turned. He grinned widely and burst into peals of laughter, but just as abruptly, he cut his laughter short and frowned.

Mayada quickly cast her eyes down to avoid the guard's look, and the man spun around. She followed, willing her body to move while she tried to keep her mind free of both hope and terror. But any hope ended at a door a short way down the long hall. Mayada heard a murmur of low moans through the metal door. This was the door to the prison torture chamber. Some poor soul was being quietly tortured there now.

"Wait here," the guard ordered before he walked away.

Monitored by the younger guard, Mayada was left to stand in the hallway for a long time. The waiting just multiplied her apprehension.

Mayada tried not to listen to the moans that came from the torture room. To keep her mind from imagining the scene beyond the door, she studied the young guard's face. She noted his pale complexion and light gray eyes. He had a pleasant look about him. He was no more than twenty years old—just a child, really, Mayada mused.

Feeling her stare, the young guard turned and narrowed his eyes. For the first time, he looked straight at Mayada. She bore his gaze as he gave her a malicious sneer. "What are you looking at, you old bitch?"

Mayada averted her eyes, longing to ask him how one so young had become so filled with hate. But she didn't.

The door to the torture room flew open. The largest human being Mayada had ever seen was framed tight within the doorway. He was so tall he had to stoop to pass his head under the door frame. His broad chest forced him to contort sideways to continue through. At his hurried approach, even the young guard jumped aside, reacting as nervously as Mayada. She saw that the man bore an unconscious prisoner across his sloping shoulders. The door slammed noisily behind him.

Mayada drew back, and stared at the limp prisoner with frightened eyes. His face was pale and slack, and his head wobbled from front to back. His limbs were twisted in an unnatural way. A large wet circle covered the front of his trousers. In his fear and pain, the poor soul had obviously urinated on himself.

Mayada turned her gaze to the huge man, closely watching every expression displayed on his face. When he looked back at her, Mayada knew for certain that she had not been called for release. She was going in for torture.

Everything changed in a moment. Without a word of warning, the huge man hurled his unconscious prisoner at the young guard, who staggered under the weight.

Mayada instinctively turned to bolt, but the huge man pounced on her, yanking her arm with such force that he lifted her off her feet. He dragged her behind him and into the torture room. Mayada cried out, but immediately the giant man ringed her throat with one huge hand.

With his hand around her throat, Mayada's only desire was to hold on to her life. Fay and Ali needed her. She fought her fear and tried to keep her wits about her. She focused on her physical surroundings. The torture room was not much larger than cell 52. Men she had never seen before stood in dark corners of the room, and they soon began to stream toward her. Mayada had never been so frightened in her life, not even on the first day of her arrest.

One of the torturers greeted Mayada with a hard kick to her lower body as the giant threw her to the floor. She cried out in surprise and he laughed as he said mockingly, "Welcome, Mayada Nizar Jafar Mustafa Al-Askari."

Mayada longed to discover the courage to fight back, but she was hopelessly outnumbered.

The giant man threw her into an old wooden chair that was worn with scratch marks. Before she could protest, two men jumped forward and bound her to the chair with a number of white plastic bindings.

Within seconds, her arms and legs were immobilized against the chair frame. She struggled in vain against the nylon restraints. Now she was truly helpless.

She was blinded by a bright light.

Although quivering with fear, she focused her attention on the one face she could see looming in front of her. An ugly man with a large, flushed face on and oversized head set upon a small body stared at her.

"So, you are a supporter of the Shiite!" he accused, swinging his rubber truncheon close to Mayada's head.

Another angry voice from the back of the room denounced her. "She plots with them."

Another voice called out, "Such actions bring unpleasant consequences."

The accusation puzzled Mayada. She had been raised by moderate Sunni parents, who enjoyed friendships and business associations with people of every religious affiliation. Mayada had never felt prejudice against any Iraqi—Sunni, Shiite, Christian or Jewish. Her employees were Shiite. In her printing shop, she accepted business from any person or company, as long as the printing order was not illegal. And from the day she had opened her shop, no one had ever asked her to print anything against the government.

But Mayada now had a sudden flash of memory: Several months earlier, she had accepted an order to print some simple Shiite prayer books. Were those prayer books the problem? If the printing of prayer books was illegal, she had never been informed. Still, Mayada

knew Saddam's government hated everything associated with Iraq's
Shiite population.

Keeping her face free of the panic she felt, Mayada protested in
vain. "I have done nothing wrong."

Her terror grew as she detected movement behind her. Mayada
sensed that she was surrounded.

"This is what happens to supporters of the Shiite," the big-headed
torturer said, as he stepped forward and slapped Mayada's face three
times hard.

She cried out in surprise.

The torturer gestured with his hand, and an unseen man slipped a
blindfold over her eyes.

Despite her fear, Mayada spoke clearly, so all could hear: "I am an
innocent woman."

In response, she heard only loud laughter.

She was slapped once again.

She was kicked on her shins.

The truncheon came down on her fingers.

She shrieked.

Another slap, followed by, "Shut up!"

Surrounded, her heart began pounding so loudly that she heard
each beat clearly.

Mayada felt her sandal being slipped from her right foot. The big
toe on that foot was squeezed in a clamp. A rough hand yanked back
her hair covering, and a second clamp squeezed her right earlobe.

Through the pain of the clamps and the disorientation of the
blindfold, she heard heavy equipment scrape against the floor as it
was moved closer to her. Something ominous was being readied.

She began to pray, "God let me live, for Fay and Ali."

One man suddenly threatened, "This is what happens to traitors."

Mayada heard the hum of machinery. Immediately, the first burst
of electricity coursed through her, and her head jerked backward as the
electricity rolled down her neck and into her armpits, and up her leg

and into her groin. She wondered if her body had been set afire. "Ah-hhhhhhh. . . ." She gasped for breath, crying convulsively.

The voltage was sent through her body again and again. Tremors and spasms seized Mayada, convulsions so forceful they threw her head against the back of the chair. The pain grew unbearable.

She screeched for mercy. *"Please! Stop!"*

She heard loud laughter.

"Please! No!"

They stopped the electricity for a minute.

She was so weak that she couldn't speak, but she could hear a demanding voice ask, "Tell us about the Shiites who are conspiring against Iraq."

She groaned and shook her head. When she tried to speak, nothing came from her mouth but a wild chattering. Her tongue would not function properly.

"You decide. Give us names."

She shook her head again.

She heard the sound of someone walking and then the roar of the machine once again. Even before the electricity struck, she screamed loudly.

She screamed and cried as the current struck deep into every part of her body.

Mayada's blindfold closed her world to everything but the fire that rolled up and down her veins, deep into her sinews.

Just as she thought the agony would never end, Mayada heard a woman's high-pitched shriek from far away, a howl of pain unlike anything she had ever heard. Before she blacked out, she mumbled a heartfelt prayer for the suffering creature who had let loose that spine-tingling scream.

An hour later, cell 52 was unlocked and Mayada was tossed to the concrete floor.

She was unconscious, and the shadow women were unable to rouse her.

For Mayada, the following hours passed in a dazed twilight.

It was a sunny day and she was in Beirut, eating a flavored ice cream. She glanced up to the balcony of a rose-tinted villa. There stood Jido Sati and her father, side by side, each with a wide smile and a pair of waving arms that motioned for Mayada to come running, to run into the comfort of their open arms. Mayada hurried her pace to reach them quickly, but no matter how fast she ran, she failed to shorten the growing distance between her and them. As her father and grandfather drifted farther and farther away, Mayada began to weep in disappointment, then to scream in fear as dark events overwhelmed her: Cigarettes were snuffed out in her eyeballs; she was handcuffed and a length of wood was inserted between her elbows and her knees; she was suspended from a hanging hook; she was placed inside a tire and rolled around and around; she was tied to a table and her bare feet were beaten; two belts were tied to her arms and she was hung from a ceiling fan that spun round and round and round, turning back time, carrying her back to her childhood.

Like most upper-class Iraqis, Mayada's parents lived in Baghdad from September through May; during the hot summer months of June, July and August, they traveled throughout the Middle East and Western Europe.

When not traveling, Mayada lived with her mother and father and her nanny in a lovely old house on the banks of the Tigris. A line of beautiful homes housed Nizar's mother and his three brothers, Tarik, Zaid and Qais. A cooling breeze wafted off the river through the open windows of the houses and into the peaceful, tree-shaded gardens that surrounded them. Their lovely little neighborhood felt so safe that the family's nannies were confident enough to allow Mayada and her cousins to run happily from garden to garden without close adult supervision. Their little black Scotty dog, Scottie, was always on their heels.

Those childhood days were the most carefree of Mayada's life. Swimming was a favorite pastime, and Mayada was good at it. Abdiya was an excellent diver. After many days of swimming in the sunshine, the girls' little bodies were tanned bronze; their father jokingly called them his "two little fishes."

Salwa wasn't a housewife in the traditional sense, as she had never learned to cook or clean, but she was an expert in guiding servants so that her house ran in perfect order. Most happily for her children, Salwa gave the best parties in Baghdad.

She always gave her girls a double birthday party before school was out, so that the sisters could celebrate with their Iraqi friends and cousins before the family left for their summer travels. Those birthday parties were the talk of Baghdad, because Salwa meticulously prepared them many months ahead. Fireworks were sent from Lebanon and cake decorations were ordered from London. While the girls were allowed to choose the flavor of the cake filling—usually chocolate, orange, vanilla or lemon—Salwa chose the theme. One year, the theme might mean a heart-shaped cake, the next year a cake in the shape of a train. Salwa even ordered special baskets from Harrods of London to hold the many presents.

She also cleverly arranged games galore. There would always be a treasure hunt, in which the children searched for hidden toy animals. The child who discovered the most animals would win a prize, usually a great toy. Salwa organized pin-the-tail-on-the-donkey, or suspended a papíer mâché sack, filled with sweets and candy bars. The children were blindfolded and given a baseball bat so that they could send candy flying through the air.

But never far beneath the veneer of gaiety bubbled the bitter conflict of Iraqi politics. Iraqis could not seem to make their peace last long. Since Jafar's death many years before, Iraqi governments were plagued by violent overthrow, and political coups continued to wrack the nation's modern history. This tumult affected every Iraqi's life. During her childhood, Mayada was moved back and forth between distant homes, as her parents were forced to heed political tensions and migrate for the safety of the family.

After the 1958 coup, in which the entire Iraqi royal family was massacred, Mayada's family moved to Beirut. The family's 1961 return to still-tense Baghdad was quickly cut short, and Nizar took his wife and daughters back to the safety of Beirut.

Although Iraq was mourned, life in Beirut was good for a time. The family lived in a roomy apartment on Hamra Street over the Al-Madina Pharmacy, next to a French chocolate store named Chantie. The chocolate aroma drifted through the building and into their apartment, so that Mayada and Abdiya's youthful memories were wonderfully flavored.

Mayada was only six when a more serious problem arose. Her mother one day unexpectedly pulled Mayada aside and presented her with a beautiful pearl ring. She told her that she was to keep this ring until her mother and father returned from a long trip. As the oldest sister, she was to watch over Abdiya and keep her safe. Mayada was frightened. She stared into her mother's rich brown eyes, fearful at this unexpected turn of events. She wondered why she was being left behind. Even Grandfather Sati could not lift Mayada's spirits when she and Abdiya and their two nannies were left with Sati. Frequent rains curbed their outdoor activity that year, and Mayada spent long, lonely hours fingering that pearl ring while she peered past the balcony, aching to see her parents return.

It was years before she knew that a diagnosis of colon cancer in her forty-year-old father had spurred her parents' lengthy trip. Nizar's greatest fear was that he would leave his young children without a father, as he had been left without his own father, Jafar—who had also been left without his father, Mustafa. Nizar even began to express his fear that there was a curse of early death for the Al-Askari men.

Although the family was happy in Beirut, their passion for Iraq had never cooled. Hoping that the days of drama were over, they packed their belongings and returned to Baghdad in late 1962. Within days, the family had resumed the good Baghdadi life, and Nizar felt his spirits lift for the first time since 1958. Then, the winds of fortune shifted again and disaster struck on February 8, 1963, when the Baath Party seized control of the Iraqi government. Although the family survived without personal injury, the military seized some of Nizar's private property. Nizar was not a cowardly man, and he confronted the Baathist leaders. He insisted firmly that his property was not available for the taking. Although they assured Nizar that the situation was temporary, their tone was unwavering. They let Nizar know he had no rights to his own property, and he understandably worried that Baathist promises of fair play were nothing but lies. Surrounded by armed men and wanting nothing more than to live for his daughters, Nizar accepted what he could not change.

In the Nizar Al-Askari household, illness eclipsed the importance of politics when Nizar's colon cancer returned. He struggled to live, but in Room 52 at the Nun's Hospital in Baghdad, he realized that his time on earth with his wife and daughters was quickly running out.

Nizar's three girls, as he called them, surrounded his bedside at every opportunity. His determination to live extended his time, and Mayada and Abdiya came to visit him every afternoon after school. When he was near death, he was allowed to go home for a while, where Mayada assisted the nurses with his injections and medication. But Nizar soon returned to Room 52, where he died one morning after graciously thanking the nurse who held his vomit pan. Mayada and Abdiya were in school when their mother sent word of their father's death. In the principal's office, Mayada stood shocked. The pain was so acute that it felt as though her father had fallen dead unexpectedly.

Now in her delirium in Baladiyat's cell 52, Mayada thought of Fay and Ali. She did not want them to lose a parent like she had lost her father. She called their names, "Fay! Ali! Come to me."

"Mayada! Mayada! Can you hear me? Open your eyes, Mayada." Samara leaned over Mayada's face and softly dabbed it with a wet cloth. "Mayada. Wake up."

Mayada's tongue lightly explored her lips. A strange taste lay in her mouth—something like burned wood. She felt someone lift her head and place a glass against her lips. She sipped a few swallows of water. She was confused. Where were her children? She didn't know where she was. She opened her eyes and saw a multitude of female faces pressing forward, staring kindly at her.

"Mayada. This is Samara. You are back with us. In cell 52."

Still confused, Mayada mumbled, "Who are you?"

"I am Samara," the woman hovering over Mayada murmured with a faint laugh.

Mayada opened her eyes a second time. "Samara?"

"Yes. I am here, little dove."

Mayada groaned as she shifted. She was sore all over. "What happened? Where are Fay and Ali?"

Samara shared a worried look with Dr. Sabah.

"You are alive. That is the only thing that matters. You are alive."

Mayada looked up once again. Many worried faces stared down at her. She saw Dr. Sabah and Muna and Wafae and Aliya and Sara and many others. But her stomach plunged when she remembered that she was a prisoner at Baladiyat.

"What am I doing on the floor?"

Samara whispered, "You were taken from us—for a short time. But you are safe now."

Dr. Sabah and Muna sat down beside Mayada. Wafae and Aliya and the other women crowded in close.

Dr. Sabah asked, "What did they do to you?"

"I don't know," Mayada answered honestly. "My head aches. My arms hurt." She cautiously touched her leg. "Everything is sore. I cannot remember what they did."

Dr. Sabah examined Mayada, checking her face and arms and legs. "Look at this," she exclaimed to the gathered women. "The flesh on her right earlobe is depressed, as is her right big toe. They gave her the electricity."

"Anything else?" Samara asked Dr. Sabah, worry quickening her voice.

"Nothing that I can find. Muna?"

Muna gently lifted Mayada's feet and examined the bottoms. "Her feet were not beaten. That is good."

Samara touched her cheek. "As bad as it was, you were treated lightly."

Mayada began to weep. "I remember something now. I was kicked in the stomach. And I was slapped in the face."

"Her cheeks *are* red," Muna acknowledged with a gentle brush of her hand.

"Someone kicked me," she said with a sob.

"Do you have the taste of wood or metal in your mouth?" Aliya asked.

"Wood."

"That is the result of the electrical shocks," Aliya said with certainty.

"Help me raise her head," Dr. Sabah said to Muna.

Their gentle hands dampened the back of Mayada's neck with a cold cloth. Dr. Sabah then laid the cloth across Mayada's forehead. "This will help your headache."

Slowly, Mayada began to remember the nightmare of the electrical torture. She trembled with small sobs. "I cannot take this torture. I will die in Baladiyat."

"Shhhh." Samara patted her hand. "Listen to my words. I know what I am talking about. You will be released sooner than most. You are a special case."

Mayada didn't believe her, and wept louder.

"Mayada, I want you to think of this. Your torturer was careful. Not one mark was left on your body. They did not beat your feet—or your back. They can deny everything you accuse them of. I have no doubt: They have received orders to be light with you."

Mayada was sick of dashed hopes, and she refused to be consoled.

"I will never see my children again. No. Never again. My children will be without a mother."

Samara's face showed patience. "Mayada, you have a degree from a university. I have a degree only in Baladiyat. I know this place. I know these men. You will be released soon—as soon as the orders come down. I feel it in my bones."

Mayada remembered something else. "I think I was tied from the ceiling and rotated on a fan. Then they put me in a tire and rolled me around the room," she sobbed.

Samara continued to comfort her. "No, my sweet. Those ghastly things occurred only in your nightmare. Your body is clean of any torture but for a kick and a few slaps and the electricity. You went into a delirious state after you were returned to us. This delirium happens to most of us. Especially in the beginning." Then she grinned widely. "Besides, few of us would fit into a tire."

At any other time in her life, Mayada would have laughed. She was indeed too large to fit into an automobile tire. She must have been hallucinating.

Muna confirmed, "I was tied by my arms when I first came here. And spun around from the ceiling. My arms rotated right out of my shoulders. It was weeks before I could lift either arm." She raised both of Mayada's arms to prove her point. "See, your arms are uninjured. You were not hung from the ceiling." She paused before giving Mayada a sweet smile. "And we all thank God for that."

"And I was hung from a hook and beaten. I can see this did not happen to you," Dr. Sabah verified with a light touch on Mayada's face.

Mayada looked slowly from one shadow woman to the other. Every face was worn with worry—for themselves, for their children, for the lives they left outside Baladiyat, but also for Mayada's well-being. She had never met such kind women. And despite the fact that each woman in cell 52 had been treated more harshly than she, none of them begrudged Mayada her better fortune.

Samara insisted, "Now, you must eat a few bites of bread, then take a spoonful of sugar. The bread will help to erase the wooden taste from your mouth, and the sugar will relieve the weakness that still lingers in your limbs."

Before Mayada could respond, everyone was startled by the opening of their cell door and the sudden appearance of three guards. A tall, skinny man with a bushy mustache whom Mayada had never seen called out in a small voice that piped out of his nose, "We are here for Safana."

Muna jumped to her feet so quickly that her shiny brown hair bounced up and down. She looked toward the back of the cell with alarm.

Mayada was unable to turn her head to search for Safana's face, but she knew that Safana was a young Kurd, in her late twenties with a dark, smooth complexion marred by black circles under her eyes. She was very short and stout. Safana had been arrested with Muna, and the two women often wept on each other's shoulders. Both women had worked in a bank before being arrested. Mayada knew little else of Safana, but had often wondered about her story.

Safana stumbled from the back of the cell, her fist in her mouth, tears welling in her eyes.

Muna asked fearfully, "And me?"

The tall skinny guard stared at Muna, his lips snarling back from his teeth. "Only one goose to cook today," he piped in his nasal voice, before snatching Safana by her short arm and pulling her from the cell.

Muna's beautiful eyes swam in tears. When the cell door closed again, Muna crumpled onto her bunk, crying bitterly. "Safana is only a witness. She has done nothing. Nothing."

Mayada looked at Samara with a question in her eyes.

Samara raised herself into a sitting position. Mayada noticed that the effort had caused sweat to bead on Samara's upper lip. Samara had not yet fully recovered from her own torture session.

"Be careful and don't exert yourself," Mayada said gravely, thinking that with this escalated pace of torture, cell 52 would soon house only wounded women.

Samara wiped the sweat from her face with her hand. "Poor Muna and Safana are nothing but witnesses in a bank embezzlement case. The bank's director general was a thief."

"They are not even accused?" Mayada asked.

"No. Let me tell you the complete story. Then you will understand."

"Please speak slowly." Mayada warned her, "My head has not yet cleared from the electricity." This was true. Mayada still suffered from ringing in her ears and her head.

"I will." Samara looked down at Mayada's spoon lying on the floor, still half-filled with sugar. "Eat that. Then your head will clear."

"I cannot."

"Okay, then." Samara carefully lifted the spoon and licked it clean before she began the sad tale.

"Our sweet Muna came from a poor family that got poorer still after the disaster of 1991. Her father's house is in Al-Horiya Al-Uola. Muna attended public school and university and graduated at the top of her class. In school, she met a very nice young man, though he was from a family as poor as her own. The two of them fell in love, but her father resisted their union. He wanted something better for her. But Muna was in love, and she convinced her father that the couple, armed with a pair of university degrees, could carve out a prosperous life. So the father finally agreed.

"Muna married and moved in with her husband in a little house close to the Kharkh side of the Tigris, in a neighborhood called Al-Rahmaniya. It was densely populated, with one house built right next to the other. But Muna and her new husband were very happy. When investment banks began to open in Iraq, Muna was so smart that she was quickly hired.

"Now, as for our harmless little Safana," Samara said with a deep sigh. "Safana, as you might have guessed, is a Kurd with a Persian background. She's never married, and she is an only child. Safana and her mother live in the poor area of Habibiya, not far from the main Secret Police building. Her father died during the war with Kuwait, although he was not a soldier. So Safana and her mother tried to run the little food shop that they had inherited from him. Mind you, Safana was a student at the same time. So she went to school during the day and managed the store until bedtime.

"But after the sanctions were laid on, they could not afford to stock the store, so it stood empty. But Safana was also smart, like Muna. She had studied economics and commerce at the University of Baghdad. She couldn't think of marriage, because all she did was go to school, study and work in the store. And without a father or any siblings, she knew she would be responsible for her mother, who had been sickly for many years.

"Safana got lucky and found a full-time job at the same bank where Muna worked, although they didn't know each other before meeting there. Safana was happy, because she would finally have enough money to buy food and medicine for her dear mother, who was by that time an invalid. She wore diapers, like a newborn baby. Every morning before work Safana fed her mother, cleaned her, changed her diaper, placed plastic under the bed and left her mother a lunch snack on the table beside the bed. After work, Safana rushed straight home to tend to her mother's needs.

"Safana worked so hard and well at her new job that she was promoted to department head at the bank, which was a happy, happy day for her.

"Meanwhile, our Muna has gotten pregnant. She and her husband are so excited that they decide that she will take the full maternity leave, to stay with her baby as long as she can. She has her baby, a little boy they name Salim. Muna is home with Salim one day when the neighbor rings her doorbell. She tells Muna that bank officials are on the phone, and that she must take the call immediately. Muna's husband is still at work, so she runs to the phone, with Salim swinging in her arms. The person on the line is the security officer at the bank. He tells Muna she must come in, that some important documents are missing. Muna tells the man she has no one to leave her baby with, but he insists. He tells her to bring the baby with her. A worried Muna rushes to the bank with Salim.

"When Muna arrives, there sits Safana and two other men she has never seen. They all sit in the security office, where the officer tells Muna to take a seat. Muna and Safana will be taken to the head-quarters of the Secret Police, he tells her. Muna senses something terrible has happened, and she begs the man to tell her what is wrong. He refuses to explain. She asks if she can deliver her baby to her mother and father. The man rebuffs her plea, telling her the baby will go with her. She begs to use the phone, and the man says no. Muna is allowed to do nothing but sit and cry.

"Safana's hands are tied behind her, but they allow Muna's to be free, so she can hold her little Salim. Then without a word of explanation, the three poor souls are brought here and dumped into our cell. I was here when they arrived, and both women were even more frightened than you, Mayada, on the day of your arrival. A week later, the interrogations started. That is when Muna and Safana discovered the truth. Both were asked to give a full account of their director general at the bank. Both women told what they knew, which was basically nothing. He was a kind boss to both of them. The truth of the matter is that the director general had written himself a check for 15 million Iraqi dinars [around $7,000 in 1998]. He had been stealing money from the bank for several years. When Muna and Safana said that he was a good man, and failed to say he was a thief, they were beaten. Of course, neither had a clue that he was a thief, or they would have said so."

"Oh, God, where does this end?" Mayada asked.

Samara leaned close and her voice came as a whisper. "That is not the worst thing. The story gets much sadder. After a week of imprisonment, Muna's little Salim starts crying all the time. Muna had been smart—she had taken a big supply of milk to the bank—but this was soon gone. We gave little Salim sugar water for a few days but it began to make him sick. That poor baby screamed night and day. Finally the guards came in one morning and told Muna to hand over her baby. Of course, Muna put up a fight. They hit her with an electric prod and she fainted. When she hit the floor, the guards grabbed little Salim and rushed out the door. We haven't seen her baby since."

Mayada gasped, "Do you believe they killed the baby?"

Samara shrugged and nudged Mayada's arm, then gestured with her head toward Muna, who was softly crying. "I pray they took the baby to Muna's husband, or to her mother. The guards refuse to tell Muna anything."

Mayada met Samara's eye. "And Safana? She is always weeping, as well."

"The reason that poor Safana weeps all the time is because no one knows the condition of her mother. When she told the guards that someone had to check on her mother, she got slapped in the face. Safana now assumes her poor mother has been forgotten in her bed and has starved to death.

"Think of that: Two helpless creatures in diapers—one old, one young—and no one to take care of them."

Mayada was horrified. She closed her eyes and began to pray, because she knew of nothing else to do.

A rolling groan spread through cell 52 when the door flew open once again and yet another shadow woman's name was called. "Sara! Show yourself!"

Mayada looked up as Sara slowly walked past. Sara was one of the youngest women, only twenty-one years old, a student of pharmacology who was in prison for no good reason, as far as anyone knew. Now she was going from the safety of cell 52 into the hands of a guard eager to take her to torture. Her eyes glittered with sheer terror. At the door, she turned to the women. "Samara, remember what I told you," she said. "If I die, someone must contact my mother. I am her last living child."

Samara reassured her, "You will not die, little Sara. Be strong. We will be here praying for you."

The guard cursed, and Sara turned and walked away. The door slammed behind her.

Samara raised herself from the floor and issued explicit instructions. "Soon we will have two women who will need us. Let's get Mayada to her bunk and arrange two beds for Safana and Sara."

With Dr. Sabah by her side, Mayada walked in silence to her bunk. After settling in, she closed her eyes. She shivered, as though she had a fever. She willed herself to regain her strength. She wanted to be strong enough to assist Samara with Safana and Sara when they returned.

Lying quietly, she thought of her old life, the life she had once believed to be nothing but work and worry, a life she had been forced to give up in a single day. But now that old life of work and worry seemed so wonderful that the thought of leaving it was terrifying.

She heard Samara's quiet voice giving instructions to the other women. What would they do in this cell without Samara? She was like a mother to every one of them.

She remembered Samara's words, that the shadow women must survive for their children. And survive she would, for Fay and Ali.

8

Dr. Fadil and Mayada's Family

Mayada thought about her two children, trying to imagine what they were doing at this moment. Were they eating? Sleeping? Where were they living? Were they still in Baghdad? If so, were they with their father's father, the only grandfather they had ever known? Or had they fled to Jordan, where they were now under the protective wing of her mother, Salwa?

Stung by the idea that she didn't even know where her children were, Mayada's eyes seeped large tears, which rolled down her face and soaked a widening circle on her blanket. Mayada trembled at her helplessness, but recalled Samara's advice upon her arrival at Baladiyat: build a mental fence around her children and keep them safe inside, or else she would be unable to manage her grief. Samara was right, of course. Knowing she would go mad if she concentrated on Fay and Ali, Mayada instead sketched an imaginary line to separate herself from her two children, and forced her thoughts elsewhere. Her mind threw a second image onto the prison wall, the face of a man once among the most powerful in all of Iraq: Dr. Fadil Al-Barrak. Dr. Fadil was a physically attractive man—tall and dark, with brown hair and dark eyes. He had a lovely voice, and usually spoke with a dancingly happy tone. While Mayada now understood that he had a double personality, she had rarely seen his dark side.

She knew only one thing for certain: If Dr. Fadil was still alive, her world would still be normal, and she would be at home with her two children.

Mayada's thoughts drifted back to 1979, to the first time they had met. Just as she closed her eyes to slip away to the past, however, one of the shadow women quietly approached and laid a small white hand on Mayada's face.

Mayada rolled over in alarm.

"It is me," Samara said gently, as her familiar green eyes gazed intently at Mayada.

Mayada's ache for her children was so great that she felt as though her heart had been scooped out of her chest. "You know something, Samara, I *know* I am going to die in this cell," Mayada said obstinately.

"Stop it!" Samara insisted.

Mayada explained, "It seems that we Al-Askaris have always been pursued by the number 52. My father died in room 52 at the Nun's Hospital, when he was 52 years old. His father, Jafar, was assassinated at age 52. Now here I am in cell 52—the cell that will be my tomb." Mayada stared up at Samara and said with conviction, "My death will be linked to the number 52. It is written."

"Don't be so morbid." Samara scolded her in a gentle voice. "I say that you will be released—soon. Long before you reach age 52."

Mayada suffered a new thought. She whispered with certainty, "I am being punished."

Samara snorted. "Punished for what?"

Excited with her new insight, Mayada pushed herself up on her elbows. She twisted to peer behind Samara, to see if any other women were lingering within earshot. Satisfied, she whispered to Samara, "Dr. Fadil Al-Barrak was our protector—for many years."

"And?"

"For ten years Dr. Fadil ruled such places as Baladiyat."

"The name *is* familiar."

"Of course you have heard of him, Samara. Dr. Fadil Al-Barrak was so powerful he could order the release of anyone from prison. And he did that, for me, more than once." A long silence lay between the two women before Mayada continued. "But don't you see? Without even knowing it, my mother and I were protected for many years—and now I am being punished for that protection."

Samara pulled back Mayada's blanket and sat on the edge of her bunk, examining Mayada solemnly. "I see," said Samara. "Did you help him torture people, Mayada?"

"No! Of course not. I didn't even know the extent of his duties. At least, not at first." Mayada paused, then offered, "You know, even now, I find it difficult to believe he was capable of carrying out torture. This was a man who thrived in academia. He was a scholar who talked about books all the time. But to reach the highest position in security, surely he *had* to have participated in the torture and killings. Saddam would have never appointed him, otherwise."

"So? I still do not understand why you believe yourself responsible," Samara insisted.

Mayada lowered her eyes. "My mother and I should have fled this country—and denounced Saddam's government—the moment my father's body was lowered into the ground."

"You are working yourself up, Mayada. Don't do this. You need to keep up your strength."

Mayada spoke quietly but firmly. "No. I am being punished for remaining here with my mother. The Al-Husri presence in Iraq lent credibility to Saddam's government, on Sati's behalf. I see that now."

"Well, Mayada, you didn't know then what you know now. Were you a fortune-teller? How could you have known any of this?"

Mayada considered Samara's words, and replied with utmost conviction. "I heard once that Dr. Fadil's nickname was Beria, after the Russian torturer. Why did I let that allusion pass over my head?" She whispered feverishly, "You know, Dr. Fadil was the Iraqi Military At-taché to the Soviet Union before he became Iraq's Director General of Secret Police. In the Soviet Union he must have learned sophisti-cated torture methods."

"No. I know little about the man."

"Well, he was greatly feared by many people." Mayada rapidly patted her index finger against her cheek, thinking, then looked at Samara. "Are you interested in hearing about Dr. Fadil?" she asked.

Samara looked around the room, smiled vaguely and gestured with her hand across the small cell. "Of course I am. What more im-portant tasks are waiting for me?" She settled sideways on May-ada's bunk.

Mayada strained to whisper. "I heard about Dr. Fadil before I met him," she said. "It was 1978 and I had just returned from Beirut. The civil war was raging in Lebanon and the fighting there had heated up so much that my ears whistled from the continual shelling. So I left school and returned to Baghdad. I couldn't find a suitable job, so I de-cided to continue my studies. I was accepted at the Institute for Archives and Librarian Studies. It was a night school; classes began at five o'clock each afternoon. One afternoon a very shy student, a lovely girl named Fatin Fuad, walked up to me and said, 'My sister's fi-ancé knows your mother, but he has lost her telephone number. Can you please give it to me?'

"A bit wary, I asked her who the man was. She told me, 'He's Dr. Fadil Al-Barrak Al-Takriti.'

"The name meant nothing to me. I was uninvolved in the Iraqi government, and I had lived outside the country for a few years. But this Fatin was a sweet-faced young woman who could win your trust with a single look. So I gave her our home phone number. After class, I went home and mentioned the name to my mother, and although a look of surprise crossed her face, she didn't indicate how powerful a man this Al-Barrak was. I didn't bother to ask more, since my mother knew everyone who was anyone in Iraq.

"The following morning, the telephone woke me up. I didn't recognize the caller's voice. Still half asleep, my conversation with Fatin had slipped my mind. The caller asked to speak to my mother. I replied in a cold tone that Salwa was at work. He asked, 'Who am I speaking with?' and I said, 'Her daughter.' He asked, 'Which daughter?' " and I told him, 'The eldest.' After a measured pause, he laughed out loud and asked me, 'How do I get you to say your name?' I thought the man was flirting with me, so I told him nothing, but instead I instructed him to call back later. Before hanging up, he requested, 'Tell your mother that Fadil Al-Barrak called. Give her my private number.' I've never forgotten that number.

"Later that day, I saw Fatin at school and asked her about her sister's fiancé, who I imagined was trying to make a pass at me. Fatin quickly told me, 'No, I don't think that is the case. He speaks that way with most people. But he is a very unusual man.'

"Then Fatin pulled me to a corner of the school corridor and confided, 'Let me tell you an amazing story. My sister's fiancé should be *my* fiancé.'

"Noticing my shocked expression, she said, 'Let me explain. Dr. Al-Barrak is a prominent man, and my father, who is a judge, accepted his offer of marriage for me. My father is old-fashioned, and I had not yet met my fiancé; but I was set to do so on the day of our official engagement. Dr. Al-Barrak came to our home on the appropriate day, and there I was, dressed in my finest clothing, about to become officially engaged. Then my younger sister, Jinan, walked into the room. You should see my sister, Mayada. She is truly the greatest beauty in Baghdad. Anyway, my fiancé, Dr. Al-Barrak, took one look at my sister and was so dazzled by her blinding beauty that he turned to my father and shocked us all by saying loudly, "I want this one." My father was so astonished that he couldn't speak. I just stood there, frozen in shame, and Jinan ran out of the room. Well, I had *no* desire to marry a man who wanted my sister, so I told my father that I didn't care. Let him marry Jinan if that's what he wants—and what she

wants. Considering the circumstances, my sister was initially reluc-
tant. But I assured her that it would not affect our close relationship,
or affect our family. I reminded her that I had only met the man, so I
had no feelings attached to the engagement. Further, Dr. Al-Barrak is
a powerful man in the security services and my father was wary of an-
gering him. So my sister will soon marry my former fiancé.' "

Samara shook her head from side to side.

"Samara, I watched Fatin's face very carefully while she told that
story and I could tell that the poor girl was humiliated, regardless of
what she insisted. Fatin was a beauty in her own right. She had green
eyes and a round, pretty face. Her hair was long and thick, and a
beautiful chestnut color. I doubted her sister could be any lovelier."
Mayada threw a brief look around the cell before returning her gaze
to Samara. "Then I saw Jinan. Samara, that girl was the most beautiful
woman I had ever seen. I understood Dr. Fadil's reaction. Fatin's sister
was very tall, and blessed with an unforgettable face. She resembled a
young Brooke Shields, the American model and actress. She had
deep, blue-green eyes and the longest black eyelashes I've ever seen.
Truly, she was so stunning that every woman around her paled in
comparison, even her pretty sister Fatin. She was so beautiful, in fact,
that Dr. Fadil soon stopped taking her with him to government functions. One of Saddam's half-brothers, Barzan Al-Tikriti, lost his mind
over Jinan the first time he saw her. Dr. Fadil grew anxious that Barzan
would ask Saddam to intervene and force Dr. Fadil to divorce his
beautiful young wife."

Mayada paused and Samara interrupted the story. "How does
your family know Dr. Fadil?"

"His contact with my mother was solely for access to Sati's books
and private papers, which Mother kept at our home. The first time I
met him in person, I was startled when he took a familiar key from his
pocket and twirled it around his finger. We had a very distinctive
house key and I wondered, good grief, where did he get our key? He
saw my eyes pop in surprise. A mischievous grin passed his face, and

he explained that my mother had given him permission to come into our home anytime to study Sati's papers. I didn't like that idea very much, but there was nothing I could do. Dr. Fadil sent some men to our home to spray all of Sati's documents with a special chemical that would prevent them from being destroyed by insects. After that, he began to make frequent visits to our home. I slowly grew accustomed to a man from outside our family visiting alone in our library, although I never grew accustomed to the handgun he always left on our foyer table. Dr. Fadil treated his weapon as casually as I would handle a cup of water."

Mayada stopped and thought for a moment. "Samara, thinking back, I believe that Dr. Fadil was a man who existed in two worlds. He was a scholar who adored books, and he could speak for hours on the most interesting topics. Yet he ruled Iraq's prisons. I will forever believe that the dark part of his life bothered him, because he *always* wore a burdened look on his face. The only times I ever saw him relax was when he held one of his five children in his arms, or when he was in our library, cradling a treasured book."

Mayada continued, noting the surprised look on Samara's face. "During this same time, I had gotten a job writing for a children's publication called *Majalaty Wa Al-Mizmar* [*My Magazine and Al-Clarionet*]. One afternoon I received an unexpected call from Lutfi Al-Khayat, a prominent journalist at *Al-Jumhuriya*. This was the most widely read paper in Iraq, although it was not a party newspaper. Being young and eager to advance, I was thrilled to get the call, although I couldn't imagine why this man was contacting me. When I arrived at *Al-Jumhuriya*, Lutfi led me into his big office, where I was nearly faint with excitement. One of my biggest dreams was coming true: I would be taken seriously as a writer. Lutfi told me he had been reading some of the articles I'd written for children, and he wondered if I had a similar ability to write for adults. I was so thrilled that I didn't want to lose this opportunity. So I confided to him that I was writing a book of short stories for adults. Lutfi hired me. I was even given a weekly column, called "Itlalat" ["Overviews"]. Then soon after I was hired, I was told that Dr. Fadil Al-Barrak had asked for me to come and interview him. The newspaper's editor-in-chief, Sahib Hussein Al-Samawi, was excited because the Iraqi secret police simply didn't give interviews. While Sahib was excited, I was momentarily devastated. I knew then that I had not gotten my dream job on my own merits, but that Dr. Fadil had been behind my sudden journalistic advancement. When I went home, I telephoned Dr. Fadil to ask him if that were true. He laughed and said, 'Of course.' He explained that he wanted me to become an excellent writer and asked, 'What better way than by writing?' So to prove I was up to the task, I worked harder than anyone else at that newspaper. And I believe I proved it.

"From that time until the day Dr. Fadil was arrested, our lives were filled with 'little' miracles. But the best aspect of our acquaintance with Dr. Fadil was that I was in a position to help others—and in some cases, even save lives."

"See, I told you," Samara said as she wagged one finger, "you used your association with Dr. Fadil for good. That made the friendship virtuous, Mayada."

Mayada closed her eyes for a moment, opened them, and closed them once again. "I pray that is true, Samara. I am haunted that I should have done something differently."

"I would tell you if that was the case. I am an honest woman," Samara insisted with a light in her eyes. "Tell me about some of the people you were able to help."

Mayada hesitated.

"Go on, Mayada, I'm waiting," Samara urged with a small smile.

"All right. Sometime late in 1979 or early 1980, after meeting Dr. Fadil, I was still living with my mother. One morning, I was getting ready to leave for work when the doorbell rang. Um Aziz, our maid, answered the door and came running up the stairs to tell me that Dr. Saib Shawket's wife, Jalela Al-Haidari, was at our door, dressed in her

nightgown. Jalela Al-Haidari was a very distinguished lady, a true aris-
tocrat, so I knew immediately that something was terribly wrong.

"I went to greet her and found her standing at the front door,
looking like a woman roused from sleep in the middle of the night.
She was in tears. I pulled her inside, trying to calm her, which was difficult because she began to weep in earnest. Finally I convinced her to
talk. For a few moments, I thought she was losing her mind, because
she first started telling me about the family farm in Al Dora. She
elaborated, explaining that the farm was a huge spread with palm
trees fifty years old and with beautiful orange groves planted beneath
the palms. Then the woman shifted to describe a large water pump.
She spoke so glowingly of that pump that I thought for one crazy moment she wanted to sell it to me. She said the pump was purchased
from England, and was so huge it could irrigate half the land.

"Then she related a wild tale about the mayor of Baghdad,
Khayrallah Tilfah, who was Saddam's uncle and the man who raised
Saddam from childhood. She told me that Saddam's uncle kept visiting Al Dora, pressuring her husband to sell him the family farm. Dr.
Shawket, who was eighty-three at the time, didn't want to sell his
farm, and he knew he would never see any money from this man even
if he said yes. Every Iraqi knows that Saddam's relatives are famously
greedy; they always ask to buy something and then simply take it. Dr.
Shawket knew he would likely lose his farm sooner or later, so he offered to give this powerful uncle of Saddam's half of the farmland.
Khayrallah accepted the offer, but claimed he must have the half with
the water pump. Dr. Shawket had paid a lot of money for the pump,
and he knew his trees would die without its water. He rebuked
Khayrallah's insistence for the half of his farm that bears the pump.
Then Khayrallah changed his mind once again, and insisted that nothing but the entire farm would satisfy him.

"The morning that Jalela appeared on our doorstep in her nightgown, the secret police had arrived at their home and arrested the

doctor. They had taken him away in his pajamas. Samara, this doctor was Iraq's top surgeon and the founder of Iraq's first medical college, as well as one of Iraq's first Ministers of Health. His arrest was a terrible shock to us all.

"I didn't know what to do about this catastrophe, so I called my mother, who was already at her job. She was very upset and she instructed me to call Dr. Fadil immediately. She was afraid that the elderly Dr. Shawket would die of a heart attack if he was not rescued quickly.

"So I called Dr. Fadil and told him the story. He paused, then said, 'You call our Vice President now. His hot line is open. Tell him the whole story.'

"I was surprised, but I followed his instructions. I called Saddam's number and he answered after a couple of rings. I told him who I was and that I was speaking on behalf of Dr. Saib Shawket's wife. Then I relayed part of the story, about Dr. Shawket being arrested because of the land. Saddam listened quietly. He said little more than that I should reassure Dr. Shawket's wife that everything would be handled to her satisfaction. I was to advise her that her husband would return shortly. I was also to tell her that Dr. Shawket should come to the presidential palace at four o'clock that afternoon.

"Within five minutes, my telephone rang. The caller was Dr. Fadil. He told me, 'Tell Dr. Shawket's wife that her husband has just left prison and is being returned to his home as I speak.' He hung up without saying goodbye.

"Later I understood the reason Dr. Fadil had told me to make that call. It would have been awkward for Saddam to hear from one of his assistants, like Dr. Fadil, that his uncle was a thief, but to hear the story over the telephone on behalf of the victim was less embarrassing for him.

"I was waiting with Dr. Shawket's wife when he returned from prison. The doctor was still in his pajamas, of course. The poor man was in a state of shock. I remember his first words. He stood there with an astonished expression on his face and said, 'That was an impolite group of men at that prison. Can you believe that they slapped me?' He stood there, stooped and frail, patting his reddened cheeks in disbelief.

"But Dr. Shawket gathered himself and got properly dressed and left for the presidential palace. I remained with his wife, for the entire day, because she was still scared to death." Mayada's indignation returned as she told the story, even after all the intervening years. "These were two old people—people who had served Iraq from the modern nation's first day. It was a scandal."

"What happened at the palace?" Samara asked as she leaned forward, brushing a few locks of her black-and-white-streaked hair from her eyes.

"Dr. Shawket was gone for over an hour, but when he returned, he told us what had happened. Dr. Shawket said he was met at the door by Barzan Ibraheem Al-Hassan Al-Tikriti, Saddam's half-brother from his mother, the man who was married to Sajida's sister. Barzan greeted Dr. Shawket in a polite manner and told him that Abu Uday (Saddam) was also in the room. Dr. Shawket swiveled his head around at this news, but as far as he could see, the two of them were alone. He looked at Barzan puzzled, and Barzan pointed to a table in the center of the room. 'There he is,' Barzan explained. 'Saddam is on that table.' Dr. Shawket is old, mind you, and can't see too well. So he walked over to the table. 'I still don't see him,' he said, confused. Barzan laughed and picked up a tape recorder. 'Here he is,' he explained, hinting that Saddam would be listening later to everything that was said.

"Dr. Shawket said he was a bit bewildered after that ridiculous episode, but he tried to explain to Barzan in the most delicate words possible what had happened. He was cautious in his wording because his tale shed unflattering light on Khayrallah, who was Barzan's uncle and the man who raised Saddam. The family link is even stronger because both Saddam and Barzan were married to Khayrallah's daughters.

Fully understanding all these family connections, Dr. Shawket realized that there was an invisible line over which he shouldn't step, or he might end up back in prison.

"Finally Barzan told Dr. Shawket, 'Doctor, tell Saddam and me exactly what happened, and do not concern yourself with good manners.' He patted the old doctor on his shoulders and reassured him it was safe to speak openly. Barzan insulted Saddam's uncle, and his own, when he joked, 'Believe me, if Abu Uday had not been called and informed of your situation, our uncle and father-in-law would have confiscated everything you own, even the jacket you wear on your back.' Barzan shocked Dr. Shawket further when he admitted, 'Our uncle is a greedy old man. We are forced to watch him carefully.'

"Dr. Shawket was incredulous that the nephews of Khayrallah would admit such a thing, but he was delighted to hear it.

"So Dr. Shawket's valuable land remained intact. Afterward, the doctor and his wife visited us in our home. The couple was so grateful for my intervention that Dr. Shawket offered to give me a few acres of the farm as a gift, but of course I refused to accept. I told him that seeing his face was gift enough for me. I suggested instead that he give me an interview for *Alef Ba* magazine about his work as a physician from the earliest days of Iraq's formation. He happily agreed.

"The interview was published, and it was read by Saddam Hussein. A few days after the piece ran, Saddam's staff called Dr. Shawket and told him that his medical work was so important that he would be decorated by Saddam. A very pleased Dr. Fadil called and told us to watch for him on television. Dr. Fadil had a good laugh, saying that I was responsible for getting Dr. Shawket a medal in exchange for a prison term.

"As part of a televised event, Dr. Shawket was decorated. When the program ended, I traumatized my mother when I leapt from the sofa and somersaulted across the Persian carpet. I ended in a split, laughing up at Mother. I was so happy to have played a role in the agreeable outcome. Mother, too proper at times, was so shocked by my shenanigans that she scolded me and urged me to act my age. But I smiled for weeks over the outcome, knowing that a single phone call had essentially saved Dr. Shawket's life."

"See, one life saved," Samara congratulated Mayada, holding up a delicate white finger. "Without you, that poor man would never have seen the light of day again."

Just remembering that day helped Mayada overcome her despair over her current situation in Baladiyat. Then she half hid her face in her hands and laughed quietly. "Can you believe that Saddam's uncle never gave up on that land? Dr. Shawket died a natural death six years later, in 1986. That sorry Khayrallah was still waiting for the land, despite the fact that he was old and ill and had lost both his legs to gangrene. Khayrallah was ready for the grave himself, yet he couldn't get that farm and that water pump out of his mind. After Dr. Shawket's funeral, Khayrallah went straight to the grieving widow and sat outside her house in a parked car. When Jalela came to investigate, he called her over and bluntly asked, 'Now are you willing to sell the land?'

"Dr. Shawket's widow was so brave. Even knowing what had happened to her husband six years earlier, she screamed, 'Never!' and walked away. The widow glanced back to glare at Khayrallah, a man accustomed to getting almost anything he wanted. He gave her a filthy look as he ordered his driver to pull away. But he was afraid Saddam would be notified if he pursued the farm further, so there was nothing more he could do. That land remained in the family, where it belonged."

"Knowing that you might call Dr. Fadil helped to keep the widow's farm safe, I bet."

Mayada was plunged into faraway thought. "Well, I even saved my husband Salam's life once, believe it or not."

Samara joked with soft laughter, for Mayada had told her about Salam's past conduct. "You *are* a saint, then!"

"This happened later, in 1984. I had been away for two months on an official trip to Sudan. When I arrived at Baghdad airport, I called to check on Fay, who was only a year old. During the call, I was told that my husband had just been taken away by the army's secret police.

"Salam was serving his compulsory army service as a soldier in the Iran-Iraq war. One night he was ordered by his commander to transport a soldier who had deserted. This soldier had stupidly gone straight home, to a place called Qalat Sukar in Umara, in the south, and was quickly apprehended. After this deserter was arrested, Salam was told to take the man to army headquarters.

"Despite being a useless husband, Salam is not a violent man. So he good-heartedly transported the man without restraining him. Well, when Salam stopped at a red light, the deserter seized the opportunity to open the car door and run away, disappearing into the night. Because of this incident, Salam was about to be sentenced to life imprisonment.

"So I did the only thing I knew to do: I called Dr. Fadil. I shared the devastating news. He told me to remain at the airport; he would send a car and driver for me. By now it was late at night, but Dr. Fadil met me at his office. I rushed in and he asked me for the name of Salam's army unit. He pressed a button on a switchboard and was connected instantly to Salam's commander. Dr. Fadil asked him about the incident. He then asked where Salam had been taken. He was informed that Salam was already in jail. Dr. Fadil ordered the commander to drop all the charges and release Salam immediately. Further, he told the commander to return Salam safely to his home within the hour.

"I remember that night as clearly as yesterday. Dr. Fadil looked at me with a sweet smile. He tilted his head and scratched his temple, saying, 'Do not worry. Your lovely husband will soon be with you.'

"Then, right before my eyes, this kind man turned into an unfeeling monster. He called the commander back and barked, 'Tell me about this deserter.' The commander told him the deserter was from Qalat Sukar. Dr. Fadil then telephoned the secret police in that district and ordered the commander there to go to the soldier's house and arrest every relative, down to the last child. The family was to be held until the son turned himself in.

"I was astonished to see this man do a good deed and then instantly flip to do such an evil deed. I remember I urged him, 'Please, do not arrest more innocent people.'

"With a hard look on his face, Dr. Fadil told me that other than Salam, nothing else in the affair was my business.

"So, for me, a painful sting was attached to Salam's return: All I could think about was that innocent family. But there was nothing I could do. A very happy Salam returned home within the hour. Salam later learned that the deserter turned himself in to the authorities within the hour, as well."

Samara spoke in an unusually intense and somber manner. "This Dr. Fadil *was* a strange man. I wonder how he could turn back and forth so quickly between good and evil."

"That's the mystery, Samara," Mayada agreed. "Dr. Fadil even saved me from imprisonment twice. The first time, I had foolishly posted a Khomeini photograph in my bedroom—which was discovered. And nothing happened to me, because of Dr. Fadil. The second time was in 1985. I was married, Fay was two years old, and I was pregnant with Ali. I was working with the Arab Labor Organization and was so naïve that I had no idea that just about everyone working there, but me, was working for Mukhabarat.

"Every employee was ordered to listen for remarks that could be misconstrued. One of my coworkers wrote a negative report about me. The report insisted that I did not have enough respect for the President and that I talked too freely to everyone. Further, the report described that I did not use Baath slogans in my speech.

"So one day I was surprised by a telephone call from the secret police. A man by the name of Abu Jabbar was on the line, and he ordered me to pass by his office that morning. I had no idea what the man wanted, but I knew it couldn't be good. So I called Dr. Fadil and told him about my summons. Dr. Fadil found the situation strange, as well, but he told me to go ahead and keep the appointment. Meanwhile he would do some checking. Dr. Fadil stressed that I was to call him the moment I returned from the appointment.

"I went to the appointment, although I was not frightened because I knew Dr. Fadil was aware of my goings and comings. I knew that if I didn't call him within a few hours, he would seek the reason.

"I walked into Abu Jabbar's office and there he stood, a fat man with a bald head. On his face were the thickest eyeglasses I've ever seen, which magnified his eyeballs and gave him the appearance of a frog. I sensed immediately that Dr. Fadil had already phoned this Abu Jabbar, because the man was more nervous than I was. Before Dr. Fadil's call, Abu Jabbar had most likely planned to arrest me, but now he knew I was poison to him. The man didn't know what to do— he had to make up some excuse that wouldn't anger Dr. Fadil for bringing out this heavily pregnant woman who was obviously well-connected. He kept mumbling, pacing and shaking his head. I asked him what was wrong and he repeated, 'Nothing, nothing,' over and over. Finally he explained that he had asked me over for a cup of coffee. I couldn't believe my ears. My voice grew shrill as I complained, questioning if he had really asked a woman eight months pregnant to come over for a cup of coffee. Feeling brave with Dr. Fadil's power behind me, I asked, 'Do you realize that I was up all night worrying and could have had a miscarriage?'

"Abu Jabbar stopped pacing, stared at me and said, 'You must be joking. Why should *you* be frightened? Have I offended you in some manner?'

"I asked again, 'Tell me why I was summoned!'

"He was so stressed by this time that he raised his voice. 'I am *sorry* that I summoned you. Forget the coffee. Now go home and relax.'

"I left in a huff and went home to call Dr. Fadil. He told me of my coworker's report about my attitudes, and lectured me that I was criticized because I didn't talk 'Baathist speak.'

"Looking back, I suppose I should have adopted some of their ridiculous phrases, such as 'Plant and eat,' or some other similar nonsense that they so highly prized. Every word they spoke was a waste of good breath, in my opinion.

"Dr. Fadil told me that everyone in that place reported on one another. He told me I should keep my flippant mouth shut and tend only to business. He urged me not to trust a single colleague. This sort of insight made my time at the job less than pleasant, but I became more cautious. I refused, however, to join them in quoting socialist verses.

"Samara, Dr. Fadil was always there for us."

"God will have a hard time deciding whether Dr. Fadil will rise up to heaven or plunge down to hell," Samara said with a slow shake of her head.

"Yes. You are right. He is a man that mingled good acts among a skein of the darkest deeds. Do you remember when the Iranian Tabaeya document deportations began? In 1980?"

Samara gazed dismally at her hands, before looking back up at Mayada. "I knew something of it. Shiites were the ones marked for deportation. I heard about that, but never quite knew what was happening or even why it was happening. I had neighbors who were caught up in the deportation. What was that about?"

"Being Sunni of Ottoman descent, I was not touched by it," Mayada explained. "At least not in the beginning. But I soon learned that many Iraqis were getting into serious trouble with their Nationality Certificate. This document was instituted in 1921, when the modern Iraqi state was created upon the collapse of the Ottoman Empire. When the earliest census was taken, Iraqis were given the choice to declare whether they were of Ottoman origin or Iranian origin. If they described themselves as Iranian, their sons would be exempt from the army. Therefore, to protect their sons, many families chose to declare they were of Iranian origin, even if they were truly of Ottoman origin. Within a single family, sons might be declared Iranian and daughters Ottoman. Sadly, after the Iranian revolution, these choices came back to haunt many Iraqi families.

"When Khomeini returned with acclaim to lead Iran, Saddam decided to deport anyone in Iraq whose nationality papers were marked, 'Tabaeya Iraniya.' Saddam deported these people despite the fact that they were wholly Iraqi, many from as long ago as their great-great-great-grandfathers.

"I know of cases in which people were thrown out of their homes with no prior notice, forbidden to take anything with them. Those poor people were deported on foot and abandoned at the Iranian border. Anyone who tried to return was shot. Whole families were treated in this manner. It didn't matter if the people were old, handicapped, sick or pregnant. Mothers with infants were not allowed to take as much as a baby bottle to feed their babies.

"Iranians under Khomeini were distrustful of these Iraqis, too. They feared Saddam was sending a lot of spies into Iran. But after a time, the Iranians relented and built some refugee tent cities to house the poor deported Iraqis.

"The strangest part of the entire affair was that few people even knew it was happening. Saddam's enforcers quietly went from family to family, kicking them out of Iraq. Although this practice started slowly, it gained momentum. By 1981, horrified whispers murmured in the streets about what was happening. Then, another great crime was instigated against people I knew.

"I was in my office at the Arab Labor Organization when one of the department heads came in. Right behind him was a man by the name of Jaweed, one of the organization's drivers. Jaweed was a nervous wreck. He told me he had just received a frantic telephone call from home; his family told him a truck filled with people was nosing through the neighborhood, with soldiers checking documents to demand that anyone with an Iranian background marked on their papers immediately vacate their home. He was told to go home and join his family. They were being deported. To where? Jaweed didn't know.

"We took him in to see the Director General of the organization, who told Jaweed he could do nothing. But feeling sorry for the fellow, the Director General asked the personnel department to give Jaweed a year's salary. The accountant was away from his desk, however, so the personnel head went person to person among the employees, urging us to empty our pockets for Jaweed. Jaweed left our offices with a year's salary. He was not seen again.

"No newspapers wrote about it. No one outside of Iraq seemed to even *know* about it.

"Then the war started, which made Saddam even more determined to deport anyone with an Iranian connection. Any Iraqi with the words 'Tabaeya Iraniya' on their documents Saddam considered an enemy spy.

"Then in December 1982, this persecution struck members of my husband's family.

"Once, after a business trip, I went to visit Salam's parents. Salam is one of four brothers and five sisters. At his parents' home, I found his entire family in desperate conference. Nibal, one of Salam's sisters, was there, along with Nibal's small sons, three-year-old Wissam and the baby, Bassam. The three looked as forlorn as refugees. I asked the problem, and Nibal began weeping. She told me that her husband, Dr. Kareem Al-Saadi, had been taken into detention.

"Dr. Kareem was fifteen or sixteen years older than Nibal, but she had chosen to marry this man above all suitors because he was educated, having earned a Ph.D. in inorganic chemistry in the United States. Nibal had explained to her family that an educated man accustomed

to Western ways was bound to treat his wife better than an uneducated Iraqi who had never been out of the country. So they let her
make the decision.

"Nibal's home was in Hai Al-Jamia, the University District, and
early that morning three men had rung the family's doorbell. They
said they were taking Dr. Kareem for detention because 'Tabaeya
Iraniya' was marked on his nationality papers.

"Now, Dr. Kareem was no more an Iranian than Saddam Hussein
was. But because both of his parents died young and left him four
younger siblings to support, he had written 'Tabaeya Iraniya' on his
nationality papers. Saddled with adult responsibilities, he couldn't
leave his family to serve in the military. Before the revolution and the
war with Iran, Iraqis thought nothing of marking their papers so.

"This Dr. Kareem was the hardest-working Iraqi I've ever known.
He had worked his life away, studying nights and working days and
winning such good grades that he was sent on a scholarship to America.
There he worked equally hard, obtaining a master's and a Ph.D. Then
he came back to Iraq and supported his family, insisting that his siblings gain good educations. He accomplished this feat amazingly
well: Two sisters earned medical degrees; one brother became a dentist and another a civil engineer.

"Dr. Kareem postponed marriage and a family so that he could
educate his siblings. But now he was paying for having avoided
the army.

"Nibal said the men who arrested Dr. Kareem were unnecessarily
brutal—they forced her husband out of the house in his pajamas.
They then ordered Nibal to take her two boys and vacate the home.
They wouldn't allow her to take a single item. They even took the
house key from her. Nibal was put onto the street in shock, with two
babies in her arms. She watched as those men locked her home and
stamped the outer door with red wax.

"She was terrified that she was going to be arrested with her
two babies, but instead, the men informed her that she had the right

to divorce Dr. Kareem in any court of law. He was an Iranian, they told her.

"Dr. Kareem argued with the men, explaining he had changed his papers after his parents died so that he could support his younger siblings.

"Nothing Dr. Kareem said mattered to the men. The last Nibal saw of Kareem was his face through a car window as he was driven away, leaving Nibal and the boys standing on the side of the road like refugees.

"Well, I knew I had to do something, but wasn't sure who could help with this situation. I thought of Dr. Fadil and decided that it couldn't hurt to ask him. He had asked me to bring him back some books from the Iraqi Embassy in Khartoum. I had also bought him some ebony statues as a small gift. This gave me a good excuse to see him and bring up Nibal's situation.

"I called Dr. Fadil the next day and told him that I had some things for him. He said he would pass by our home after work.

"As soon as he arrived, I gave him the books and gifts and then told him that there was an urgent matter. I related the whole story— that Dr. Kareem was not an Iranian nor was he of Iranian origin. He was caught in a terrible situation only because he had changed his documents years before so he could provide for his younger brothers and sisters.

"Dr. Fadil was not moved. He shook his head and muttered, 'Too bad. He shouldn't have done that.'

"When he saw my look of dismay, Dr. Fadil added, 'Besides, by now he is deported and there is nothing I can do.'

"I told Dr. Fadil I had good news. It wasn't too late. Nibal had learned that her husband, because of his stature as an esteemed scientist, had not yet been deported. He was still held in detention.

"Dr. Fadil didn't look so pleased to hear that the situation was still open. He paused and agreed to look into the matter.

"I called him the next day and he said he was too busy.

"I called him the day after, and he gave me the same excuse.

"I called every day, for nine days. During this time, Nibal was going crazy with fear. She couldn't return home. Her boys cried all the time. By now, the secret police had started arresting Dr. Kareem's younger brothers. Although their papers were marked to indicate Ottoman descent, they would suffer the same fate as their relative— deportation. Then the husbands of Dr. Kareem's sisters were told they had to divorce their wives.

"Nibal was a high school teacher. The school's principal was told that if Nibal didn't divorce Kareem, he must fire her.

"The lives of everyone in that family were being destroyed. For *nothing!*

"Dr. Fadil was avoiding me. He didn't return to our home again for over a week. But I was persistent. The tenth time I telephoned Dr. Fadil, the tone of his voice made it clear he was displeased at my perseverance. I told him I was not calling about Dr. Kareem, so he relaxed and we talked for a few minutes. At the end of our conversation, I asked him, 'Dr. Fadil, if I have a baby boy in the future, will he be allowed to enter an Iraqi military academy?' 'Of course, Mayada,' he countered in his smooth voice, 'why do you ask?' I told Dr. Fadil I was concerned that if my son's uncle was deported, the boy's future would be somehow stunted.

"Dr. Fadil didn't speak for a long time. Finally he drew a deep breath and said, 'I'll call you back later.'

"I didn't expect to hear back from him for a few days, but he called back before lunch. Dr. Fadil spoke rapidly, saying, 'Dr. Kareem will be released within the hour. Tell his wife to go to the reception area of the secret police to get her house keys.'

"I started to thank him and he said, 'Mayada, don't bring this subject up with me again.' And he hung up. He was irritated with me, but he solved the problem.

"Sure enough, Dr. Kareem returned from prison. Samara, never have I seen a man who had aged so rapidly. He had lost fifty pounds.

His hair had turned completely white. He refused to speak about his detention—he was terrified to do so, in fact.

"Dr. Fadil saved members of my husband's family, but thousands of Iraqis died in this manner," Mayada said angrily. "For absolutely nothing."

"Did Dr. Fadil ever ask you or your mother to spy on people?" Samara asked curiously.

"Not me. Not ever. I was foolishly bold in those days." She smiled. "My youth pushed me to correct injustices, you know. Anytime I heard a tragic story, I called Dr. Fadil and harassed him until he helped. He understood that I used his friendship to help others—never to spy or to hurt others—so he was a bit wary around me. He was careful never to tell me anything of real importance. But my mother was a different story.

"As you know, since Saddam came to power, Iraqis haven't been allowed friendships with foreign diplomats. But they made an exception to this rule when it came to my mother. She was probably the sole exclusion in all of Iraq. It was a highly irregular arrangement.

"Mother was so cosmopolitan that she gave the foreign diplomats a good impression of Iraq. She spoke fluent English, French, Italian and Turkish. She was so skilled as a hostess that she could entertain fifty people with only an hour's notice. Saddam and Dr. Fadil admired this in her and encouraged her to lend Iraq a good name with her foreign friendships.

"But Dr. Fadil grew so confident in his relationship with my mother that he made a mistake: He asked her to report on people. She turned him down flat; she told him she was not an agent and never would be. Once Dr. Fadil asked my mother to plant a bug at our home so when foreign diplomats came to visit, there would be an automatic record of every conversation, but she reacted angrily and he quickly dropped the subject. My mother was all for Iraq—not for the government of Iraq. Saddam's government thought it was a feather in their cap that Sati's daughter chose to live in Iraq under the Baathist rule. They didn't want to anger her; they didn't want to lose the Al-Husri name. And more than one good thing came from this recip-rocal arrangement. Because Saddam and Dr. Fadil trusted Mother, she played a role in saving one British woman's life."

Samara hunched her back and leaned forward, asking in a startled whisper, "A Brit? How?"

"Well, the story made international headlines. One man was hanged and one woman received a long prison sentence."

Samara shook her head. "I do not remember this."

"Yes, you do. Don't you recall the Bazoft incident in 1989? The British journalist, Farzad Bazoft, who worked for *The British Observer?* The one convicted of spying for Israel while he was working on a story about an explosion at the weapons complex? He was tried, con-victed and hanged. But lots of people forget that there was also an in-nocent woman involved in the story."

A light of memory came into Samara's eyes. "Yes, I remember now. That was a big scandal. It made all the papers."

"That's the one. When the incident took place, the Iraqi govern-ment had little doubt about Bazoft's guilt. But they were less certain about the woman who drove him to the complex, a British nurse by the name of Daphne Parish. During this same time, my mother was a good friend of the British ambassador's wife, Lady Terence Clark. In conversations with Lady Clark, my mother came to realize that Daphne Parish was innocent of all wrongdoing. The British nurse, who was fa-miliar with Iraq, had simply offered to give Bazoft a ride. Mother knew that Saddam was furious about the incident and that more than likely the man was going to hang. Mother was concerned that Sad-dam would order the woman hanged, as well. So she called Dr. Fadil and, for the first time, told him about her personal conversations with Liz Clark. Mother pressured Dr. Fadil to protect the British nurse. Dr. Fadil believed Mother, and after a flurry of meetings in which her conversations with Liz Clark played a major role, it was decided that Daphne Parish would receive a prison sentence, rather than a death sentence. This course left the option open to Saddam and his officials to pardon the nurse at a later date.

"So when Bazoft was tried, found guilty and put to death in March 1990, Daphne Parish was given a fifteen-year sentence. During the subsequent investigation, it was discovered that Miss Parish was indeed innocent, just as Mother had said. She was pardoned in six months, in July 1990, and allowed to leave the country.

"Mother was shocked when, for alerting his government about her conversations with the British ambassador's wife, Saddam presented her with a beautiful two-story house in a residential area called Al-Sullaikh, which overlooks the Tigris. When my mother left Iraq for good, she gave me the ownership documents. So I put the house up for sale. Before selling the house, the broker asked me to come by to discuss the previous owners of the house. He asked me if I knew them. I didn't. He told me that the house had belonged to a family of 'Tabaeya Iraniyas.' The broker said that the entire family had been taken away in the middle of the night, imprisoned and killed, even before they could be deported.

"I rushed home to call my mother in England. I explained as well as I could what had happened to the true owners of the house. Mother is not a highly religious person, but she has high morals and ethics, and she insisted that she couldn't profit from such a gift. She said it would be like holding a piece of burning coal in her hands. She asked me to search for relatives of the now-dead family. I tried, but couldn't locate anyone.

"After a few weeks, I told her that there were no relatives that I could find. So she told me to sell the house and to donate the proceeds to the poor, saying such a gift would honor the souls of the home's rightful owners, who were robbed of their house and their lives. I did what she asked. I distributed the money from the sale of that house to the poorest people I knew."

"That's a beautiful story," Samara said in a quiet voice, clasping Mayada's hand and giving it a squeeze.

"We are not a family who could take something in such a manner."

"Take me back to Dr. Fadil. Didn't I hear that Saddam had him killed?"

"Indeed. And that was the start of everything bad, at least for me. In 1989, everything changed. My mother decided to move to England. Dr. Fadil was transferred from the Intelligence Service to the palace, where he was made an advisor to Saddam. I remember the last time we saw him. He came by the house to say goodbye to Mother, and he talked about his new job at the palace. He told my mother that he already felt retired, that his work was empty." Mayada looked past Samara's shoulder. "Knowing what I know now, I question what it was that he missed about his old job."

"We will never know all of his deeds, Mayada, good or bad. But it is enough to know that he did *some* good. Now go back to your story: Dr. Fadil was saying goodbye to your mother."

"Yes. And my mother was so happy to be leaving Iraq. That surprised me, but Saddam's government had grown to throw a great shadow over all of our lives. Mother looked forward to living in London or in Beirut, her favorite cities. As for me, I just hoped everything would be all right. I was finally divorced from Salam. The Iranian war was over. Iraqis could travel freely again, so I knew I would be able to travel, to visit my mother in England when I felt like it. Dr. Fadil still held a powerful position in the palace. Or at least I thought he did."

Mayada edged a little closer to Samara, choosing her words carefully.

"Then one day, Dr. Fadil just disappeared. I called his home. I got a busy signal. I kept calling. For days I called, and I got nothing but a busy signal. Then I called Fatin, his sister-in-law. There was no answer. Rumors began to swirl that Dr. Fadil had been arrested. His entire family was missing, even his beautiful wife Jinan and their five children. It was as though he and his entire family had been shipped off to the moon." Mayada paused. "For more than a year, I heard nothing about any of them. Then, over the following years, I slowly pieced together the puzzle that was the truth of Dr. Fadil Al-Barrak's disappearance.

"In June 1991, after the first Gulf War was over, my mother purchased a home in Amman. She asked my children and me to come for a visit, and we got tickets to Amman on the Businessman's Bus Line, which is so much better than the regular buses.

"The bus was filled with people, but I particularly noticed one interesting woman—an elderly lady in black clothes. She had such a dignified look. Her skin was snow white against her black clothing. She looked out of the ordinary to me.

"But I said nothing to her. After we passed the Iraqi border, Fay and Ali fell asleep and I sat thinking about our lives, pondering what we were going to do next. The bus driver then played a tape of a very old Iraqi song, a sad melody about a woman who had lost her son. The elderly lady I had earlier noticed began to weep quietly, covering her face with parts of her head scarf. She was so anguished that just watching her brought tears to my eyes.

"I wanted to help her in some way, so I offered her a cup of water. She drank a bit, but her tears continued to flow. She finally asked the driver to turn off that song. I knew she must have lost a son. So I asked her what was wrong.

"We were no longer in Iraq and she felt safe, so she poured her heart out to me. She said that she once had a wonderful son named Sabah, a son who treasured his elderly mother. She added that he had been detained for two years in Al-Hakimiya, a prison known for its harsh brutality. Two weeks before her trip to Amman, she was informed by government authorities that her son was finally going to be released, and that she should come to collect him and take him home. She was further ordered to bring a music band with her so that she and her son could celebrate his homecoming. The woman was ecstatic. She hired a special band and appeared at the prison, as instructed, to bring her son Sabah home.

"Imagine her horror when, instead of seeing her son walk out of the prison, she is presented with a casket that houses her son's body. After this, the woman grew so miserable in Iraq that she decided to live in Amman for a while.

"Then she spoke her son's complete name: Sabah Al-Ani. I was so stunned I couldn't speak. I knew that her son was Dr. Fadil's best friend. I blurted without thinking, 'Do you know anything of the fate of Dr. Fadil?'

"Um Sabah [the mother of Sabah] immediately grew cold and withdrawn. She questioned me, 'Who are you?'

"I told her that Salwa Al-Husri was my mother and that she was a good friend of Dr. Fadil's. I told her my family had been frantic over Dr. Fadil's whereabouts since he disappeared. We had no knowledge of her son's arrest.

"At my words, that mother broke down completely. She told me that Dr. Fadil had been killed along with her son.

"When I arrived in Amman, I rushed to tell my mother the story. Then she told me that she had just met with the former Egyptian ambassador to Iraq and that he had provided her with even more details of the story. He claimed he had credible information that Dr. Fadil had been framed, accused of spying and treason and all sorts of serious crimes. He added that someone high up in Saddam's inner circle had wanted Dr. Fadil out of the way. This person had the connections to set up a Swiss bank account in Dr. Fadil's name before telling Saddam that Dr. Fadil was working for the Germans as a spy and that the Germans had paid him a large sum of money. My mother and I knew it was all a lie, because we knew that Fadil Al-Barrak loved Iraq more than his own life. But Saddam was so paranoid that when he uncovered a Swiss bank account in Dr. Fadil's name, nothing could save Dr. Fadil.

"But still, we knew very little about his arrest and imprisonment. Those details would come later.

"After I returned to Baghdad, I uncovered another piece of the puzzle. There is an art gallery behind our home in Baghdad. One day the doorbell rang and I answered it to find the owner of the gallery standing there. He asked me if I would sell him the two giant trees we have in our garden. I told him no, that my mother liked those trees very much. Then he asked if he could just come into the garden and look at the trees. Ali, still a small child, told me he recognized the man because his best friend lived next door to the gallery. So I invited the gallery owner in for a cup of coffee.

"We sat and conversed and stared at the trees. I discovered that the gallery owner had graduated from law school and become a member of the Mukhabarat. I quickly asked him if he knew what had happened to Dr. Fadil. Since he still hoped to convince me to let him have the trees, he opened up and confided that Dr. Fadil had been accused of some very serious charges, that he was accused of being a spy. He told me Dr. Fadil was detained for over a year in the Al-Hakimiya detention center, just as Sabah Al-Ani's mother had told me on our bus ride.

"Samara, I was truly sad when that man told me that the favorite pastime of the detention center's junior officers was to seek out Dr. Fadil so they could kick him or pull his hair or yank at his ears. He said that some of the men made it a daily ritual to spit in Dr. Fadil's face.

"Hearing such stories burdened me with sadness. I sat in my home, remembering Dr. Fadil the human being, the man who always smiled and who loved to speak of Iraq's greatness. I remembered Dr. Fadil the father, who beamed at his new baby daughter in his arms while she bit his fingers. I remembered him chiefly as a kind human being who loved his wife and children, and as a man who always helped me when I tried to right some injustice. Yet I was told later that Dr. Fadil boasted of killing thousands of Shiites from the Hizb Al-Dawa Al-Islamiya [the Islamic Convocation Party].

"Then in 1993, I received the final two pieces of the puzzle of Dr. Fadil's fate.

"A man by the name of Usama Al-Tikriti came into my offices in

Baghdad to inquire about my mother. I knew she had no plans to return to Iraq, but I didn't tell him that. He said she was needed to give lessons in protocol at the National Security College. I assured him I would pass the message to my mother. As we chatted, our conversation led to Dr. Fadil, because this man had been one of Dr. Fadil's aides. The man felt bad about what had happened: He told me that after Dr. Fadil was arrested, he was tortured until he confessed to all kinds of ridiculous crimes against Saddam. The confessions were taped. The torturers then made Dr. Fadil wear a dog collar and a leash, put him in the back of a pickup truck, and drove him to his tribe in Tikrit. His confession was read before the elders of the tribe, who all insisted that they would kill him on the spot if that is what the government wanted. But Saddam was not finished with Dr. Fadil. He was taken back to prison for more torture.

"Only later did I acquire the final bit of information about Dr. Fadil's end. It was the summer of 1994 or 1995, and I was once again visiting my mother in Amman. She had invited a lot of friends for lunch, and I had volunteered to cook all of my specialties. I had prepared a number of salads and some cooked vegetables stuffed with rice and meat, along with a roast, pasta, eggplants with minced-meat tomato sauce and cheese, and some Biryani [hot spicy rice with nuts and chicken]. For dessert I baked a Black Forest cake and Mahalabi [milk pudding], and also served some fresh fruits and tea.

"Everyone ate their fill and was having a jolly time. But I noticed one man in particular because he was so quiet and withdrawn, with the saddest face I'd seen. His name was Dr. Mohammed. When the group finished drinking their tea, almost everyone went to the television room to watch the news. This one man, however, stayed behind to help me with the dishes.

"It was a scorching hot day, but Dr. Mohammed was wearing a long-sleeved shirt. When he reached to put away some dishes, his sleeve pulled back. I saw a deep red scar on his wrist.

"My curiosity was piqued, so I asked the doctor for his medical specialty. He told me he was a surgeon. One thing led to another and he told me his story.

"Dr. Mohammed's father was a high-ranking army officer during the Iraqi-Iranian war. He was a fair man, and very popular with his soldiers. Because of his great popularity, many generals did not like him. He was accused of being too soft with his soldiers, too lenient in attacking Iranians. He was further accused of being a leader in a conspiracy against Saddam, which was a tired charge that people around Saddam always trotted out when they wanted to get rid of someone. But when Saddam heard the accusations, he turned on Dr. Mohammed's father and ordered his arrest.

"Because Dr. Mohammed's father, the head of the household, was under arrest, the Mukhabarat bugged Dr. Mohammed's home, although he and his mother did not know this.

"Because of that security bug, more trouble came their way. It was 1988 and the war was still raging. Dr. Mohammed and his mother were watching television when they saw a news report about Saddam and his family. Saddam had been visiting his wife, Sajida, and his youngest daughter, Hala, at the palace in Tikrit when an Iranian Scud missile hit the palace. The palace was almost destroyed, but the family escaped with their lives. Saddam was obviously emotional, because he kissed his wife on the cheek, and as you know, Arabs don't kiss their wives in public, no matter what has happened.

"This young doctor looked at his mother and casually commented that, 'He should know better than to kiss his wife in public.'

"Two days later, the Mukhabarat arrived. The doctor and his mother were arrested. They were taken to Al-Hakimiya, one of the worst prisons in Iraq. The doctor was put into a tiny cell with his mother. They were left there for a month. They were given barely enough food to survive. Then the prison guards began to take Dr. Mohammed out every day for torture. He told me the torture he went through was unbearable. He was made to stand in water while they shot electricity into him. His fingernails were ripped out, and electric prods shocked the raw flesh under those torn nails. This happened every day. Dr. Mohammed told me that in his years of imprisonment, there was not a single day he wasn't tortured. When they finished with their daily torture, the guards would throw Dr. Mohammed, barely alive, back into the cell with his mother. Her wails of anguish would wake him—and steel him to live—for her.

"Dr. Mohammed and his mother existed in this cruel regimen for several years.

"But he claimed that one of the worst things was the *waiting* to be tortured. In that prison, the guards had devised an especially cruel habit. Each morning, they gathered all the prisoners they planned to torture that day. Then they would handcuff them all in a line to a long metal pipe attached horizontally to the corridor. Each prisoner could see nothing but the back of the prisoner in front of him. Sometimes they had to wait for eight or ten hours to be tortured.

"Then one day Dr. Mohammed snapped. He went hysterical. He had been handcuffed to the pipe for over eight hours, and he had had no water for that entire time. He screamed that he was a doctor and the son of an army commander. No one had the right to treat human beings in such a manner, he shouted. One of the torturers, a man by the name of Abu Faisal, began kicking Dr. Mohammed, screaming at him, 'You are nothing but a piece of shit.' Then the torturer ran forward to pull a prisoner off the line. He dragged the prisoner in front of this young doctor and shrieked, 'You think you are too good to be tortured? Do you know who this is?' Then the guard yanked up the head of the prisoner by the hair. This prisoner had been so badly tortured that he could barely open his eyes. The young doctor nearly fainted when he recognized Dr. Fadil Al-Barrak, a man he knew to hold some of the highest positions in the entire government.

"Dr. Mohammed knew then that no Iraqi was safe. After seeing

Dr. Fadil's face, he lost all hope. He told me he couldn't take another day in that place. He decided to commit suicide. So after he was tortured and returned to his prison cell, he waited for his mother to go to sleep and he began to chew through his flesh, into the veins on his right wrist, the wrist that bore the scar that I saw beneath his shirt that day in Amman.

"Dr. Mohammed was serious about wanting to die. The following day when the guards came to take him to torture, they discovered him near death. They rushed him to the prison hospital and saved his life. They then held his trial, at which he was given a prison sentence of twenty years for talking badly about Saddam. His mother received the same sentence for *hearing* her son talk badly about Saddam. Thankfully, Dr. Mohammed's mother was soon pardoned.

"By this time, Dr. Mohammed's father had been executed. One of his father's friends, a high-ranking officer in the Iraqi army, General Al-Dulaimi, went to visit Dr. Mohammed's mother to convey his condolences. When General Al-Dulaimi discovered that her son was in prison, he told her of a certain jail warden who took bribes through a well-known gypsy dancer named Dollarat [meaning dollars]. This contact was immediately established and the warden accepted five thousand dollars to arrange Dr. Mohammed's escape from prison.

"Dr. Mohammed was smuggled out of the prison in one of the sacks normally used to transport dead bodies. With the help of smugglers, he crossed the border into Syria, where he met with some free Iraqi officers who had defected. Those men got him to Amman.

"So it was from this Dr. Mohammed that I received the third confirmation of Dr. Fadil's arrest, imprisonment and torture. I don't know the exact date of his execution. All I know is that he died a horrible death. And, to add insult to injury, Dr. Fadil's beautiful wife was forced to marry Saddam's half-brother, Barzan. This was the man who was married to Sajida's sister. But after Sajida's sister died of cancer in

1998, the first thing Barzan did was take the beautiful Jinan for his very own."

Samara opened her mouth to respond but the cell door flew open at that moment.

Mayada heard a thump and peered around Samara's shoulder.

Sara lay crumpled face down on the floor. Despite their own recent torture and injuries, Samara and Mayada both moved quickly and gathered with the other shadow women at Sara's side.

Iman carefully turned Sara over. Smoke billowed from Sara's mouth.

Mayada gasped and drew back. "What is that smoke?"

"Did they set her insides afire?" Muna cried out.

Samara shook her head. "I think they have killed the poor girl this time."

"What shall we do?" Dr. Sabah asked Samara.

Samara examined Sara's body. Her dress was ripped down the front. "Look, they put the current to her from many places."

Mayada looked, as well. The telltale indentations marked Sara's ears, lips, the nipples of each of her beasts, her wrists and her ankles. Remembering how jolting and painful it had been to receive current only to her toe and her ear, Mayada shook her head in disbelief. She doubted that Sara would survive the pain of her interrogation.

Samara gave brisk orders. "She's smoking from her insides. We've got to get water on her. Let's get her to the shower to cool her down."

Carefully following Samara's instructions, Dr. Sabah, Muna and Aliya lifted Sara from the floor and carried her under the single shower head, located next to the toilet.

Samara told them, "Use only the cool water."

With Sara held upright, Dr. Sabah sprayed her face and body with the cool water. Out of modesty, they kept her torn dress on her body, although it was parted and open in the front.

Under the spray, Sara began to gain consciousness. She opened her eyes and looked into the faces surrounding her, slowly realizing where she was and what had happened. When the full force of her memories hit her, she sobbed and called for her mother and father in the most pitiful manner, "*Youma! [Mama] Yabba! [Father] Come and see what has happened to your daughter! Come and see what has happened to your daughter! Youma! Yabba!*" Sara took her right hand and began striking herself in the face and on the body. "*Youma! Yabba! Help your poor daughter! Save your poor daughter!*" She sobbed so hard that she doubled over. "*Youma, Youma, help me! Help me!*"

Not knowing what else to do, Mayada began to recite verses of the Fatiha, comforting verses from the Quran, in hopes of calming the dear girl. "In the Name of Allah, the Most Gracious, the Most Merciful. All the praises and thanks be to Allah, the Lord of Alamin, The Most Gracious, The Most Merciful. The Only Owner of the Day of Recompense. You we worship and you we ask for help on each and everything. Guide us to the straight way. The way of those on whom you have bestowed your grace, not of those who earned your anger, nor of those who went astray."

Sara continued to cry, calling for her mother and her father, although he had been dead for many years.

Every shadow woman wept with Sara, a young innocent woman, unmarried, terrified and without the protection of her parents. Together, their sobs grew into a loud roar of women's wails that would have struck pity into even the hardest heart.

Samara gained control of her emotions first and told the shadow women to take Sara to her bed. There she was gently covered with a light blanket. The shadow women then took turns dabbing Sara's face and head with a damp cloth.

"Truly, this is the saddest story in the world," Samara confessed to Mayada.

Sara had talked little since the day of Mayada's arrest. So Mayada knew very few details of her background or the reason for her detention. "What brought this young woman here?" Mayada asked in a quiet voice.

"Sara is from a middle-class family. Although her father died when she was only eight, her mother was educated, an agricultural engineer. The mother dedicated her entire life to Sara and to Sara's younger brothers, Hadi and Adel. The mother refused to remarry, so the family was limited to only the mother and her three children."

Since her divorce and her mother's move from Iraq, Mayada's family was restricted to her two children and herself. She and Fay and Ali often jokingly called themselves "The Three Musketeers." So she understood completely the closeness of that mother and her children.

Samara told Mayada more of Sara's story. "Sara's mother sacrificed everything. She had big dreams for her children. She retained a plot of land left to her by her husband, telling the children that after their educations were complete, she would sell it and set them each up in business.

"Then disaster struck. Last year, Sara was in her final year of pharmacology school, dreaming of opening her own pharmacy. Her two brothers had begun medical school. Then one day Hadi ran home without his brother. He tearfully reported that members of the secret police had come to the medical college and taken his brother Adel away. When Hadi saw what was happening to Adel, he rushed to follow his brother. The secret police told Hadi that they were taking Adel for questioning, but that he would return within a couple of hours. Adel was the trusting brother, the one who believed everything, so he told Hadi not to worry. Adel assured his brother that he would likely be home for supper. Hadi was more cynical about the world, however, and didn't believe the men. Hadi began to yell in the school hallway, shouting that they couldn't take his brother. One of the secret service men grabbed Hadi's wrist and almost broke it, hissing at him cruelly, 'You mind your own business, you son of a prostitute, or you'll get it right here.'

"The next few days were a nightmare, with the family looking in every prison for Adel. They never found him.

"Then late one night the following week, the secret police came to their home. It was after midnight and everyone was in bed. Hadi ran to the door, hoping it was Adel, finally back home safe. But no, their late-night visitors were those same three secret service men who had taken Adel away. They pushed Hadi aside and stomped into the house, ordering Sara and her mother to stay in the kitchen. They then bullied Hadi into his room. When Sara and her mother began to hear loud knocking and banging, they ran out to see the three men running out the front door.

"Sara and her mother ran to Hadi's room. The room had been completely torn to pieces, as though someone were looking for something in particular. Hadi had been thrown to the floor between the bed and the wall. He had been murdered.

"Of course, Sara and her mother were beyond grief. Two boys gone in a single week.

"After the traditional seven days of mourning, Sara was still frightened to leave her home and return to college, though her mother insisted. The poor girl was fraught with nightmares that her brother's murderers were looking for her.

"At her mother's insistence, Sara went back to class. And sure enough, her nightmare came true. Within a week, those same men came for her. Forbidding Sara to telephone her mother, they arrested her and threw her here, in Baladiyat, and they have been torturing her ever since. She learned during her interrogation that someone had anonymously accused Adel of being in a conspiracy cell that opposed Saddam's regime. These men believed Sara knew the names of other conspirators. But, of course, there was never a conspiracy. Those boys were so busy with medical school that they didn't have time for such activities."

Sara was obviously listening to Samara's words, for her sobs now grew more wracking. "Youma! Yabba! Please help your daughter," she cried. "I cannot bear it! I cannot bear it!"

Then Muna interrupted, reminding them of yet another shadow woman whose fate was unknown. "Samara, I am also worried about Safana. She has been gone for too long."

"Cell 52 has become a revolving door," Samara said, looking at Mayada with the greatest sorrow.

Sara's sobs filled the room. All the shadow women gathered around her—some holding hands, others weeping softly.

Mayada sat and stared at the ceiling, praying that she was at home in bed, and that Fay and Ali were safe in bed just down the hall.

9

The Chirping of the Qabaj

The shadow women looked up anxiously when, less than an hour later, their cell door was flung open and an unseen hand pushed Safana back among them. Although she lurched through the door on her own feet, she was not the same Safana who had walked out of cell 52 earlier that day. Once inside, she stumbled two or three steps, then reached for the wall to keep from falling. Her head scarf was askew and the flaps of her abaaya hung wide open. The day's ordeal had aged her youthful face, and her once-firm cheeks now sagged, blotched and flushed. Her back was bowed into a terrible stoop, as though her spine had been twisted during interrogation. Her blood-shot eyes scanned the cell wildly.

Safana's legs trembled and bent like rubber, and Muna ran toward her with outstretched arms. Muna gripped her around the shoulders, crying out, "Safana? Are you all right?"

Confusion quivered in Safana's eyes before she wrinkled up her face to utter a low moan. Her body corkscrewed, then crumpled. Muna wrapped her arms around Safana and held tight, then called to the other women, "I need help." Dr. Sabah rushed to assist, and the two shadow women slowly pulled Safana toward the bedding they had prepared for her.

Samara stood watching, her eyebrows narrowed in concern. "Look at her back," said Samara with a small shake of her head. "Blood is seeping through her dress and her abaaya." She nodded toward the bedding on the floor. "Lay her on her stomach."

The three women slowly lowered Safana. Once she was down, Samara carefully slipped her bloodstained dress off her shoulders and lowered it down to her waist.

Mayada was overcome with pity and wanted to assist, but when Samara saw Mayada fumbling with her blanket and leaning forward to get up, she ordered, "You stay where you are, Mayada."

Mayada did as she was told, but sat propped on her elbows, examining Safana's back. From the base of her neck to the top of her buttocks, Safana's back was a mass of bloody tissue.

She had been viciously beaten with a whip.

Samara busily tended to Safana's wounds. First she probed gently, dabbing the wounds with a dry cloth, then she gently washed them with a damp cloth. She rinsed the reddened cloth in a small pail of water.

Safana grimaced in pain, groaning, "Oooooooh. . . . Oooooooh."

Samara, too, looked pale and tired, but she paused in her ministrations long enough to whisper consolingly in Safana's ear before proceeding.

Mayada lay and watched, letting her eyes travel slowly around the small cell. All of the women were gathered around Safana, and Mayada saw that every woman's cheeks were wet with tears.

Safana's friend from the bank, Muna, silently wept while she clung tightly to one of Safana's hands.

Rasha squatted on the floor a few feet away, her legs tucked beneath her, rocking back and forth.

Dr. Sabah watched as the women tended to Safana. The ever-widening crinkles around her eyes and lips revealed her fifty years.

Mayada glanced over at Sara, and feeling Mayada's gaze on her, Sara's eyelids flew open. The two shadow women exchanged a long, sad look. To Mayada, Sara seemed like a child among all the shadow women. If Mayada was allowed to select just one prisoner to set free, she would choose Sara—she was, after all, only a few years older than Mayada's precious daughter, Fay.

Sara had shed all the tears her tortured body could produce, but nothing relieved her physical torment. She had overheard other shadow women whispering about the smoke that had billowed from her mouth. She had been thinking about that smoke for a long time. Now she haltingly explained in a muffled voice, "Rather than quick short blasts, they set the machine for a low voltage and shot the electricity into my body very slowly and for a long time. After a while, I could not even force my eyelids to close. My eyeballs swelled so large that I felt them pushing against my eye sockets." She sobbed, "I thought my eyeballs would pop out of my head. They were frying my insides. That's why that smoke came out of my mouth."

Samara looked up and said, "Someone give Sara more water. Sara, you need to drink as much water as you can. That is the only thing that will heal your insides: cool water. And stop thinking about that smoke."

Iman pushed her thick eyeglasses back up on her nose. She stooped to pick up a glass of water and shuffled to Sara's side with it. With her thin brows twisted in concern, Iman convinced Sara to drink down the full glass. Iman remained by the young woman's side, affectionately patting her back with one hand while she held the now-empty glass in the other.

Iman, who was fifty-four and married, was one of the older shadow women. She was plump, with extremely pale skin. Iman had arrived in Baladiyat because she tried to do good for her community. Though she had never joined the Baath Party, she was selected as a member of the people's council for her district. She accepted the appointment with enthusiasm, eager to improve her community. But

Iman was uneducated and naïve. She didn't realize that complaining about uncollected litter could trigger serious trouble for her in Saddam's Iraq. Iman was arrested for making "trivial" criticisms of the government.

Wafae, the shadow woman nicknamed "Tomatoes" for her hair color—a cross between a ripened tomato and golden wheat—dashed back and forth between Samara and the toilet, where she emptied the small pail of water that had turned pink from Safana's blood and refilled it with fresh water. Wafae had been seized by the secret police because her brother had escaped to Syria.

Anwar was a tall woman with strong shoulders. She was very attractive, with blond hair, hazel eyes, a delicate nose and thin lips. She puckered her lips as she leaned over Samara, offering her opinion on how to best stanch Safana's blood flow. Mayada was not familiar with Anwar's story because she was an intense, silent woman who rarely complained about her own problems. Mayada knew that she had a degree in the arts, and that she taught social sciences. Mayada also recalled that Anwar's sister was an invalid, and that the two women together took care of their combined families.

Anwar was the only woman in cell 52 who had actually committed a crime. Her job required that she travel to Yemen to teach some courses at a Yemeni school. Anwar that she couldn't afford to pay for a passport, so she borrowed her invalid sister's passport, since they looked so similar. A relative who wanted to curry favor with the local secret police had reported her transgression. Anwar had been warned to expect a long prison sentence. Now her biggest concern was that she'd left her invalid sister to manage their family alone.

Two other inmates of cell 52—Hayat and Asia—stood side by side, their fingers interlocked. The two women had been imprisoned together seven months earlier over two missing boxes of floor tiles. The pair had been arrested at their office in the QaQae Establishment for Construction Materials, a company hired to build most of Saddam's many palaces. When two boxes of floor tiles disappeared from the establishment, Hayat and Asia were blamed. Hayat had signed the document that verified two cartons had left the company's inventory. Asia's signature confirmed that those same two boxes had been loaded onto the delivery truck.

Hayat was a thirty-two-year-old unmarried woman who had previously lived with her brother and his five children. She had a sharp, thin face, and her body was emaciated. Hayat could never speak calmly, and she constantly paced and wept. With frightened eyes that continually darted from one corner of the cell to another, she reminded Mayada of a rabbit caught in a trap. Hayat once admitted she was scared to be set free: She claimed that her brother would be so angry that her arrest had brought suspicion onto the entire family that he would beat her.

Asia, on the other hand, was a forty-two-year-old woman who had been the happily married mother of three young boys. Asia was always in a state of anxiety, desperate for her children. She wept night and day, explaining that the faces of her three boys never left her mind's eye. Her steady tears had left permanent violet patches under her eyes.

Overwhelmed by loneliness for her own two children, Mayada wrung her hands, wondering if she would live to see Fay or Ali again. Or would she die under torture, like poor Jamila? While Mayada didn't fear death from old age, death today or tomorrow terrified her. She simply couldn't die until her children were grown. They were young and needed their mother.

Yearning for the touch of her children, to breathe the scent of their fresh-smelling hair and to stroke the soft skin of their faces, Mayada lifted a finger and brushed aside a tear. She then turned on her side to stare at the wall. But she was unable to sleep, for the light was always bright in cell 52 and the noise never ceased.

Mayada had been in Baladiyat for less than a week, but that week felt like a lifetime. The long days and longer nights dragged endlessly, reminding her of her former full life, when she didn't have enough hours in the day to accomplish all of her chores. Now, in prison, there was not enough life to fill the long hours. Time became Mayada's enemy as the days and nights merged together.

Every twenty-four-hour period was the same. At night, the women were either subjected to torture or forced to listen to others being tortured. At dawn, they would rise for the first prayer of the day. They would then take turns using the toilet and the small shower. Next came breakfast, which consisted of tasteless lentils and moldy bread. If they were lucky and no one in the cell was called out for torture, the women would spend the morning weeping or praying or reminiscing about the loved ones central to their lives. After noon prayers, the women were served dirty rice in a watery substance, an unappetizing mush. Occasionally they were served warm bread, which smelled of moss because it was intentionally made of rancid flour. Their afternoons were the same as their mornings: talking and praying and waiting for torture or nursing the ones who had been tortured. After evening prayers, they received a final meal for the day—once again, lentils and bread. Then the dreaded nighttime lay on them once more, when the prison rang with screams.

Of all the shadow women, only Samara kept busy, maintaining a strict schedule of daily tasks. Unless she was incapacitated by torture, she cleaned herself or organized her belongings or tended to whatever other women needed her attention. Samara was so particular about personal cleanliness that she made a daily routine of washing her one set of clothing and her abaaya. While other shadow women ignored vomit splashes on their clothes or bits of food stuck between their teeth, Samara could not abide such untidiness. Each morning before bathing, Samara would remove all of her clothes and scrub each piece by hand. As soon as she showered, she would slip the wet garments back on, leave the toilet and walk briskly around and around in the small cell, her abaaya flapping, claiming to the smiling shadow women that her rapid movements dried her garments as efficiently as a brisk wind.

Mayada spent her days moping, daydreaming about her children, studying the faces of the other women or staring at the door in feverish expectation. While other shadow women were called out for questioning and torture, it appeared that the torturers at Baladiyat had forgotten Mayada Al-Askari. She was not taken back to torture, nor was she called for questioning. It seemed her case was being neglected.

Afraid that no one on the outside knew where she was and that she would die in Baladiyat, Mayada's will began to sag. She felt pushed down into a pit of depression. She was forced to confront death as a new and unanticipated issue in her life. The topic was so discouraging that after two weeks of waiting to hear about her case, she began to emulate Asia and Hayat, crossing her arms and walking around and around in the small cell, pacing and weeping during all hours of the day and night.

Samara, who was naturally sweet and kind and always eager to offer an answer to every problem, now tried to lift Mayada's wretched sadness. "Listen, I want you to believe me," Samara told Mayada. "*No one* at Baladiyat goes without torture for weeks. Our jailors have discovered that you are poison for them. One day you will be released," she snapped her fingers, "just like that."

Mayada looked sidelong at Samara, and seeing her confident face staring back with such affection, Mayada smiled apologetically before bursting into tears anew.

Samara hugged her and said, "You cannot lose your energy for this struggle to survive. You must hold fast to your emotions."

But Mayada was too disheartened to act with conviction.

Then one Thursday morning, everything changed in a flash.

Mayada was lying quietly in bed, staring at the ceiling. Her eyes drifted to the small, barred window at the top of the back wall. She waited for the sun to rise and to stretch a few kind rays of sunlight into cell 52.

Then Mayada thought she heard the chirping of a qabaj, a kind of partridge.

An old Iraqi folk tale says that to hear a qabaj singing is a sign you will soon move from your current place.

Mayada's heart skipped a beat. She sat up. Confused between her dreams and the reality of Baladiyat, she looked around the cell to see if anyone else could confirm the qabaj's welcome cheeping. Mayada had been in this ugly room for nearly a month, and today was the first time she had heard a bird of any sort.

The qabaj continued singing. A light breeze pushed the bird's song through the barred window. Its welcome notes spread through the cell.

The bird's song roused the other women from their beds. It sounded as though it had been piped through the open window like an extraordinary message straight from God. The happy song circled the room and filled every woman's heart with hope. One by one, the inmates of cell 52 sat up and scanned each other's face with fresh optimism. Each woman prayed that the qabaj sang his message for her.

Samara then echoed musical time with the bird, singing an old Iraqi song that matched the bird's pace. As the qabaj continued its trilling, Samara jumped from her bunk. "Listen to that persistent qabaj. It is right outside our window. Someone is leaving Baladiyat, and soon." Her green eyes flashing, Samara twirled around once. She halted her spin with her right arm extended and her finger pointing at Mayada. "And that would be our Mayada."

For days, Mayada had been too despondent for conversation, and she resisted Samara's gaiety now. But she loved this wonderful Shiite woman and couldn't bear to hurt her feelings. She smiled faintly. "Thank you, Samara, for trying to raise my hopes. You are very kind.

But I have been forgotten. I will die in this place. It is written. I fore-saw that my fate was to die here the moment I saw I was locked into cell number 52. This cell will be my tomb."

Samara stared at Mayada with her pretty, steadfast face. "This is a feeling I have had for days—this qabaj is confirming it," said Samara. "You are going home—and soon. Mayada, you must start memorizing our telephone numbers, our addresses and the names of our family members. Now. Today. There's no chance for any of us unless one of us is released. It will be you, and from outside, you can help us all."

Deeply miserable, Mayada shaded her eyes from the overhead light with her scarf. She was too depressed to accept Samara's hopeful prediction. She knew she would never be freed from cell 52.

But the qabaj kept singing, its little voice never once faltering.

After morning prayers, Samara cornered Mayada and insisted qui-etly, "I will say this again, Mayada. I feel it deep in my heart. You are leaving Baladiyat, and soon." Samara always had a plan. "Now, you must pretend you are a parrot. You must learn many names and num-bers. Repeat this number for me: 882-6410."

Mayada listened quietly. The qabaj bird still sang, and it began to kindle her hopes. For the first time, she wondered if Samara might be right that her release was imminent. So she obediently repeated, "882-6410."

"Here are your instructions," Samara told Mayada. "You will call 882-6410 and here is what you will say: Samara is rotting away in the Amin Al-Amma [the main security building]. She needs your help. Sell every-thing you can and bribe a guard. That is the only way." Her eyes gleamed as she thought of every possibility. "My family will need to know that you were truly sent by me, so here is a secret code: How is Salma's husband?"

"882-6410. Samara is in Amin Al-Amma. She needs your help. Sell everything you can and bribe a guard. That is the only way. The code is: How is Salma's husband?" Mayada repeated Samara's message like a well-trained parrot.

Asia called out, "Samara, that bird is still singing."

Both women stopped and listened. The qabaj *was* still singing. This unusual event had been going on for nearly an hour now.

Just then, the cell door opened and a guard spoke, saying in an unusually humane tone of voice, "Mayada. Get ready. The judge will see you now."

Samara squealed with joy and jumped forward. "Who is this judge? Is Mayada being released?"

"Mind your own business."

Mayada ran to wash her face.

Samara followed her and murmured happily, "If a judge has come to this building to see you, you will be released."

Mayada began to sense a miracle in the making.

During the few minutes she spent at the toilet, hopeful shadow women filed by, passing her phone numbers or whispering addresses and names.

"In case you leave straightaway, without coming back to the cell," Dr. Sabah explained, as she lifted Mayada's skirt and painstakingly wrote her telephone number on Mayada's slip with a half-broken ball-point pen.

The guard shouted, "Mayada! Come!"

Mayada rushed forward, names and numbers and addresses ringing in her ears.

When she stepped out from the cell, Mayada noted that another guard waited in the hall. This unattractive officer was very tall and heavyset. His skin was yellow-tinged, and when he opened his mouth to speak, Mayada noticed that his large teeth were as yellow as his face.

The officer dismissed the guard and turned to Mayada to ask, "How are you, Um Ali?"

Mayada questioned him, "Have I seen you before?"

The officer did not answer, but instead quickly whispered, "My name is Mamoun. I have a special interest in your case. I saw Ali and

Fay yesterday. Their father, Salam, will be back from Hilla tomorrow to be with them. You are going to a judge that knows your family. He has orders to close your case. You should be released from Baladiyat within a couple of days. Once you are released, do not leave your home until I come and visit Ali." In the Arab world, a visit with the man of the house is a sign of respect. Ali, though a young teenage boy, was considered to be the man of Mayada's household.

Mayada raised her hand to her scarf and adjusted it. She brushed the front of her dress. The single most important meeting of her life awaited her, yet her clothes were dirty and she smelled. She felt a momentary flash of envy for Samara's hygiene discipline. What kind of an impression could she make on a judge in her filthy clothes and unclean body?

After walking a short distance down the prison hallway, Mayada and her ungainly escort turned left to confront an unmarked mahogany door.

Mamoun held up his hand and ordered Mayada, "Wait here." He knocked before he entered the room and pulled the door closed behind him. Very soon, the door opened again and Mamoun stepped out, this time commanding, "Come in."

Mayada walked into the room. A distinguished man sat behind a wooden desk. He looked vaguely familiar to Mayada.

He spoke. "My name is Judge Muayad Al-Jaddir."

Mayada instantly knew that this man was a nephew of Adib Al-Jaddir, Iraq's Minister of Information during the mid-1960s.

The judge was polite. "How is your mother, Salwa?"

A fleeting smile crossed Mayada's face. "Before I was brought here, she was fine. Now I do not know. But thank you for asking."

"Mayada, my uncle Al-Jaddir was a very good friend of your mother, and of your father. He considered himself the spiritual son of your grandfather, Sati Al-Husri."

Mayada nodded slightly, feeling more confident by the minute that this man was here to help her.

Judge Jaddir then shuffled some papers, lifted a pen and began signing documents. He looked up at her and said, "Mayada, this was a mistake. I want you to go out and live and forget this experience. Wipe these days from your mind."

The shadows of the pain she had endured for the past month passed through her body, but she bit her tongue to keep from telling him that she would *never* forget Baladiyat and the thousands of innocent Iraqis who suffered inside its walls. Instead she asked, "Do you know why I was arrested?"

"Yes. I do. Someone working for you printed some leaflets against the government. But this shows that justice prevails in this good land. All of this is best forgotten."

"Will I be released today?"

"This will be taken care of very soon. For now, go back. Take comfort from knowing that you will be released." Then he put his pen down and said warmly, "You know I visited your home in 1980, with Abu Ali." He was referring to Dr. Fadil Al-Barrak, whose eldest son was named Ali.

Mayada nodded again, now dimly recalling the social visit. She also recognized that this man referred to Dr. Fadil as "Abu Ali" because Saddam had deemed Dr. Fadil a spy. No clear-thinking person in Iraq would flaunt an association with a man accused of treason and put to death.

The judge was ready to dismiss her. "You may go now, Mayada," he said. "The next time you speak with your mother, please convey my best wishes."

Mayada said, "Thank you. Goodbye." And she stepped back out through the wooden door.

Mamoun was there. He told her, "Wait here." The large man entered the room once again and quickly returned with Mayada's file. He leaned close. Despite his new pleasant manner, the man's face still intimidated Mayada. He told her, "Your paperwork must be processed. Another guard will take you back to cell 52. I will come to get you when it is time for you to go home."

Mayada was frantic to know when she was going to see her children and risked asking, "When will you come back?"

Mamoun's face twitched with impatience and he pulled himself up to tower over her. He barked at her over his puffed-out chest, "As I told you, when your paperwork is processed. Today, or tomorrow, or the next day. Go back and wait." He snapped his fingers at another guard to come and take her and then he walked away.

Walking back to cell 52, Mayada couldn't believe the day's events. First the qabaj bird and now the judge. For once she kept pace with the fast tread of the guard, eager to share her news with Samara and the other shadow women.

The moment Mayada entered the cell, the qabaj bird ceased its singing.

Every woman there quickly shot a glance at the cell's small, barred window, puzzled over the bird's singing—and at its sudden cessation.

Roula, who had been jailed for reading the Quran at work and praying too much, said, "That qabaj bird was sent from God. To remind us of his power."

Several women nodded in agreement.

Samara stepped forward with a bright smile and open arms. "We cannot stand the suspense. Tell us," she said.

Mayada announced, "Samara was right. That qabaj bird delivered God's message. I am leaving!"

Samara twirled around and around on her toes, like a trained ballerina.

A small roar rose to fill the tiny room as the shadow women began hugging and crying. In the turmoil, Iman's glasses were knocked off her face and she indulged in a moment of hysterical searching for them until they were recovered, unbroken. "I would be blind without them, you know," Iman said with a smile as she replaced the heavy spectacles on her nose.

Even Safana and Sara, both still weak from torture, sat up in their bunks to smile and congratulate Mayada.

Sara whispered, "Will you call my mother for me?"

Mayada smiled. "Yes, Sara. I will call your mother."

Samara was seized with a joy so profound she couldn't stop jumping around. "She will call all our mothers." She grabbed Mayada by her arm. "Tell us. Tell us. Did they say when you are leaving?"

"The judge did not say. He signed the documents while I was there, but an officer told me that my paperwork had to be processed."

"Wonderful," Samara replied in a sing-song voice. "Then you can expect no more than ten days."

Mayada frowned over that answer. "Ten days? I thought I might go today or tomorrow. I cannot bear ten days more."

Samara wrapped her small hands around Mayada's face. "Only ten days, Mayada?" She nodded toward the other shadow women. "Each of us would give a limb," she smiled affectionately, "or perhaps *two* limbs, to learn that our time here was limited to only ten more days."

"It's as though you've been given all of Iraq's riches," Muna said with a small, happy smile.

Not one shadow woman appeared jealous of Mayada's good fortune. No one was angry that she was leaving while they were forced to remain behind.

Mayada was ashamed of her insensitivity before these selfless women. And her heart contracted as she gazed around the cell at them. As desperately as she wanted to walk out the prison door and rejoin Fay and Ali, Mayada was heartbroken to leave these good women behind.

Mayada believed that Samara could read minds when she said, "Mayada, you must not feel guilty. We are glad you are leaving, although we will hold you in our hearts. Mayada, you *can* help us from out there."

Other than Sara and Safana, all of the shadow women began to gather around Mayada.

Muna voiced what they were all thinking. "Mayada, do not forget us when you get out of here. You must swear by Allah that one day you will tell the world what has happened in this cell."

Mayada hugged Muna and pledged, "I swear by Allah that one day the world will know all our stories, Muna."

Samara, always sensible, looked from Muna to Mayada. "It is good if the world knows, but for now, the most important thing is for Mayada to call our families," she said. "Now that we know Mayada is leaving, we must seriously begin her memorization process—now," she persisted. Samara looked at Mayada with a smile that lit her face with hope. "You are our only chance, Mayada."

Since Mayada clung to the wish that her release would come sooner than Samara predicted, she decided to start memorizing numbers as soon as possible. "Yes, Samara, you are right. Let us start, tonight."

"The important thing is to call our families and tell them exactly where we are being held. That is the first key to our release. Then, tell them that the only way to get us out of here is through bribery. They must sell land or cars, if that is what it takes. Practically every guard here will accept a bribe.

"But Mayada, when you do call, make it quick. As you know, all telephones in Iraq are bugged. Say what you have to say and hang up. Do not wait for questions, and do not answer questions. Never, ever, speak your own name. If you are tempted to comfort our loved ones, know that your kindness will get them arrested, as well."

Samara was thinking of every angle. "You will memorize as many phone numbers and addresses as you can today. The rest, tomorrow. Then every day until you leave, I will test you. We want you to remember all these numbers," Samara said with determination.

It was an unusual night. Mayada was taken to the furthermost corner of the cell, so no guard in the corridor could hear the odd reciting that emitted from cell 52.

Aliya was first to line up behind Samara's shoulders, her beautiful face bright with anticipation. Her imprisonment had separated her from her baby daughter, Suzan, whom she had not seen for over a year. The prospect of Mayada's release had conjured a happy vision of reunion with her darling Suzan.

Rasha was next. She proffered her information to Mayada in an aggressive whisper and wore her usual scowl, despite the happy possibilities of the occasion.

Mayada was determined to remember every number, every word, the two women urged on her. Mayada knew that Aliya and Rasha had now been in prison for nearly three years, and that no end to their imprisonment was in sight.

Dr. Sabah, serious but kind, checked Mayada's slip to ensure that her number was still visible there. She needlessly entreated Mayada not to wash the slip until Mayada had called Dr. Sabah's family.

Iman twisted her glasses in her hands and spoke her information to Mayada clearly and slowly.

Wafae wrung her handmade worry beads as she earnestly repeated her information for Mayada over and over, until Samara urged Wafae to move along, that she would test Mayada's memory later.

A woman named Eman came next. She was only twenty-eight, pretty with her Elizabeth Taylor coloring: pale skin, jet black hair and deep, sapphire-colored eyes. Eman was so petite that she looked no older than a pubescent girl. Along with her contact information, Eman related again to Mayada the story of how she came to be imprisoned. "I never thought of breaking any Iraqi laws, but these torturers claim I criticized Saddam Hussein," Eman reminded her. Mayada knew that condemning Saddam was a crime that would cost Eman her tongue, so she prayed she could contact Eman's family in time to save her.

May was a dark-skinned, thirty-five-year-old woman with short brown hair, attractive sloping eyes and delicate features. Her crime, she had been told, was "favoring communists," but as far as May knew, she had never even *met* a communist. May sat with Mayada for the longest, concerned Mayada would forget her number, 521-8429.

It was after midnight when Mayada's concentration faltered. Samara promised the waiting shadow women, "Tomorrow. You can give Mayada your information tomorrow."

When Mayada retired, her spirit was surprisingly low, considering the day's happy events. She was plagued by the sad realization that Saddam's prisons offered no guarantees. What if the decision to free her had been reversed? Mayada would remain skeptical of her promised freedom until she walked out of Baladiyat.

The following morning she awoke to find her cheeks wet with tears. She had awakened from a nightmare in which a man wielding a dagger held her apart from her children.

That morning bore yet another surprise. As soon as dawn prayers ended, the door to cell 52 banged open and a guard bellowed, "Mayada! Out!"

Mayada was so shocked that she was unable to move.

He shouted once again. "Mayada! You are released!"

Samara, remembering that Mayada had not yet memorized all the telephone numbers of the shadow women, quickly thought of an excuse to keep Mayada another few moments. "She just told us she had to use the toilet. Give her a few minutes."

The guard looked at them disgusted and slammed the door. "Five minutes. No more!"

In a flurry of activity, Samara pulled Mayada to the back of the room and urged, "Repeat the numbers you have memorized, quickly. I will gather the remaining shadow women." Samara looked panicked. "Do not let that Al-Askari brain of yours fail us!"

Mayada was so familiar with most of the women's stories that she had no need to be told the names of their towns or neighborhoods. Instead, she urged them to focus solely on critical contact names and telephone numbers. While Samara lined up the remaining women to brief Mayada, Mayada thought of Sara, who was still unable to walk. Mayada rushed to Sara's bedside, tugging at the young woman's shoulder. "Sara, tell me how to contact your mother. Quickly!"

Sara slowly raised her head. "Oh, yes, Mayada, yes. Please do tell my mother that I'm here. Tell her to save me. Call her at 422-9182. Tell her that I told you she keeps the house key under the yellow pot, next to the cactus plant. She will know then that I have sent you."

Sara was so weak that her head now began to wobble on her shoulders.

Mayada assured her, "Your mother will bribe someone, I am sure of it. She will get you out of here, Sara."

Sara's sweet face broke into a smile. "Yes. My mother will arrange it. She will sell the land and pay for me to leave. She will do that if she only knows where I am." And Sara slumped back onto her bed. "Tell her I am waiting on her. I am waiting."

By now Samara had arranged all the remaining shadow women into a short line.

"Mayada! Come!"

Mayada moved quickly.

Roula was the first waiting and she bent down to cling to Mayada's neck.

Roula was a twenty-five-year-old single woman with a simple-hearted appearance, who stood accused of being an Islamic activist. She hastened to unburden herself, reminding Mayada that her co-workers had reported her as an activist because she read the Quran too much and prayed in her office during prayer times.

Mayada promised Roula she would do the best she could.

Amani was a married woman of thirty-two with dark skin, rosy cheeks and light brown hair. Like Rasha, Amani could trace her imprisonment to having once lost her passport.

Anwar was next, thanking Mayada more than once.

Hayat and Asia stood together, their eyes bright with hope.

Mayada tried to memorize all these numbers in a matter of minutes.

With a sinking heart, she realized she would likely never remember them all. She told Samara, "Get that pen from Dr. Sabah. I will write the rest of the numbers on my slip."

Samara quickly returned with the pen, but the instrument would barely write. Its ink supply was nearly emptied.

The door banged open again.

From the doorway, a different guard—not Mayada's intended escort—snorted maliciously, "Samara! You are wanted." Samara was being called to torture. Every shadow woman was jolted by this turn of events, and a low groan swept through the cell.

The guard that had earlier come to escort Mayada appeared now at the new guard's shoulder to shout, "Mayada! Come! You are released!"

The last moments Mayada would spend with the shadow women in cell 52 slipped by, one by one. Samara's beautiful face was grave as her green eyes met Mayada's. The two women looked at each other with sincere love. Samara held out her arms and pulled Mayada to her. They kissed, first on one cheek and then on the other, and as they clung to each other, Mayada whispered, "Samara, you are the most unselfish person I have ever known. Thank you for everything. I will never forget you. And I will help you from the outside. I will!"

Samara's eyes filled with tears. "I will miss you, Mayada, and your wonderful stories."

"Samara!" the guard bellowed impatiently, as he marched to the back of the cell to snatch Samara from Mayada's arms.

Samara's feet left the floor as she was dragged along by the angry guard.

Mayada quickly followed, touching each of the shadow women she passed on her way out. Tears of grief stung her eyes. Her freedom would wrench her away from these magnificent shadow women, and she and they would now live in wholly different worlds.

The last thing she heard as the door slammed was Muna's low voice calling out, "Mayada, please do not forget us."

Fighting back sobs, Mayada knew that if she lived forever, she would never forget these women.

The same officer she had met the day before, the large man named Mamoun, waited in the hallway for Mayada. "It is Mamoun, once again," he said. "We will get your things and I will take you out of here."

Mayada's ears listened to Mamoun's voice as her eyes followed Samara, who was only a few steps ahead. She noted idly that a knot of black and white hair had escaped from under Samara's scarf, and Mayada's heart sank to think that the two friends now walked toward such disparate fates.

Feeling Mayada's eyes on her, Samara turned to share one last look. All of her emotions were concentrated in her vivid eyes as she stared levelly at Mayada. She mouthed something, but Mayada could not discern the words.

At the end of the corridor, Samara was pushed toward the torture room.

Mayada was helpless to save her.

The guard looked at Mayada, speaking rapidly. "Salam is waiting. We will meet him. He will take you home."

Mamoun quickly marched Mayada back into the same room she had visited on her first day in Baladiyat, nearly a month before. Nothing had changed—the same gray man sat behind the same circular desk. He searched through a cabinet and handed Mayada her bag. He grunted and pointed to a document, instructing her, "Sign here." After signing, Mayada peeked into her bag and saw that everything was there: her ring, watch, wallet, workbook, telephone book, identification card, keys and even the note written to her by Fay.

Mayada slipped on her watch and then her ring. The ring spun loosely around her finger. She had lost a lot of weight. Mayada put the ring back into her bag.

"Follow me," Mamoun ordered, as they retraced steps she had

trod the day she was first arrested. Everything seemed surreal to
Mayada as she walked quietly behind Mamoun.

On her way out of Baladiyat, Mayada followed Mamoun into the
prison's entrance hall. The large room was crammed with hundreds of
men, all squatting on the floor with their hands tied behind their
backs. Although the men were waiting to be processed, and none had
yet been tortured, acute misery was etched on every face in the room.
The men's wide eyes reflected the terror that writhed inside each
of them.

As they cautiously wove their way through this nest of trapped
men, Mayada's gaze moved among them.

She whispered at Mamoun's striding back. "What is this about?"

He turned his head slightly and answered in a low voice, "Later, in
the car, I will tell you."

Mayada knew when to keep quiet. She followed Mamoun out
through the door of Baladiyat prison and marched briskly down its
broad stairs. When she cleared the steps, she paused and through eyes
bright with excitement she peered up at the sky. The sunlight was
blinding. It was beautiful. Mayada's face quickened into a smile that
pulled at her eyes and her mouth and her heart. She was truly free.
She held out her hands, welcoming the warm August sun on her face
and hands. She heard a flock of birds squawking and searched the sky
to see their flight.

"Come now!" Mamoun commanded.

Mayada walked as briskly as she could. The best was yet to come.
She was going home. To Fay and Ali.

"My car is parked in the car park," Mamoun told her. "Let's hurry."

Knowing that someone might be watching their departure, and
knowing that if she appeared too friendly with Mamoun, she might
be arrested once again, Mayada lowered her head and walked deter-
minedly. "Here we are," Mamoun announced as they arrived at a
white, 1990 Toyota Corolla.

"Get in the backseat," he instructed her, nodding with his head.

Mayada's heart pounded as the chief gate of the prison compound was soon framed in the car's windshield. This time she was traveling in the right direction, *out* of Baladiyat. She glanced back at the photographs of Saddam that flanked the gate. She wanted to spit at the evil dictator. But of course, she didn't.

Mamoun slowed at the exit and showed a few documents to a guard there before he and Mayada passed through the black gate of Baladiyat.

The moment they were rolling on the highway, Mayada began to laugh, a wild unrestrained sound that she couldn't control.

Mamoun turned around and stared. "Salam said you were a jolly one," he remarked.

Not wishing to irritate this man, Mayada managed to curb her noise and instead threw back her head into a soundless laugh. Abruptly, though, concern for the unknown fate of the hundreds of new Baladiyat prisoners jolted her upright.

"What about those men? Has there been an attempted coup?"

"No. Someone passed out leaflets against the government in the Kadumiya district. All of the men walking in that area were arrested earlier this morning."

Mayada knew that Kadumiya was a Shiite district in Baghdad.

"Why would the secret police arrest all the men? Only a few were passing out leaflets, I'm sure. Most of those men are innocent, nothing more than passersby, men running small errands or the like. Why is our government like this?"

Mamoun replied sternly, "Don't ask me. I am my master's slave. I do what I am told." He twisted his head around. "Listen to me, sister, all Iraqis are under arrest. They take turns picking us up and bringing us in. Even I have been locked up and tortured on two occasions."

Mayada nodded in agreement. Not one Iraqi was safe. She would leave this country as soon as she could arrange it.

Then Mamoun spoke again. "This is important. Your husband is waiting for you, at Baghdad Al-Jadida." Al-Jadida meant "New Bagh-dad," and Mayada knew that this was a neighborhood about thirty minutes from Baladiyat.

She quickly set the record straight. "I am divorced," she said. "Salam is my ex-husband. But my home is next to his father's home and we have two children together, so we are still on speaking terms."

"He's not your ex-husband for long," Mamoun said with a smirk.

Mayada was baffled by his comment, but Mamoun gave her no time to ask for details. "Listen to my instructions," he said. "You are not to leave Iraq. I will come and talk with you in a day or two and tell you what you must do. Remember, you cannot leave. This is a tempo-rary release only. If you want to stay out of Baladiyat, you will have to do what I say."

Mayada knew instantly that Mamoun was threatening her with blackmail. She had heard many stories from Samara about the routine extortion of former prisoners. By blackmailing released prisoners with the threat of new detention, many guards became rich.

She pushed this new worry out of her mind for the moment, telling herself she would deal with it later. Mayada refused to let her joy over her release be diminished by this guard's forewarning. Be-sides, regardless of what anyone urged, she would take her children and leave Iraq as quickly as she could arrange it. Her mother would help her.

Mamoun quieted as he tended to his driving. Mayada longed to reach over his shoulders and blow the horn and shout out the win-dows that she was free. But she didn't.

Instead she sat back against the car seat and stared out the win-dow. She hummed quietly behind her closed lips so Mamoun couldn't hear her. She slumped down to peer at the sky, seeing a few white fluffy clouds.

How she longed to leap from the car and breathe the fresh air! But she couldn't, at least not yet. Instead, she straightened her back and studied the shop windows and the people walking past. She cast her gaze from side to side with pleasure. Baghdad was unfolding as new, as though she had never seen it before. Outside a supermarket, people pushed their shopping carts expectantly toward the entry door. Mayada noted a grandmother with graying hair. The content-looking woman walked holding the tiny hand of her grandson, who toddled along with the pleasure of new life. Three or four teenage boys peered into a shop window filled with sports equipment. Nearby, two men walked side by side, laughing, gesturing and talking.

Four major traffic lights slowed traffic between Baladiyat and Baghdad Al-Jadida. The main street was filled with shops and super-markets, and the side roads led to quiet suburban homes. It would take another ten or fifteen minutes to reach Baghdad Al-Jadida.

Mayada saw a whole family of women walking together down the street. She felt a tug at her heart. These lucky people—walking and talking and living full lives—were unaware that at this very moment, only a few miles away, a beautiful Shiite woman named Samara was being brutally tortured.

Mayada sat quietly and reviewed the shadow women's telephone numbers and special code words.

Soon she and Mamoun arrived at the Baghdad Al-Jadida neigh-borhood, where Mayada quickly saw Salam. He sat in his white Olds-mobile outside a flower shop called Al-Khadrae, or The Green. He wore dark sunglasses and sat slumped in his car. Mayada laughed hys-terically. Salam looked like an undercover cop.

She leapt out of the car as Salam stepped out of his.

She cried out, "How are the children?"

Without answering her question, Salam began shouting at May-ada, furious that she had been arrested. "You stupid! Getting yourself arrested! Now, get in the backseat," he ordered.

With a wave of his hand at Salam, Mamoun roared off.

Mayada was so happy to be free that even Salam couldn't upset her. She was one step closer to her children.

As he started the car, Salam told her, "We must get remarried. Soon."

Mayada's eyes widened. "What are you talking about, Salam?"

"Mayada, this is a temporary release. You will be arrested again. I have to take you and Fay and Ali out of Iraq, to Jordan. You cannot go alone."

Mayada saw his point. She had no *Mahram* to accompany her out of Baghdad. If she wanted to leave Iraq—and she did—she would need that marriage document. She capitulated quickly.

"Well, this will be only to get the children out of Iraq. We get divorced the minute I arrive in Amman."

Salam didn't answer.

"Salam? Only if you agree to an immediate divorce once we arrive in Amman. Otherwise I'll find someone else who will agree to marry me, only for the sake of leaving Iraq."

"All right. I will do it," he agreed. "But we must hurry. Your stupidity at getting arrested will have the secret police on all our heads."

Mayada sat and glared at the back of his head. She was glad she was no longer this man's wife. And she would not remain his wife a moment longer than it took for her to move her children out of Iraq, to a safe country.

"Salam. You didn't answer my question. How are Fay and Ali?"

His voice was filled with impatience. "They are fine."

As they approached her house on Waziriya Place, she sat up in the backseat and stared through the front window. She didn't see either of her children waiting for her return, though she did see a small, thin boy who stood miserably beside her former father-in-law's garage. She supposed he was one of Ali's many friends.

The moment the car stopped, Mayada didn't bother saying goodbye to Salam but quickly jumped out and hurried up the walkway. As the car drove away, she heard Salam shout out the window, "We get married tomorrow!"

The skinny boy looked up and then came running toward Mayada. Could it be that this child was her Ali?

"Mama! Mama!"

"Ali!" Mayada's lips trembled with his name.

Ali leapt into her arms, crying and exclaiming, "Mama! Mama! You are home!"

Mayada was choking on her tears. "Ali! Let me see your face! Let me see your face!"

Her chubby young boy with the smooth baby-face had disappeared. In his place was a serious young man with dark circles under his blue eyes.

"Mama, I thought I'd never see you again!"

Mayada lifted Ali off the ground. Her child was frail and small. She sobbed, knowing how her children had suffered without her.

Ali hugged her tight, then pulled at her face. "Mama, I took your nightgown with me and tucked it under my pillow. Every night I asked God: Get me back my mama. Get me back my mama. That's all I want, for the rest of my life. Just my mama."

"Your mama is back, Ali. And I'll never leave you again."

Mayada glanced behind him. "Where is Fay? Where is your sister?"

"Our father took her to stay with Uncle Mohammed."

"Why?" Mayada felt a flicker of anger. Fay should have remained with her paternal grandfather, close to her own home.

Mayada pulled Ali with her. "Let's go to your grandfather Mohy." He was her former father-in-law, Mohy Al-Haimos. "He'll get Fay back."

Mayada and Ali went into Mohy's home without knocking, and she found Mohy standing there in his white dish dasha (Iraqi men's attire). When he saw Mayada, his face broke into a wide smile. "Hella, hella, hella [welcome back]," he cheered. Mohy walked up to Mayada and kissed her on both cheeks. Mayada's former mother-in-law, Jamila, heard the noise and walked out from the kitchen. "Am I dreaming? Is this really Mayada returned to us?" She looked into Mayada's face and smiled happily.

Mohy told Jamila, "Call Mohammed and tell him to bring Fay home. Her mother has returned.

"While we are waiting, sit down, Mayada, and tell me everything that happened to you."

With Ali hanging on her arm, Mayada told the old couple something of Baladiyat, leaving out the most ghastly parts to protect her young son.

"And do you wish to stay in Iraq?" Mohy asked Mayada, as her tale wound down.

"No. There is danger here for us." Mayada paused. "Uncle Mohy, my children and I can no longer live in a country filled with houses of torture."

Mohy nodded his head in agreement. He had once been arrested on a bogus charge and had spent a year under house arrest. He hated Saddam Hussein and everyone associated with his government. "I will help you do what is best," he promised.

From the beginning of her marriage, Mayada had loved her wise father-in-law. Mohy was a fine gentleman.

Just then Mayada heard the roar of an engine and ran to the door. She saw Fay, who excitedly jumped from the still-moving car being driven by Salam's brother, Mohammed.

Mayada stepped outside. "Fay!"

Fay ran to her, shouting, "Mama! Mama!"

"Fay!"

When Fay saw her mother, she shrieked so loudly that neighbors walked outside to see what the commotion was all about.

Mayada called out to her former in-laws, "I am taking the children home. I will see you soon."

Holding her daughter under one arm and her son under the other, Mayada walked quickly to her home. "Inside. Inside," Mayada warned them. "Let's not make a scene."

The moment they walked in the door, Fay suggested, "We must make a prayer. We must thank God you are home, Mama."

As soon as Mayada put down her bag and the three of them washed their faces and hands, they stood in a straight line, facing Mecca. They kneeled and touched their foreheads on the floor and thanked God for returning Mayada from Baladiyat.

And Mayada's world was good, once again.

10

Dear Samara

IRAQI LIBERATION DAY:
APRIL 9, 2003

Mayada Al-Askari
Amman, Jordan

Dear Samara,

A glorious day has dawned.

Last night my twenty-year-old daughter, Fay, sat up all night watching television, waiting to hear that Iraq had been freed. This morning she woke me at fifteen minutes before six and whispered, "Mama. Get up. I think it's over."

I knew instantly what my daughter was telling me. After thirty-five years of cruel and capricious tyranny—from July 17, 1968, until today—Saddam Hussein's steel grip on my beloved Iraq had finally been smashed.

I jumped out of bed and ran into the living room to hear the wonderful news with my own ears. When the newsman said that Iraq's Baathists were on the run, and that many of them had disappeared into thin air, I laughed with an abandon I hadn't felt in years. In joy and in triumph, Fay tilted back her head to loose a chant of Halhoula, howling in celebration. I immediately joined her. The two of us created such a commotion that Ali jumped out of his bed to investigate. When he too heard the news that Iraq had been liberated, he slipped off his T-shirt and twirled it above his head, whirling a dance of freedom.

Our hearts were bursting with happiness. After exhausting ourselves in jubilation, the children and I washed and prepared for prayer. Together we faced Mecca and thanked God for putting an end to our country's long nightmare.

After our prayer, I told Fay and Ali a little about the precise moment when I realized the nightmare had begun. I was only thirteen years old. The Baath revolution of 1968 had taken place the week before. My father was still alive, and we were still living in Baghdad. One of my father's dearest friends, Haqi Al-Berezenchi, an Iraqi Kurd who was the ambassador to India at the time, was a dinner guest that warm July night, as we all sat in the garden overlooking the Tigris. Because of the recent Baath revolution, politics was the only topic of conversation that evening. My father was worried sick for Iraq and for Iraqis, but Haqi assured him, "Don't worry, Nizar, this is nothing but a wolf's wedding. Like brief copulating animals, this revolution will end soon enough."

With all due respect to Haqi, that wolf's wedding led instead to a long, stormy, thirty-five-year marriage in which a vicious beast had gripped the Iraqi people by the throat.

Samara, I am so happy that I am ashamed, for I know there are many Iraqis who have suffered terrible losses during this battle for freedom. We have been reminded in the cruelest manner that freedom does not come cheaply.

Samara, no day passes that I don't see a vision of your beautiful face, and the faces of the other shadow women in Baladiyat's cell 52. Every morning now in Amman, when I walk from my apartment to my place of work, my steps slow as I scrutinize the face of every woman sitting among the sidewalk vendors. I wonder if you escaped. I wonder if you made it to Amman, and renewed your once-lucrative cigarette business. A few times, my heart has contracted with hope and I have rushed to embrace a woman with black hair streaked with white—like yours. For a brief moment, I am flushed with the belief that you got out of Baladiyat alive. But so far, I have met only disappointment.

Where are you? Are you celebrating Iraq's freedom with your family? Or have you paid with your life for this freedom that I embrace? Were you murdered by Saddam's torturers at Baladiyat, long before this war started? Were you unaware that freedom was soon coming to Iraq? And where are the other shadow women? Which of them lived? Who died? These questions haunt me daily.

As you may have guessed, I now live in Jordan with Fay and Ali. As I write this letter, I'm sitting on my roomy terrace in Amman. It's a balcony that brings me cheer, for I can look east, toward Iraq. We are on Jabbal Amman, off the Fifth Circle, if that means anything to you. To my left, I can see a dim outline of the road toward Iraq. To my right, I see the road that leads to Jerusalem. Many buildings and villas surround us—beautiful white stone buildings with red sloping tops, a world mingled with sunshine and trees and beautiful homes. After dark, the sky fills with a million brilliant stars, and the shimmering lights of Amman glitter.

You would like sitting on this balcony with me, Samara. It seems such a paradise after Baladiyat.

The terrace is furnished with four white chairs, a round table and a bench. Beautiful flowering plants—colored red, white, pink and yellow—ring the terrace and lift their perfumed aroma into the air. These many-colored plants also dangle down the side of the balcony, where they attract vivid butterflies and industrious honeybees. The children and I often eat on the terrace. We stare off at the skies over Iraq and talk about days long past, when living in Iraq meant sunny days sitting by the beautiful Tigris, strolling through green gardens and living the good life.

Occasionally we'll even bring the television set onto the terrace and watch a movie on the video player. When the weather is warm, Ali, now seventeen, sometimes sleeps there.

So you know already that my biggest worry did not come true. My children were not arrested. Nor were they physically harmed. For that, I thank God every time I pray.

As was her habit, my mother saved the day. She got me released from Baladiyat.

As you know, Mother knew practically everyone of consequence in Iraq. Luckily, she still had the private telephone number of the man who headed Saddam's Presidential Office: General and Dr. Abid Mahmud al-Tikriti, the man who filters every call to Saddam (known as Dr. Abid Hmoud to those who know him well).

Mother had met the man years ago, when he invited her to the ceremony at which he defended his Ph.D. thesis. After Dr. Abid received his degree, he encouraged Mother to call him if she ever needed anything. Anything at all, he said. And so she did. He came through for her, as promised.

After some investigation, Dr. Abid told Mother why I was arrested. It seems that *someone* in Baghdad had printed leaflets against the government, but the secret police had no clue where they originated. So they arrested the owners of ten print shops in the area. It didn't matter if the one arrested was guilty or innocent. I fear I am the only one of the ten ever released, although all were most likely innocent.

Dr. Abid told my mother that he had spoken with Saddam and that Saddam agreed to allow him to sign the papers for my temporary release, but that Saddam wanted my mother to give him her word, through Dr. Abid, that I would not try to escape Iraq. If it was found that the leaflets had originated from one of my computers, I would have to be brought back in for further questioning—so that they could find the real culprit. This was a national security situation, Saddam wanted her to know, although he believed I had nothing to do with the crime.

I've never known my mother to lie, not once. But faced now with this deadly choice, she didn't mind lying one bit, she told me. So my mother gave Saddam her word, through Dr. Abid. She told him the blood of my father ran in my veins and that I would never commit a crime. She assured Dr. Abid that if I tried to flee Iraq before the investigation was complete, she would wash her hands of me.

Unfortunately, no one at Baladiyat knew that my release was working its way down from Saddam and the Presidential palace until the day after I was tortured, or I might have been saved that horrifying and painful experience. Once the order had been given, I was simply ignored until the paperwork received all the necessary signatures. So you were right from the first minute, Samara. I would have been tortured daily had the Baladiyat officials been unaware of my upcoming release.

Once my imminent release was common knowledge in Baladiyat, the blackmail started. When that rascal Mamoun saw the paper ordering my discharge, he rushed straight to my home. He assured my children that he could arrange my release if they would give him five hundred dollars. The children were frantic, and sought the help of their grandfather, Salam's father, who gave them the money. That money was turned over to Mamoun.

Thankfully, the children received financial assistance from our neighbors, who had learned of our misfortune. At night, Fay told me, people would slip around to tuck anonymous envelopes stuffed with cash inside our glass outer door.

On the drive home, Mamoun said I was not to leave my house until he came by to settle matters. I had no clue that he was laying the groundwork for weeks of intimidation and blackmail. Daily he came to my home, wanting money for this or that. He told me I would be arrested soon if I didn't "keep the machinery oiled." When he learned through the children's father that I was making plans to leave the country, he warned that my name would be put on a "blacklist" of former prisoners forbidden to leave the country. These names are released to all government agencies and sent directly to the border police.

To satisfy his demands and keep him from reporting me to the authorities, I had to sell the pictures off my walls and borrow money from everyone I knew. And at the last minute, he concocted an additional scheme and held Fay ransom for $50,000! I'll come back to this sorry tale later.

I'm happy to report to you that there was at least one good soul toiling among the staff in Baladiyat. That young doctor, Dr. Hadi Hameed, did telephone the number I outlined in the dust of his black plastic sheeting.

Besides safeguarding my children, only two compelling tasks held me in Baghdad as I made my plans to leave: I needed to contact the families of the shadow women, and I had to visit my father's grave a final time.

I spent the first day of my release from Baladiyat calming my poor children.

The second day after my release I spent trying to contact relatives of the shadow women.

And on the third day of my release, I bade farewell to my father.

Samara, I believed you when you warned that every phone of every prisoner's home would be kept under surveillance. So knowing that my own telephone was most likely listened in on, I went to the only place in Baghdad that boasts a pay phone: the old Alwiya Club in Baghdad. This social club, located next to the Sheraton and Meridian hotels in Al-Firdous Square, was established by the British in 1924. In those days, few Iraqis were even allowed inside the club. Of course, Jafar, Nouri and Sati were a few of the rare exceptions. Since members of my family ranked as some of the more prominent early members, I've often been accorded access there.

The pay phone at the Alwiya Club no longer uses coins, but it now offers a constant dial tone. An operator, hired by the government, listens to all calls from the phone, but the children and I developed a plan. (After learning about the shadow women still imprisoned in cell 52, the children insisted on helping me. I let them help, despite the danger. If I learned only one lesson in Baladiyat, it was that every Iraqi should fight Saddam's tyranny, in whatever way possible.)

A few days before I was arrested, I had thrown Fay's sixteenth birthday party at the Alwiya Club. There Fay and Ali had made friends with a few staff members, including the doorman and the pool lifeguard. I knew I would need a distraction to make the phone calls, so I baked a beautiful cake and urged Fay and Ali to offer some to the operator who listens to calls. The children gathered all the staff together, and after I heard noisy conversation and loud laughter there, I slipped over to use the phone.

I called Sara's mother first and was relieved that she answered quickly. I told her, "Sara is at Amin Al-Amma. Sell the land. Bribe an official. Get your daughter out. *Now.* She needs you."

Sara's mother screamed in surprise and asked, "Is my daughter all right?"

I urged her, "You must get her out. Sara needs to get out and soon." Then I remembered your caution to make every call short, so I told Sara's mother one last thing before hanging up, "Sara says that the key is under the yellow pot next to the cactus plant."

Although I wished I might risk a long talk or a visit with Sara's mother, so I could stress to her the importance of fast action before Sara succumbed to torture, I forced myself to hang up.

Then I went down the list, calling every number I had memorized. As you recall, the morning of my release came so suddenly that I was unable to get the phone numbers for Asia and Hayat and Anwar. Some of my phone calls were answered by children who didn't understand me, and who refused to call an adult to the phone. Some calls were answered by frightened adults, who hung up the moment they realized a former prisoner was making a forbidden call. I'm sad to report that I made reliable contact with only five families.

Samara, I'm also devastated to tell you that your telephone number was no longer functioning. I was unable to contact anyone for you. That's one reason I have been so worried for your safety.

The third day after leaving Baladiyat, I went to visit my father's grave. It's at the Bab Al-Muaadam cemetery, not far from my childhood home on the Tigris. Over the years, I've rarely visited my father's burial place. Much sadness surrounds his gravesite for me. Even after all this time, I find it difficult to believe that my father is a dead body lying in a dirt grave.

Despite my sorrow, I felt a strong need to bid my gentle father farewell, for I knew I would never return to Iraq as long as Saddam ruled, which might stretch for my entire life.

Father had been laid to rest next to the grave of his mother, Fakhriya Al-Said. His burial place is a restful spot, shaded by a large palm tree. His tombstone is simple, just as he requested. The flat white marble headstone reads,

> *Here lies Nizar Jafar Al-Askari,*
> *born in 1922 and died on March 2, 1974.*
> *May Allah rest his soul in Paradise.*
> *(Al-Fatiha on his soul)*

Because it had been some time since I had been at my father's grave, I was shocked by something extraordinary that I saw there on this visit.

In 1955, the year I was born, my mother ordered an African jasmine plant for our garden at the house on the Tigris. It was a beautiful bush with white flowers centered with a violet blush. The leaves were thick and dark green.

That African jasmine was the healthiest little plant, and it grew and grew and grew. Within a few short years, the bush had grown huge. Even before Saddam confiscated our homes on the Tigris, that little bush had grown into a massive one. It was so large that many people thought it was a tree.

When I was a child, our gardener complained of it, saying he had never seen a bush grow so rapidly. That old man swore that the African jasmine was a magical plant that was going to take over the entire yard and cover the house. And I had heard several years ago that the little plant had actually spread all over the area, becoming a bush of legend that carried itself from garden to garden.

Can you believe that that bush had reached my father's grave? As if by magic, the same African jasmine I had often seen my father admire and caress—the bush from which he often plucked a flower for one of his "girls"—now peacefully entwined his grave.

The message-song of the qabaj bird, the mindful African jasmine plant . . . Samara, I'm beginning to believe in miracles.

After saying goodbye to my father and reading prayers for his soul, I returned home and began to seriously plan my escape.

Samara, there was much bitterness attached to leaving. I was forced to remarry Salam, since I would not be allowed to travel outside Iraq without that marriage certificate. It was so traumatic to remarry him that I refuse to think about it. I did what I had to do to save myself and my children.

After marrying Salam, I had to buy my way out of Iraq. Mamoun extorted money for every little thing. When he put that huge price on Fay's head, believing that I could somehow come up with $50,000 to ransom her escape from Iraq, I despaired. I feared I would have to remain in Iraq with Fay, and so run the real risk of being arrested and returned to Baladiyat. But Fay was so terrified that I would be taken away from her again that she insisted she remain behind with her father's family while I fled. She encouraged me to flee, and explained I could arrange her escape once I was safe in Amman.

I was in a terrible bind, just like that good doctor at Baladiyat. My head told me to leave, but my heart urged me to stay. It was a terrible struggle and I didn't know what to do. And then a little miracle happened: You, Samara, came to me in a night's dream and encouraged me, "Mayada, flee. Take your son, Ali, with you, and negotiate for Fay from a stronger vantage point. You can do nothing for either of them from Baladiyat." As the image of your form slowly faded, I heard your voice again. "Flee, Mayada, flee."

As horrified as I was at leaving Fay behind, I felt that the dream was a true omen. I understood you were warning me not to risk Baladiyat, cautioning me that I might not survive a second visit. Knowing that you are the most sensible woman in the world, I decided I had better heed your advice, even if it was delivered in a dream. I knew I could move mountains if I could only leave Iraq.

Samara, the saddest day of my life was the day I went to the bus station in Al-Nadha to board a bus for Amman. The station was crowded with people and vendors, and the walls were covered with ugly pictures of Saddam. I saw a dozen signs reminding Iraqis to wash their faces in the morning or brush their teeth at night. Those infantile slogans so irritated me that I wanted to slap somebody, preferably the Baathist who posted them there. The bus station teemed with families surrounded by tattered luggage. It was obvious from all the boxes and bags that most of the people boarding buses were leaving Iraq for good. And who could blame them?

Imagine our terror when the station door burst open and in walked Uday Saddam Hussein with his entourage. Even though Uday hobbled with a cane, he held an enormous Asian tiger on a leash. Everyone in the station pushed to get away from that dangerous creature, which growled and bared its huge fangs. I truly feared that Uday might turn the tiger loose on the crowd. I had heard of several Iraqis who, while dining in a Baghdad restaurant, had had to fight off Uday's tigers. One man said the only thing that saved him was his expensive lamb dinner, which in desperation he threw into the tiger's mouth.

Samara, I stood near my luggage with my jaw hanging open. I could scarcely imagine that after all I had survived, I would be mauled to death by a tiger in the Al-Nadha bus station. Surprisingly, Uday kept the beast on the lead, although two grown men protecting their families got swatted hard by a large paw.

Uday hobbled through the station, spitting on people and screaming at them. He called everyone a traitor for leaving Iraq. Thankfully, Ali and I were at the back of a long line and the madman couldn't get to us. I was terrified that Fay might be attacked, however, as she and her father had been separated from us by that frantic pushing crowd. But she didn't.

Uday spat until he exhausted himself and left the building. Everyone then began boarding buses, praising God they had survived yet another day in the zoo that was Iraq.

Ali and I finally got on our bus, and I was blinded by tears when I looked out the bus window to wave at my weeping daughter. Poor Ali, only twelve at the time, was tearful that he had been unable to say goodbye to a single friend. Unfortunately, Salam had to travel with us, making the trip to Amman even more miserable.

Both Ali and I were so struck by grief and confusion and relief that we barely said a word, to each other, or to Salam. I stared out the bus window for hours, watching the desert pass, entranced by the sparkling sand that glittered like pearls under the moon. I mused that the land remains the same, no matter what is happening to the humans living on the land.

As we neared the Iraqi border station, I got the same chest pains I had experienced my first night in Baladiyat. I knew that Mamoun was fully capable of tricking me. What if he had notified the authorities at the border that a certain Mayada Al-Askari was illegally leaving the country? If so, Samara, I knew that Ali and I would be detained in the same prison at Ramadi that held you before your transfer to Baladiyat. I cannot describe the fear that knotted in my throat when the border guard asked, "Why are you leaving Iraq?" I lied, "My mother is ill in Amman and I am going to take care of her." Salam stood smirking, without offering to support my story. The guard glared at me like I was a murderer, but he stamped my passport and we were on our way.

After our passports were stamped and we passed into Jordan, a huge burden lifted from my heart. I had escaped Iraq. Now, I told myself, I could spend all my energy raising money to pay for Fay's escape, too.

I'm sorry to report that Salam returned to Baghdad, without giving me the divorce he had promised.

But, Samara, I found that even more bitterness awaited me in Amman.

After my searing time in prison and the anxiety of our plot to escape Iraq, it was wonderful to see my mother again. She is the strongest-willed woman ever to live. Yet I still faced many serious problems. Shorn of the privilege I had always enjoyed as the granddaughter of Sati Al-Husri and Jafar Al-Askari, my weakened finances now limited my options. My mother had spent a great deal of money on me and my children over the years, and I knew that she now had to think of her old age and how she was going to live. So I could not bear to ask her for money. I ended in a terrible bind, trying to pay my son's tuition and at the same time find the funds to pay Fay's ransom. I learned that Mamoun was still blackmailing her, claiming she would find trouble if the authorities discovered that I had fled the country.

But luckily, my life has long been mingled with both miracles and tragedy. Just as I was about to give up, a new miracle appeared. About a year after I left Iraq, a dear friend heard about my dilemma and gave me $25,000 for Fay's ransom. Mamoun greedily agreed to this sum, and my daughter soon came to join me in Amman.

Fay and Ali and their mother were together once again.

Then I was hit with yet another tragedy. Not long after Fay arrived, my mother was diagnosed with breast cancer. At the time, she was seventy-seven years old, although she looked forty and kept the schedule of a young woman. Her illness came as a shock to her, and to me. Sadly, the cancer spread quickly and I nursed my mother through a dreadful year. She suffered greatly. But I was with her when she died, and for that I am grateful.

With all these deaths, and with my sister living far away in Tunisia, our little family has now shrunk to three.

While suffering through many struggles, we were happy to be together, free in Jordan. Few things could diminish our joy for long.

Then something unusual on the political front began to bubble: renewed talk of freeing Iraq. When American President George Bush and British Prime Minister Tony Blair first began to speak of liberating Iraq from Saddam Hussein, we thought it was the same tired talk we had heard many times before.

But now, after a few short weeks of war, my fellow Iraqis have been freed.

Hot tears stream from my eyes when the vision of cell 52 comes to my mind. But I await yet another miracle, the miracle that you and the other women survived. I promise you this, that as soon as it is safe to leave my children and travel into Iraq, I will come to look for you and the other shadow women. If you are alive, one day I will be united in happiness with you, and with every shadow woman I came to know and love.

I greatly anticipate that day.

Your loving friend,

Mayada

After signing the letter to Samara, Mayada rose from the chair and walked to the edge of her terrace. She propped her elbows on the railing and gazed thoughtfully to the east. To Iraq. She was free to go home now, for the first time in four years. After the darkest of nights, the sun had risen triumphantly over her country. Tasting total freedom, she felt as close as she could to complete happiness.

And behind the turmoil of war and recent victory, Mayada could feel the presence of Sati Al-Husri and Jafar Al-Askari. Both of these great men had served Iraq long ago, during another pivotal time in

Iraqi history. Mayada hoped there would arise similarly noble-minded men—men who truly cared about Iraq, men who would rise to this historic time of great need, men who would work for the good of Iraq's future.

This was only the second time in the history of modern Iraq that a blank page had been opened in the nation's book—a page on which the annals of history waited to be written, a page that would describe Iraq's future.

Mayada gazed to the east as she prayed, "May Allah guide the hand that writes on that blank page."

APPENDIX I

EXTRACT FROM SPEECH IN THE HOUSE OF COMMONS
BY THE RT. HON. WINSTON CHURCHILL, M.P.
ON JUNE 14TH, 1921

The Arab army is already partly formed under the administration of Ja'far Pasha, the present Mesopotamian Secretary of State for War. I do not know whether the Committee have in their minds the romantic career of this man. I have no doubt my Hon. and Gallant Friend the Member for the Wrekin Division (Sir C. Townshend) is well acquainted with it. He began the War fighting against us at the Dardanelles, and he achieved a German Iron Cross. He then came round to the Western Desert where he commanded the army of the Senoussi against us. He fought, I believe, three battles, in two of which he was victorious, but the third went amiss from his point of view, and he was wounded and pursued by the Dorsetshire Yeomanry and finally caught in the open field, taken to Cairo as prisoner of war and confined in the citadel. He endeavoured to escape, but, being a somewhat ample personage, the rope by which he was descending from the wall of the citadel broke and precipitated him into a ditch, where his leg was broken. While he was in hospital recovering from these injuries he read in the papers that King Hussein, the Sherif of Mecca, had declared war upon the Turks and he immediately saw that he was on the other side to what he had hitherto thought. He therefore made representations to the Arab leaders at Mecca, and after some hesitation he was given a command in their army. He very speedily rose to a position of high confidence and distinguished himself greatly in the fighting which took place in the next two years. He was finally given the Companionship of St. Michael and St. George by Lord Allenby in a hollow square of British troops composed almost entirely of the same Dorsetshire Yeomanry which had ridden him down. Such is the personality of the Mesopotamian Minister of War, and he is of course a devoted adherent of the Sherif of Mecca.

OBITUARY
JAFAR PASHA
IRAQI SOLDIER AND DIPLOMATIST

General Jafar Pasha el Askari, the Iraqi Minister of Defence, who was shot after the *coup d'Etat* last Thursday, had had an extraordinary career in the War, first against and then with the British. He was twice Iraqi Minister in London and five times Minister of Defence in the Iraqi Cabinet. He was a shrewd, kindly, and capable soldier, a good organizer, a careful diplomatist, and a most joyous and amusing companion, who had many friends in this country.

The Pasha was a Baghdadi. He was born in 1880 and was trained in the Turkish Military College in Constantinople. In the War, in which he won the German Iron Cross, he was selected by Damad Enver Pasha for the difficult task of organizing the Senussi of Libya (who were then not yet subjected to the dominion of the Italians, who had acquired that province from the Turks during the war of 1912) so as to threaten Egypt from the Western Desert. He was landed hazardously on the Libyan coast from a German submarine and succeeded in persuading the Senussi to accept his authority and obey his orders. He was therefore for some time able to wage successful desert warfare against the British until he was ridden down and captured by the Dorset Yeomanry during the fighting at Agagia on February 26, 1916.

As a prisoner of war he was lodged in the citadel of Cairo. One night he contrived a rope of knotted blankets and was on the point of escaping; but one of the blankets parted under the Pasha's great weight and the fall injured one of his ankles so severely that he was unable to get away. He had, however, established excellent relations with his captors, and insisted on paying for the torn blanket. As soon as he had recovered from his injury he was released on parole, and when he learned of the outbreak of the Arab Revolt against the Turks joined the Army of King Husain in the Hejaz and served with the Emir Feisal and Lawrence in command of the Hejazi regular troops in the campaign up to the fall of Damascus.

Before the end of that campaign the Pasha had been decorated by General Allenby at his Headquarters at Bir Salem in Palestine in the middle of a hollow square composed of his captors, the Dorset Yeomanry, whose selection as a guard of honour on that occasion delighted Jafar, who had a keen sense of humour and insisted on wearing his Iron Cross at the ceremony.

After the capture of Aleppo he was appointed its Governor, and when the Emir Feisal became King of Iraq he served as Minister of Defence in the two Cabinets headed by the Naqib of Baghdad from August, 1921, to November, 1922. The Pasha was then appointed first Iraqi Minister to the Court of St. James's, and in that capacity attended the Peace Conference at Lausanne, where his vast and jovial presence made a great impression on the diplomatists and others who were gathered there.

In November, 1923, King Feisal recalled him to Baghdad to be Prime Minister until August, 1924, when he returned to his Legation in London. He was again Prime Minister and also Minister for Foreign Affairs from November, 1926, to January, 1928, and on his way back to London in March of that year to resume his diplomatic career was very nearly captured by Wahabi raiders while his aeroplane was delayed at Ramadi. On his return to London the Pasha read for the English Bar, and was called by Gray's Inn on January 15, 1930. In the following month he was the guest, with Lord Allenby, at a reunion dinner of the Dorset Yeomanry, for whom he had the highest esteem, and in March, 1930, was again recalled to Iraq to become Minister of Defence until October, 1932, in the two Cabinets of General Nuri Pasha es Said, whose sister Jafar had married. Once again Jafar became Minister in London, where he greatly enjoyed being, from November, 1932, until December, 1934, when he was appointed a Senator and returned to Iraq. In March, 1935, he entered the Cabinet which has just fallen as Minister of Defence, his fifth tenure of that office.

IRAQI HEADS OF STATE SINCE IRAQ'S FOUNDATION IN 1921

King Faisal I (1921–1933)
Died of heart problems

King Ghazi I (1933–1939)
Died in car accident

King Faisal II (1939–1958)
Assassinated

Abdul-Karim Qasim (1958–1963)
Assassinated

Abdul-Salam Arif (1963–1966)
Died in a helicopter accident

Abdul-Rahman Arif (1966–1968)
Still alive in 2003

Ahmed Hassan al-Bakir (1968–1979)
Died of natural causes in 1982

Saddam Hussein (1979–2003)
Fate unknown at time of publication

Courtesy Dan Hajost

IRAQ TIMELINE

April 1920:

San Remo Peace Conference of Allied Powers endorses the British and French mandate over the Middle East.

August 23, 1921:

King Faisal is crowned King of Iraq. Mayada's paternal grandfather, Jafar Pasha Al-Askari, is appointed Minister of Defense. Mayada's maternal grandfather, Sati Al-Husri is appointed advisor to King Faisal on matters of education. Mayada's father's uncle, Nouri Pasha Al-Said, is appointed Chief of Staff.

1927:

British strike oil at Kirkuk, Iraq.

November 16, 1930:

Anglo-Iraqi Treaty is ratified with Nouri Pasha Al-Said.

October 1932:

Formal independence is given to Iraq.

September 8, 1933:

King Faisal I dies. His son, Ghazi, is crowned king.

October 1936:

Mayada's grandfather, Jafar Pasha Al-Askari, is assassinated during Iraq's first military coup.

August 11, 1937:

General Bakr Sidqi is assassinated in Mosul.

December 1938:

Nouri Pasha Al-Said becomes Prime Minister of Iraq.

April 1939:

King Ghazi I dies in an automobile accident. His four-year-old son, Faisal II, succeeds. Prince Abd al-Ilah is appointed Regent.

April 1, 1941:

Nouri Al-Said and the six-year-old king are forced to flee after a military coup.

June 1941:

Civil order breaks down in Baghdad. There is a pogrom against Iraqi Jews, with loss of life and injury.

July 14, 1958:

Military coup in Iraq led by Abdul-Karim Qasim. King Faisal II, members of the royal family, and Prime Minister Nouri Al-Said are assassinated.

October 7, 1959:

First Baathist coup fails. Saddam Hussein flees to Egypt.

June 19, 1961:

Kuwait declares its independence from Great Britain.

February 8, 1963:

Baathist coup succeeds.

November 18, 1963:

Countercoup overthrows the Baath Party.

July 17, 1968:

After repeated coups in Iraq, Ahmad Hassan al-Bakir brings the Baathists back into power. Saddam Hussein is second in command as Bakri's deputy, although he is the real power in Iraq.

July 16, 1979:

Saddam Hussein replaces Ahmed Hassan Bakri as the President of Iraq. There is a purge in the Baath Party and many members are put to death. (Bakri dies in 1982.)

April 1, 1980:

Pro-Iranian al-Dawa Party attempts assassination of Tariq Aziz, Iraqi Deputy Prime Minister of Iraq. Iraq blames Iran for the attempt. Saddam Hussein expels Iranian-born Shiites from Iraqi soil.

September 1980:

Iraq and Iran go to war.

June 7, 1981:

Israel bombs the Iraqi Osirak nuclear plant near Baghdad.

May 21, 1987:

USS *Stark* attacked in Persian Gulf, killing 37. The United States blames Iran, although the *Stark* was attacked by two Iraqi missiles.

1987:

Saddam Hussein uses chemical warfare against Kurdish villages, killing thousands.

February 1988:

Iran and Iraq resume the "war of the cities," attacking each other's civilian population.

March 16, 1988:

Iraq again uses chemical weapons against the Kurds, killing thousands more.

July 3, 1988:

An Iranian airbus passenger aircraft is shot down by the USS *Vincennes*. 290 civilians are killed.

August 20, 1988:

Formal cease-fire in the Iran-Iraq war.

September 1989:

Farzad Bazoft, a British journalist, is accused of spying and is hanged in Baghdad.

August 2, 1990:

Iraq invades Kuwait. UN Resolution 660 calls for Saddam Hussein to withdrawn his troops.

August 8, 1990:

Iraq annexes Kuwait as its nineteenth province.

January 17, 1991:

Operation Desert Storm begins.

February 28, 1991:

Cease-fire.

April 3, 1991:

UN Security Council Resolution 687 establishes the terms of the peace. All Iraqi troops are out of Kuwait. Economic sanctions and Iraqi disarmament commence.

December 12, 1996:

Uday, Saddam Hussein's eldest son, is seriously wounded in an assassination attempt.

November 1, 1998:

All UNSCOM inspectors withdrawn from Iraq.

January 30, 2002:

President George Bush calls Iraq part of an "axis of evil" during his State of the Union address.

September 12, 2002:

Bush calls for action against Iraq. Iraq says it will allow international weapons inspectors to "return without conditions."

October 10, 2002:

Congress adopts a joint resolution authorizing the use of force against Iraq.

October 16, 2002:

Iraq renews offer to UN weapons inspectors. Saddam Hussein wins another seven-year term as President—receiving 100% of the vote.

January 28, 2003:

President Bush says that Saddam Hussein is not disarming.

February 5, 2003:

Secretary of State Colin Powell uses satellite photos in a bid to win over international opinion during a UN Security Council presentation.

March 5, 2003:

France, Germany, and Russia release a joint declaration stating they will not allow the UN resolution authorizing military action in Iraq to pass in the UN.

March 7, 2003:

The United States, Great Britain, Spain and Portugal meet in the Azores, issuing a one-day deadline for diplomacy. The leaders warn that the war could start at any time.

March 17, 2003:

The United States and Britain withdraw their Security Council resolution draft. Weapons inspectors are advised to leave Iraq. President Bush issues an ultimatum to Saddam Hussein. The Iraqi President is given forty-eight hours to leave Iraq.

March 20, 2003:

Coalition forces launch an "attack of opportunity" against specific targets in Iraq.

March 21, 2003:

Coalition ground forces move into Iraq.

March 25, 2003:

Coalition forces, mainly British, begin fighting Iraqi militia in Basra, Iraq's second largest city.

April 2, 2003:

U.S. forces reach the outskirts of Baghdad.

April 3, 2003:

U.S. forces take control of Saddam International Airport in southern Baghdad.

April 9, 2003:

Baghdad falls to U.S. forces. Statues of Saddam Hussein begin to topple.

April 13, 2003:

Tikrit, the hometown of Saddam Hussein, is taken by U.S. forces.

April 15, 2003:

Coalition partners declare the war over.

FACTS ABOUT IRAQ

Government:	At the time of this publication, Iraq is preparing for democracy
Population:	24,000,000
Capital:	Baghdad
Population of Capital:	5,000,000
Area:	168,760 square miles
Language:	Arabic, Armenian, Assyrian, Kurdish
Religion:	Muslim 95% (Shiite 60%, Sunni 35%); Christian 5%
Life Expectancy:	58 years
Literacy:	60%
Economy:	Petroleum, wheat, rice, vegetables, dates, cotton, cattle, sheep

FACTS ON NEIGHBORING COUNTRIES

ISLAMIC REPUBLIC OF IRAN

Government:	Islamic Republic
Population:	65,000,000
Capital:	Tehran
Population of Capital:	7,000,000
Area:	636,300 square miles
Language:	Persian, Turkic, Kurdish, Arabic and other
Religion:	Muslim 99% (Shiite 90%, Sunni 9%); Christian 1%
Life Expectancy:	69 years
Literacy:	72%
Economy:	Petroleum, textiles, cement, wheat, rice, grains, sugar beets, fruits, nuts, dairy products, wool, caviar, cotton

HASHEMITE KINGDOM OF JORDAN

Government:	Constitutional Monarchy
Population:	5,300,000
Capital:	Amman
Population of Capital:	1,182,000
Area:	35,638 square miles
Language:	Arabic, English
Religion:	Muslim 96% (Sunni majority); Christian 4%

Life Expectancy:	70 years
Literacy:	86.5%
Economy:	Phosphate mining, petroleum refining, cement, light manufacturing, tourism, wheat, barley, tomatoes, melons, olives, sheep, goats, poultry

STATE OF KUWAIT

Government:	Constitutional Emirate
Population:	2,300,000
Capital:	Kuwait City
Population of Capital:	850,000
Area:	6,880 square miles
Language:	Arabic, English
Religion:	Muslim 85% (Sunni 60%, Shiite 25%); Other 15% (Christian and Hindu)
Life Expectancy:	77 years
Literacy:	78.5%
Economy:	Petroleum, food processing, fish

KINGDOM OF SAUDI ARABIA

Government:	Monarchy
Population:	24,000,000
Capital:	Riyadh
Population of Capital:	4,700,000
Area:	756,986 square miles
Language:	Arabic
Religion:	Muslim 100% (Sunni 94%, Shiite 6%);
Life Expectancy:	72 years
Literacy:	78%
Economy:	Petroleum, crude oil production, cement, construction, fertilizer, plastics, wheat, barley, dates, mutton, chickens, eggs, milk

SYRIAN ARAB REPUBLIC

Government:	Dictatorship
Population:	17,500,000
Capital:	Damascus
Population of Capital:	2,200,000
Area:	71,498 square miles
Language:	Arabic, Armenian, Aramaic, French, Kurdish
Religion:	Muslim 89% (mostly Sunni; Druze, Alawite 12%); Christian 10%
Life Expectancy:	70 years

| Literacy: | 71% |
| Economy: | Petroleum, textiles, beverages, tobacco, mining, cotton, lentils, chickpeas, olives, mutton, poultry |

REPUBLIC OF TURKEY

Government:	Democracy
Population:	67,500,000
Capital:	Ankara
Population of Capital:	3,200,000
Area:	301,383 square miles
Language:	Turkish, Kurdish, Arabic, Greek, Armenian
Religion:	Muslim 97% (mostly Sunni); Christian 1%
Life Expectancy:	69 years
Literacy:	85%
Economy:	Textiles, mining, steel, petroleum, lumber, paper, tobacco, olives, livestock

GLOSSARY

Al-Askari, Jafar Pasha (1885–1936): Paternal grandfather of Mayada Al-Askari. Jafar Al-Askari was from a prominent Baghdadi family. During World War I he served with Prince Faisal and Lawrence of Arabia in command of the Hijaz regular troops. After the war he served King Faisal I and King Ghazi I, both of Iraq, in many government capacities, including Minister to Great Britain and Minister of Defense and Prime Minister of Iraq. He was assassinated while protecting King Ghazi I in 1936.

Al-Faw: A peninsula on the Iraqi Persian Gulf coast; fighting occurred at the offshore oil terminals there during the Iran-Iraq war and Gulf War II.

Al-Husri, Sati (1879–1969): Mayada Al-Askari's maternal grandfather. Sati Al-Husri was one of the first Arab Nationalists. Sati believed that Arab Nationalism was the only route out of colonialism and imperialism for the Arabs. He was an educator, a writer and a government minister. Sati was a personal friend of King Faisal I and served him in many capacities. There are over a hundred books and articles written about Sati Al-Husri. All Arab countries today have a street, a school and an auditorium named for this great man.

Al-Sa'ud: The ruling dynasty of Saudi Arabia.

American University in Beirut: University in Beirut founded by Dr. Daniel Bliss of the American Protestant Mission. With a student body drawn from all over the Middle East, the university has helped to create a class of Arab intellectuals.

Amman: Capital city of Jordan, population 1,182,000.

Arab: A linguistic group of approximately 260 million people that experts believe originated in the Hijaz region in Saudi Arabia. All Iraqis other than Kurds are Arabs.

Arab League: Iraq, Egypt, Jordan, Saudi Arabia, Lebanon, Syria and Yemen formed the League as a bulwark against Soviet expansion into the Middle East.

Arab Nationalism: Defined as the opposition to foreign rule, first against the Ottomans and then against Great Britain and France. Sati Al-Husri, Mayada Al-Askari's paternal grandfather, was considered one of the most prominent Arab nationalists.

Arab Union: Iraq and Jordan founded the Union in 1958 as a counter to the Nasser-dominated United Arab Republic of Syria and Egypt, established the same year.

Arabic Language: Arabic belongs to the Semitic language family with its sisters Hebrew and Aramaic. Arabic is written from right to left. Arabic has been a written language since the early fourth century.

Armenian: Armenians are an ancient Indo-European people originating from Eastern Turkey. In the Middle East today, Armenians mainly live in Iran and Lebanon.

Assyrians: Invaders who founded an empire in Mesopotamia from 1200 to 612 B.C.E.

Ayatollah Ruhollah Khomeini (1900–1989): A religious leader of the Shiite Muslim sect who was instrumental in overthrowing the Shah of Iran in 1979. Khomeini ruled Iran until his death in 1989.

Azhar University: Islamic University in Cairo established in A.D. 977 in the al Azhar Mosque in Cairo. It is the oldest institution of its kind in the world, and is the leading center for higher Islamic learning. Some of Mayada's ancestors attended Azhar University.

Aziz, Tariq: Iraqi politician who is a Catholic from Mosul. A member of the Baath Party, he served as Saddam Hussein's Deputy Prime Minister. He was arrested by the Coalition Forces in 2003.

Baath: The Arab Baath Socialist Resurrection Party was formed on April 7, 1947, by Michel Aflaq and Salah ad-Din al-Bitar, two Syrian university students. The tenets of the Baath Party include adherence to socialism, political freedom and pan-Arab unity. Baath parties rule in Syria. The Baath Party in Iraq was toppled in 2003 when Coalition Forces overthrew Saddam Hussein's government.

Baath Socialist Party, Iraq: The party started secretly in 1950. The party increased in size and overthrew the Iraqi government in 1963. Out of power only seven months later, the Baathist came back in 1968 and remained in power until 2003.

Babylon: One of the oldest cities in the world and a leading city in ancient times. It was situated by the Euphrates River, which has since changed course.

Baghdad: Capital city of Iraq, with a population of five million. The city is situated by the Tigris River. Baghdad was once considered the heart of the Arab Empire and was second only to Constantinople in terms of size and splendor during the city's golden age from 638 to 1100 C.E., when Baghdad flourished as a center of learning, philosophy and commerce.

Bakir, Hassan (1914–1982): Baathist President of Iraq from 1968 to 1979 and a cousin to Saddam Hussein.

Basra: Second largest city in Iraq, located by the Shatt al Arab in southern Iraq and the heart of Shiite territory.

Beirut: Capital of Lebanon. The nation's principal port, Beirut has a history that stretches back to the Phoenician era.

Euphrates: One of two main rivers in Iraq, eastern Turkey and northern Syria.

King Faisal I (1885–1933): The third son of the first king of Hijaz (modern-day Saudi Arabia), King Hussein bin Ali. Faisal was born in Taif, educated in Constantinople and linked with Great Britain's T. E. Lawrence (Lawrence of Arabia) to fight against the Ottoman Empire. He became King of Syria and King of Iraq. He was a close friend to members of Mayada Al-Askari's family.

King Faisal II (1935–1958): The only son of King Ghazi I. He was only four years old when his father died in an automobile accident. The young king was killed in the revolution that occurred on the morning of July 14, 1958.

King Ghazi I (1912–1939): The only son of King Faisal I, Ghazi was born in Hijaz and left to the care of his grandfather, King Hussein, while his father was fighting in World War I. King Ghazi died under mysterious circumstances when he drove his automobile into a lamppost on April 3, 1939. King Ghazi was a close friend of Mayada's mother, Salwa Al-Askari.

Hammurabi Code: A principle of law established in ancient Mesopotamia (now modern Iraq) that established the role of the state as an agent of justice for wrongdoing, rather than the individual.

Hashemites: The Hashemite kings came from a prominent Saudi Arabian family who descended from Prophet Muhammad and once ruled parts of Saudi Arabia. After their military defeat by Abdul Aziz Al-Sa'ud, the father of the present day rulers of Saudi Arabia, the British placed members of the family as kings in Iraq, Transjordan and Syria. King Faisal I was placed on the Iraqi throne. (The present-day king of Jordan, King Abdullah, is a Hashemite.)

Hijaz: Western region of Saudi Arabia. It is the birthplace of Islam. Hijaz was a province of the Ottoman Empire from 1517, but after World War I, it became an independent kingdom under King Ali al-Hussein. King Hussein was the father of King Faisal I, who became the King of Iraq. Abdul Aziz bin Rahman bin Sa'ud, the father of the present-day kings of Saudi Arabia, conquered the Hijaz in 1926 and declared himself king, combining the Hijaz with the Nejd into the Kingdom of Saudi Arabia.

Hussein, Saddam (1937–): The son of a landless peasant who died before his birth, Saddam was raised by his uncle, rose to power through the Baath Party and became the President of Iraq in 1979. Saddam not only led a reign of terror over all Iraqis, but attacked his neighbors Iran and Kuwait, creating war in the region. Saddam Hussein's government was overthrown in 2003 by coalition forces.

Iraq, Republic of: In 1923, a European Convention led by the British and French governments created modern-day Iraq. The country was made up by combining the Ottoman provinces of Baghdad, Basra and Mosul.

Islam: Religion founded by the Prophet Muhammad. The emphasis in Islam is on submission to the will of a single God.

Kurds: The Kurds are not Arab or Iraqi or Turkish or Persian, but are members of a twenty-five-million-strong ethnic group that inhabits areas in Turkey, Iran, Iraq and Syria. Saddam Hussein waged extensive military campaigns against the Kurds in Iraq, including gas attacks in 1988.

Kuwait: Small kingdom founded on June 19, 1961, that is located on the southern border of Iraq. In 1990, Iraq invaded Kuwait and occupied the country until the coalition forces during the Gulf War of 1991 pushed them out. There have been uneasy relations between Iraq and Kuwait since that time.

Lawrence of Arabia (1888–1935): Thomas Edward Lawrence grew up in Oxford, England, and graduated from Jesus College, specializing in medieval military architecture. Between 1911 and 1913, he worked as an Oxford archaeologist in Mesopotamia. Following the outbreak of World War I, he was assigned to military intelligence in Cairo. He developed a strong relationship with Prince Faisal (later King Faisal I of Syria and Iraq). During World War I, Lawrence organized and fought alongside the Arabs against the Ottoman armies, where he became good friends with Mayada's grandfather, Jafar, and her father's uncle, Nouri. Ironically, after surviving many close calls in the war, he died in a motorcycle accident in England. Lawrence was the author of several best-selling books about his military campaigns.

Mesopotamia: The Greek term meaning "the land between the rivers" includes the area between the Euphrates and Tigris rivers. Early civilizations emerged in this area. Today the area is in Iraq.

Mosque: An Islamic place of public worship.

Mosul: Iraq's third largest city, with an estimated population of 1.4 million people. Mosul has a long history and was a leading city in ancient times.

Mother of All Battles: Saddam Hussein's name for the ground war during Operation Desert Storm. After losing the war, Saddam portrayed it as an Iraqi victory.

Mukhabarat: Popular term in Arab countries for the secret police or intelligence apparatus. During Saddam Hussein's reign, Iraq had five intelligence agencies, all known generally as the Mukhabarat.

Muslim: An adherent of the religion known as Islam.

Nasser, Gamal Abdul (1918–1970): First independent Arab leader of Egypt; served as President from 1956 to 1970, when he died of a heart attack. During the 1950s Nasser contended with Iraqi leaders for leadership of the complete Arab world. Nasser was a great admirer of Sati Al-Husri, Mayada's maternal grandfather.

Operation Desert Shield: Military build-up of Arab-Western coalition troops in Saudi Arabia in 1990 and 1991 for the purpose of expelling Saddam Hussein's armies from Kuwait.

Operation Desert Storm: Arab–Western coalition troops began a bombing campaign against Iraq on January 16, 1991. A ground invasion followed on February 23, 1991. The ground war lasted only one hundred hours and resulted in a military victory for the coalition against Iraq.

Ottomans: Empire established by the Turkish people, which emerged in Anatolia in 1301, conquered Constantinople (now Istanbul) in 1453 and the Arab lands, including Iraq, in 1516 and 1517, lasting for four hundred years. The empire became known as the Ottoman Empire. The Ottoman Empire joined the Axis powers during World War I, and with the Allied victory, the empire formally ceased in 1918. Modern Turkey was carved from the remains of the Ottoman Empire.

Pahlavi, Shah Mohammed Reza (1919–1980): Born in Tehran, succeeded his father, who abdicated in his son's favor, in September 1941. Dedicated enemy of the Muslim cleric Khomeini, who returned to Iran and seized power after the Shah left on January 16, 1979.

Pan-Arabism: An international Arab movement that promoted Arab interests and was dedicated to the creation of a single Arab state.

Portsmouth Treaty: Treaty signed in 1948 defining the relationship between Great Britain and Iraq. The treaty was for the benefit of Great Britain, compromised Iraqi sovereignty and created outrage in Iraq.

Quran: Islamic holy book. The paramount authority of the Muslim community, the Quran is the ultimate source of Islam. The Quran is composed of the divine revelations received by the Prophet Mohammed over the last twenty years of his life.

Republican Guard: Elite Iraqi troops personally loyal to Saddam Hussein who are recruited from the Sunni sect, the ruling party of Iraq.

Shiite: Islamic sect at odds with Sunni sect over successor to Prophet Mohammed, among other things.

Sunni: The leading Islamic sect in terms of numbers.

INDEX

ABOUT THE AUTHOR

Jean Sasson is a writer and lecturer who has lived in Saudi Arabia and traveled extensively in the Middle East. She is the author of four internationally best-selling books on the Middle East, including *The Rape of Kuwait; Princess: A True Story of Life Behind the Veil in Saudi Arabia; Princess Sultana's Daughters;* and *Princess Sultana's Circle.* Jean now lives in the southern United States, although she frequently visits the Middle East.

Visit Jean Sasson at www.jeansasson.com